THE
CHICANA/O/X
DREAM

SERIES | **RACE** AND **EDUCATION**

Series edited by H. Richard Milner IV

OTHER BOOKS IN THIS SERIES

Urban Preparation
Chezare A. Warren

Truth Without Tears
Carolyn R. Hodges and Olga M. Welch

Millennial Teachers of Color
Edited by Mary E. Dilworth

Justice on Both Sides
Maisha T. Winn

Culturally Responsive School Leadership
Muhammad Khalifa

Science in the City
Bryan A. Brown

Race, Sports, and Education
John N. Singer

Start Where You Are, But Don't Stay There, Second Edition
H. Richard Milner IV

THE CHICANA/O/X DREAM

Hope, Resistance, and Educational Success

GILBERTO Q. CONCHAS
NANCY ACEVEDO

Harvard Education Press

Cambridge, Massachusetts

Paperback ISBN 978-1-68253-511-0

Library Edition ISBN 978-1-68253-512-7

Library of Congress Cataloging-in-Publication Data

Names: Conchas, Gilberto Q., author. | Acevedo, Nancy, author.
Title: The Chicana/o/x dream : hope, resistance and educational success / Gilberto Q. Conchas, Nancy Acevedo.
Other titles: Race and education series.
Description: Cambridge, Massachusetts : Harvard Education Press, [2020] | Series: Race and education series | Includes index. | Summary: "Based on interview data, life testimonios, and Chicana feminist theories, The Chicana/o/x Dream profiles first-generation, Mexican-descent college students who have overcome adversity by utilizing various forms of cultural capital to power their academic success"-- Provided by publisher.
Identifiers: LCCN 2020028295 | ISBN 9781682535110 (paperback) | ISBN 9781682535127 (library binding)
Subjects: LCSH: Mexican Americans--Education (Higher)--United States. | Mexican American college students--United States. | First-generation college students--United States. | Minorities--Education--United States. | Racism in education--United States. | Educational equalization--United States. | Discrimination in education--United States.
Classification: LCC LC2683.6 .C65 2020 | DDC 378.00868/72073--dc23
LC record available at https://lccn.loc.gov/2020028295

Published by Harvard Education Press,
an imprint of the Harvard Education Publishing Group

Harvard Education Press
8 Story Street
Cambridge, MA 02138

Cover Design: Endpaper Studio
Cover Image: iStock.com/mycola

The typefaces used in this book are Minion Pro and Myriad Pro.

For our students,
who teach us so much,
and for our Mexican immigrant parents,
who practiced unconditional radical love—
nurturing hope, resistance, and success despite hardships.
To Chicanas/os/xs who have been made to feel like atravesadas/os/xs.
In the name of social justice.

Contents

Series Foreword by H. Richard Milner, IV   ix

Introduction
The Chicana/o/x Dream Among First-Generation
College Students   1

SECTION I
Multiple Systems of Oppression Along
the Educational Borderlands

Chapter 1
The Framework of *Atravesada/o/xs Nepantleando*   *17*

Chapter 2
Engaging *la Facultad* to Explain Marginalizing Processes   37

SECTION II
The Chicana/o/x Dream in the
Community College Borderlands

Chapter 3
Navigating the Community College as Student-Parents   57

Chapter 4
Community College Students Re-envisioning Success
in STEM   85

SECTION III
The Chicana/o/x Dream in the Four-Year University Borderlands

Chapter 5
Empowerment and Success Among Four-Year University Chicano Male
Students   111

Chapter 6
Intersectional Journeys of Four-Year University Chicana Female
Students   133

Chapter 7
Conclusion   153

Appendix: Methodological Reflections   173

Notes   183

Acknowledgments   205

About the Authors   211

Index   213

Series Foreword

by H. Richard Milner, IV
Race and Education Series Editor

Hope, Resistance, and Success Among First-Generation Chicana/o/x College Students

SOME OF THE MOST PRODUCTIVE and meaningful years of my professional and personal life were spent in Pittsburgh, Pennsylvania, where I was a faculty member for five years. Bridges are plentiful and the use of them in Pittsburgh is a bit fascinating in that they seamlessly connect a city of rivers across neighborhoods. This is a powerful book about bridges. As a university professor dedicated to more deeply understanding and supporting Chicana/o/x college students, I am proud and honored that Conchas and Acevedo have chosen to include their book, *The Chicana/o/x Dream: Hope, Resistance, and Educational Success*, in the Race and Education Series of the Harvard Education Press.

This is an extraordinarily important book—one that every single higher education professional should read at two-year and four-year colleges, and a book that every single educator across the educational spectrum committed to more deeply understanding and supporting their Chicana/o/x students should read. This beautifully written book penetrates *the mind* and *the heart*. It bridges affect and the cognitive. Conchas and Acevedo carefully illustrate what is possible when theory meets reality. It eloquently bridges theory and practice. Grounded and shaped by illustrative analytic framing, particularly drawing from the work of Gloria Anzaldúa's concepts of, in their words, "*atravesado* (transgressor), *nepantla* (in-between), *la facultad* (ability to see beneath the surface), and *nepantlera* (individuals who navigate in-between spaces)," readers are engaged in perspectives and insights of first-generation Chicana/o/x college students.

But rather than focusing on individual challenges these students may face, Conchas and Acevedo showcase how these students navigate and negotiate structural and system challenges. The book bridges the individual with the systemic. Even in the midst of some of the most horrific situations that these Chicana/o/x students experienced, they persevered and succeeded despite those circumstances. How do these students build hope and resilience in the face of poverty, xenophobia, discrimination, and racism? From where do Chicana/o/x students find strength to forge forward in marginalized and inequitable school communities? Perhaps most importantly, how do we learn from the experiences of those who have experienced them in ways that teach and inform what we do in educational policy and practice? The voices that we hear and learn from in this book rely on memories and experiences of immigration, family, education, and, perhaps most importantly, love. Deeply rich in concept and content as a bridge, Conchas and Acevedo are not bashful or afraid to be vulnerable in this book—writing about their own journeys in public schools, higher education, and beyond. These authors show us what is possible when we use our lives as *testimonios* to bear witness to the ills, hatred, and hurt that minoritized People of Color experience. Similarly, the book is a bridge between *testimonios* of pain and joy experienced through success.

Demonstrating how a book can be profound in both breadth and depth, Conchas and Acevedo capture essential themes that bridge experiences outside of school with those inside, such as the school to prison pipeline, Latina mothers in community colleges, understanding and addressing stereotypes, recognizing and disrupting marginalizing structures, and the centrality of the sense of belonging. Bravo! This is a much-needed book for our field.

—H. Richard Milner, IV

The Chicana/o/x Dream Among First-Generation College Students

When Mexico sends its people, they're not sending their best.
They're not sending you. They're not sending you. They're sending
people that have lots of problems, and they're bringing those
problems with us. They're bringing drugs. They're bringing crime.
They're rapists. And some, I assume, are good people.

—Donald J. Trump, June 16, 2015[1]

THE UNITED STATES OF AMERICA was established as a land of immigrants with the idea of the American dream premised on equality, freedom, and individualistic success; that presumption, however, was erected on a foundation of coloniality, xenophobia, and racist nativism that resulted in the dispossession of Indigenous peoples and the enslavement of people from Africa.[2] Needless to say, immigrants and people incorporated through force built the nation.

Contemporary immigration from Mexico has historically been a contested issue resulting in people of Mexican descent being consigned to second-class citizens, denied access to education, and relegated to menial labor. The highly conflicted and heated political issue of immigration has presently created an overwhelming crisis—a crisis of the American heart and soul. The crisis is a profound juxtaposition between the promise of a welcoming society based on immigrant integration and one that seeks to keep out, marginalize, and further the "othering" of Chicana/o/x people with the symbol of a border wall to please a narrow nationalist base and the right-wing media.[3] The wrath of extreme racism, nativism, xenophobia, sexism, and homophobia in today's America is evident, particularly in preK–12 schools and higher education institutions. Moreover, these interrelated structures of inequality have become even more palpable during these unprecedented times of the COVID-19 global pandemic and protests against systemic racism and all forms of violence. Yet it is these most painful experiences that can also empower communities to maintain hope, resist inequality, and access resources to succeed academically. At the center of today's turbulent America are the Students of Color, who, with the support of institutional resources, challenge inequality head on and succeed despite incredible odds.

This book shares the lived experiences and perspectives of first-generation Chicana/o/x college students who—despite being affected by marginalization, immigration, poverty, and education policies—navigate successfully through inequality in US society and culture. Such experiences and perspectives divulged in the book are rooted in the understanding that feminist theories, Chicanx studies, and ethnic studies courses contribute to students' development of a critical consciousness and can also be utilized to contextualize the experiences of Chicana/o/x students in the institutions of preK–12 schooling and higher education.[4] We build on the feminist scholarship in the field of education that has interweaved Anzaldúan concepts, such as *atravesado* (transgressor), *nepantla* (in-between), *la facultad* (ability to see beneath the surface), and *nepantlera* (individuals who navigate in-between spaces).[5]

Using interviews, *testimonios*, and Chicana feminist theories, this book addresses the institutional mechanisms that shape the aspirations, expectations, and achievements of Chicana/o/x students who grew up in marginalized communities and navigated unequal school contexts. In so doing, the book looks toward the future by highlighting the actions that Chicana/o/x students take in creating bridges: they create bridges from preK–12 to college for themselves and future generations; they create bridges between their communities and higher education; and they create bridges to challenge the preestablished pathways out of education. Fundamentally, this book helps define the heart and soul of tomorrow's America and elucidates that Chicana/o/x college students maintain hope, enact resistance, and succeed against injustice—*the Chicana/o/x Dream.*

The Tales of Two Chicana/o/x UC Berkeley Golden Bears

The Chicana/o/x Dream is informed by Anzaldúan theories and represents the hope present in Chicana/o/x communities, despite the continued marginalization that results in Chicana/o/x students being treated as atravesados—transgressors—in US schools. Chicana feminist scholar Gloria Anzaldúa gave us the gift of theories to put our combined pain into action and to challenge an unjust society—especially in the realm of education: "You experience nature as ensouled, as sacred. *Este saber,* this knowledge, urges you to cast *una ofrenda* (an offer) of images and words across the page *como granos de maiz,* like kernels of corn. By redeeming your most painful experiences you transform them into something valuable, *algo para compartir* or share with others so they too may be empowered."[6] Anzaldúa's offering to current and future generations of scholars and activists provides language to explain and theorize the lived experiences of Chicana/o/x in the United States. Guided by her call for a blend of internal reflexivity and outward collaborative actions in pursuit of social justice, we take a step back to conceptualize the education system as one that contributes to both despair and hope.

The Chicana/o/x Dream serves as a clear indication that the next generation of Chicana/o/x students will continue the historical legacy of resistance to marginalizing efforts. The book serves as a framework that contextualizes both the never-ending and ever-adapting racism in US institutions and the hope and resistance enacted by Chicana/o/x students who continue to persist in education because they identify it as one avenue toward success for themselves, their communities, and society writ large.[7] We, the coauthors, exemplify such efforts as the children of Mexican immigrant farmworkers and tenured university professors.

What follows are our own testimonios of maintaining hope, enacting resistance, and succeeding against odds to introduce, illuminate, and contribute to *The Chicana/o/x Dream*. Our experiences as higher education faculty are not in alignment with the majority of Chicana/o/x individuals; in fact, our experiences are unique and far from reality. Our combined experiences attest to Anzaldúa's theorizing of borderlands, atravesados, la facultad, and nepantlera. We center the notion of hope as part of this book because, in order to survive marginalizing structures, atravesados have to maintain hope and the aspiration for a better future. We include a focus on resistance because through la facultad, Chicana/o/x students are able to see beneath the surface of marginalizing structures so as to question and challenge inequities. Finally, the (overused) term *success* is used to represent the abilities of nepantleras to use la facultad as they navigate conflicting spaces in pursuit of higher education with the end-goal of building bridges that the next generation can use. The interdisciplinary frameworks serve to provide a road map for fostering institutional opportunities and academic success for Chicana/o/x college students.

Our educational journeys have contributed to our efforts as nepantleras to foster college access and success for current and future generations of Latina/o/x students—one of us raised in a semiurban context and the other in a rural agricultural one. Our contexts have fostered hope. We have learned how to resist. Through our research, teaching, service, and activism, we develop different opportunities for Latina/o/x and other Students of Color to succeed in education and beyond. We ask that you join the journey with us and help dismantle historic racial oppression and reclaim the dream and promise of public education.

Gil's Testimonio

I was born in 1969 to my father, José, and my mother, Evelia Conchas, Mexican immigrants from San Jerónimo, a small farming town in the state of Jalisco. I am their third son and I have two older brothers, Celso and José (called Joe), one younger brother, Jessie, and a sister, the youngest—Jenny. Married in México, José and Evelia already had two sons when the elder José applied in 1966 to be a guest worker for the United States Bracero program, which legally allowed for temporary importation of Mexican contract laborers. He was accepted. Leaving his wife and children behind, he traveled alone for three or four years, throughout the Southwest, picking strawberries, tomatoes, and grapes. Later, José avoided discussing these years, but when he did, he spoke of clashes with teamsters over competition for jobs and getting sprayed by his employers with lice-killing chemicals. When the guest worker program ended, my father stayed in the United States and, no longer considered a legal worker, he began to experience police raids on top of his other ongoing issues due to his undocumented status.

Back in México, my mother went months without receiving money from her husband. She soon began taking in sewing and making cheese and yogurt to earn income. When she had saved enough, she headed for California to find her husband. Because my mother's parents were land-owners, a privileged group when it came to getting visas to visit the United States from México, she was able to fly legally to California with her two little boys.

She located the address of her husband's dwelling in San Diego and, with their two boys standing behind her, knocked on the door. José, not knowing of his family's arrival, stood frozen in shock. Evelia nudged their two sons forward—past responsibilities come to life—a resurrection of the family. Taking back its space in José's life, the family moved forward. My two brothers are what we call now the *1.5 generation*. During this period, I was conceived, and in 1969, I was born.

The family moved to southeast San Diego, to a predominately African American neighborhood near Logan Heights, where we lived through my kindergarten year. My father obtained a job as a welder, and my parents rented a cockroach-ridden, dirty duplex, which my mother feverishly sani-tized. To this day, my mother, at seventy-eight years of age, keeps her home spotless—even the dirt floor outside her home "shines" clean.

In 1972, when I was three, a woman knocked on doors throughout the neighborhood, telling parents about a new program, Head Start, that would prepare preschoolers for kindergarten. José and Evelia had third- and fourth-grade educations, respectively, but they knew the value of education and decided to enroll me. That was the beginning of an extraor-dinary venture for me—an important initiation to the power of education.

Head Start, launched in 1965, was a comprehensive program offered to families at the dawn of Lyndon B. Johnson's Great Society. The compo-nents of the program included social services, health, nutrition, education, and parent involvement. At first, I was an unwilling preschooler recruit. I didn't want to go, and my dad carried me, while I was kicking and scream-ing, to the first day of the program. But after being forced to attend, I loved Head Start. This exceptional opportunity launched the intellectual hunger—*conocimiento*—for a schoolboy born and raised in an urban bar-rio. I eventually enacted la facultad and excelled throughout pubic school, enrolled at UC Berkeley as an undergraduate, and obtained a PhD in soci-ology at the University of Michigan.

Although my father did not live to hear about my academic work as a sociologist nor especially to see his son as a Harvard professor, ten-ured professor at the University of California, endowed professor at the

Pennsylvania State University, and senior officer at the Bill & Melinda Gates Foundation, my teaching and my research represent my parents' commitment to and perseverance for equity and social justice. My parents opened the door for me, and my undergraduate experience provided the social scaffolds to acquire and activate the necessary social capital to further expand upon the limited opportunities afforded to the son of poor immigrant laborers.

All of this would not have been possible without the support and guidance I experienced as an undergraduate at the University of California, Berkeley. I was fortunate to have been part of three significant institutional processes that laid the foundation for my eventual matriculation at the University of Michigan's prestigious graduate program in sociology. The first came from living in the Chicano/Latino theme house, Casa Joaquin Murietta, on the Berkeley campus. At Casa, I was fortunate to have received the structural and cultural aspects of the undergraduate experience that privileged classes all too often take for granted. I was exposed to caring and supportive adults, peer mentoring, cultural activities, and, above all, a safe and high-achieving atmosphere. I clearly recall that as a freshman at UC Berkeley, I spent countless hours in the computer lab working on my "developmental" English class assignments. I did not pass my English essay exam and therefore had to enroll in a catch-up intensive writing course. I was such a horrible writer, and I struggled with my essays. In one semester, I had to unlearn the five-paragraph rule that I had wrongly learned in high school English classes. I was fortunate to have been exposed to peers who had a great high school education and who took the time to tutor me and guide me through the processes of articulating my thoughts on paper: they created bridges. "Gil, don't be lazy and go back down and rewrite this piece," my peer would constantly state. What a challenge, but what an experience! Had it not been for the access to computers in the first place and to being exposed to high-achieving and supportive peers, I might not have made it past Subject A English at UC Berkeley. It was this high-achieving and supportive climate that exposed me to my second and perhaps strongest influence.

Through contacts gleaned from living at Casa, after my sophomore year I was introduced to a Chicana sociologist at the University of California, Santa Barbara, where I secured an internship. The summer program, Summer Academic Research Institute, forever changed my identity. I embraced graduate school and wholeheartedly embraced an identity as a sociologist. Again, this was an important event—*conocimiento*—in my undergraduate experience that shaped my intellectual interests in research related to social equity. In addition, I believe that I impressed the professor—for one sunny day on the UCSB campus, she suggested that I apply for the American Sociological Association's Minority Opportunity Summer Training (MOST). I was consequently chosen to participate in MOST on the Berkeley campus the following summer.

MOST represents the third scaffold of my undergraduate experience. MOST sought to recruit, prepare, and help admit the next generation of Students of Color into top doctoral programs in sociology. I had the honor to not only work with renowned sociologists but also be exposed to equally impressive peers. This was an opportunity that began to mold my identity as a budding sociologist. While I did not write a formal thesis for this internship, I took several courses with other MOST peers and had the honor to dialogue with imminent professors who conduct research on race relations and social stratification. We also attended seminars and cultural events throughout the Bay Area. MOST introduced us to and prepared us for graduate school life and initiated important professional networks in academia. You have to keep in mind that the majority of MOST participants were first-generation college students. Through MOST, it was not enough to emphasize enrollment in graduate school; completion and eventual acquisition of a PhD was key.

My individual determination was not enough to complete college, obtain a PhD, and acquire tenure. I benefited from institutional bridges that mediated my engagement—*el animo*—and success. It all began with my parents' hard work and the institutional agents along the way that paved the path for me. Now, I try to mentor and create bridges for the next wave of scholars who embrace equity and social justice. I believe that we must remember those that came before us, those that opened the door for us, and those that will come after us. Let us all make our parents proud and always be *para la raza*.

Nancy's Testimonio

I was raised in the agricultural fields of Northern California. On my mom's side, my grandfather was a Bracero. With the help of her older brothers, my mother, Gloria Rivas de Acevedo, managed to *arreglar sus papeles*, against her father's wishes. Challenging gendered expectations was not new to her as she learned to resist patriarchy at a young age. She worked in the fields in Rio Vista, California, and learned to drive on its curvy roads surrounded by fields and the river. After multiple attempts, my dad, Rodimiro Acevedo, crossed the border at the age of sixteen with the help of a *coyote* and lived in Santa Ana, California, under the roof of *Doña* Altagracia, who would offer room and board for twenty-five dollars a week to recent immigrants until they secured a job. My parents married in 1983 and my mom refused to stay behind in Mexico, like so many women were expected to do. By 1986, my dad was eligible to apply for US residency through the Immigration Reform and Control Act. My parents worked in the tomato fields for many years, and we lived in the middle of the fields, in rural Yolo County.

Although there was a local Head Start program that I could have attended, my mom never wanted me to enroll, because she assumed that if I was supposed to spend so many years in schooling, I should not have to spend an additional year sitting still. At four years old, I began elementary school as an English learner. I was the first child picked up by the school bus, and I would ride the bus for an hour before being dropped off at school. I remember clearly that one day, I got home and my parents were not there. Instead of panicking, I jumped on my bicycle and pedaled to the end of the dirt road and on to the street to find my parents under the walnut trees on the side of the road. To this day, I cannot explain how I *knew* that my parents were collecting ripe walnuts off the ground; we would do this often and then sell them at the market. Reflecting back, maybe my *facultad*—that sixth sense—allowed me to think that they would be out there working. Once I arrived, I helped with the "harvest."

Although I was an only child at the time, I was not alone because I grew up with older cousins. One of my cousins, Francisco (Panchito) Rivas, was like a brother to me and would ride the bus with me every day; we were in the same class, but our educational journeys would soon diverge. The bus driver, Margaret, would say we were too loud, so she would send him to the last row with the sixth graders, and I would stay in the front row. By third grade, I was selected to stay after school for the MESA/GATE program and my cousin was not. I had no idea about the meaning of the program, but a teacher offered to drive me home on her way home. By sixth grade, we were placed with different teachers, and by junior high school, I was part of the UC Davis Aggies academy and he was not. Somehow, I was enrolled in the UC Davis Early Academic Outreach Program and would sit through college-going workshops—without really understanding what the advisors were talking about. Throughout this process, my parents reinforced the need to earn a college degree so that I could avoid the heat of the agricultural fields; they instilled in me the hope to believe that that another life was possible.

By eighth grade, my family moved, and despite being in advanced-level math (algebra), the counselor at the new school placed me one year behind, in prealgebra. Thankfully, by ninth grade, Rafael Rivera walked in to my English classroom to recruit students for admission to the UC Davis TRiO Educational Talent Search Program. I applied because I knew that I needed the support to prepare for college admission. Over four years, Rafael advised me as to what classes to take, took us on field trips to visit colleges, led college-going workshops, and supported me with both the college admission and financial aid processes.

Although I am a first-generation college, student, I have thirty cousins on my mom's side, three of whom were college graduates (at that time). Rafael was instrumental in supporting my abilities to prepare for college admissions, but it was my three cousins who were key during my college choice and transition process. My cousin, Yesenia Rivas Bejarano, had helped me in elementary school when I could not grasp the concept of fractions; years later, it was she who called me unexpectedly the day before my Student Intent to Register form was due. After her trying to convince me for what felt like an hour, based on her (partially truthful) advice that I could attend UC Berkeley for one year and then transfer "anywhere else" if I did not like it, I agreed to enroll at UC Berkeley. As I was preparing to attend college, my cousin Mane (Jose M. Mandujano) taught me that the prestige of the school I attended did not matter; if I did not gain adequate job experience during college, I would not be hired anywhere once I graduated. Thus, once I got to college, I tried my best to find a job in education, to gain career skills. My first year in college, I realized that I was not the first person in our Rivas family to attend UC Berkeley; my oldest cousin, Jose G. Rivas, was an alum. A couple times per semester, he would treat me to dinner so that we could check in and I could explore foods that were all new to me at the time.

Academically, I struggled; despite being in Advanced Placement courses in high school, I could not write an essay, resulting in a few failed courses. I had to enroll in a writing preparation course, and by luck, the printed course schedule said the course would be located in a certain classroom. But on the first day of class, I learned there was a change in the schedule and I was not enrolled in that specific section. Instead of having me figure out where the course was, the instructor allowed me to sign up for her section. It was in her course that I began to understand the basics of writing, like having to explain a quote with your own words, which to me, at the time, seemed rather pointless and repetitive because I assumed everyone would interpret quotes in the same way. By my fourth year, I was ready to graduate with a double major in social welfare and legal studies— that is, until I had courses with Dr. Blas Guerrero and Professor Josefina Castillo Baltodano. They reignited my aspirations and opened my eyes to the possibilities of pursuing a PhD as an avenue to improving the educational system for Chicana/o/x students. Seeing Josefina as a *profesora*, mother, and wife and seeing the pictures of Blas walking across the stage with his kids and earning his PhD, I envisioned the possibilities of pursuing such a pathway.

However, the key event that served as my *arrebato* (breakthrough) in my process toward *conocimiento* happened in the Chicanos and Education course, taught by Blas. I still remember clearly walking into the class. I had just come back tanned from a sunny trip to the snow and was wearing my baggy Oakland Athletics black jersey and hat that evening because I was supposed to rush to the game after class. As I stepped into the classroom in Dwinelle Hall, Blas stopped me and told me in what row to sit. This had never happened before—we were free to sit wherever we wanted—but I did not question him and just sat down. In the same manner, he chose the seat for every student in our class. He proceeded to walk us through a lesson plan, and throughout the class, he would talk to each student using different tones and would move one or two students into another row. He then asked us to look around and reflect on what was happening. Simply put, we were being "tracked." The few white and Asian students were on one end of the room, by the window; their desks were spaced out nicely so that they would not be crowded, and he spoke to them with respect and validating words. Those of us who were dressed down and/or had darker skin color were placed at the other end of the room, next to the door; our desks were crowded next to one another and we were ignored. Blas then gave us permission to change seats, if we wished, and he transitioned into discussing the readings on educational tracking. At that moment, all I could remember was my cousin Panchito and our diverging pathways. I realized that he was tracked out of the education system. There was nothing "special" about me; I was simply the quiet and shy girl who "could never" misbehave, as teachers would tell other students when I should have been disciplined for fighting. He actually learned to talk and read English well before I did, but instead of teachers recognizing his academic potential, they reprimanded him for talking. That arrebato motivated me to pursue a PhD with the intent to challenge the deficit and inequitable schooling experienced often by Latina/o/x students.

Although I had taken various education and Chicano studies courses during my four years at UC Berkeley, it was Blas's teaching that allowed me to understand the "vast veil."[8] I decided I would resist the educational inequities to the best of my abilities. At that time, it meant that, as a college advisor for a TRiO program, I would be strategic with how I advised, guided, and advocated for high school students as they prepared to enter higher education. Blas's course set me on the path toward a PhD. Although I had walked the graduation stage in May, in the summer, I ran into a friend, Gustavo Buenrostro, on my way to a third-round interview for a full-time college advisor position. We had taken education courses together, one of them being a research course. I explained that I was on my way to an interview but what I really wanted to do was pursue a PhD, which would require a letter of recommendation from a tenured faculty member. His advice was "stay as long as you can"—and I canceled my interview on the spot. Days later, I met with Laura Jimenez-Olvera, who encouraged me to major in Chicano studies because I was so close to earning that degree; as a first-generation student, it never occurred to me that I should major in something that I *actually* enjoyed. By then, I was familiar with advocating for high school students during the application process, so it was easy for me to appeal my going over the maximum number of units allowed and explain that I would complete a third major in Chicano studies.

That following spring, I processed the notion of *nepantla* (an in-between space) that I read in Anzaldúa's *Borderlands: La Frontera* book as I sat in Dr. Nelson Maldonado-Torres's class. He drew a mirror on the chalkboard to explain Anzaldúa's theories. As a college advisor, I found the Chicana feminist theories helpful when I realized that the Chicana/o/x "achievement gap" was not due simply due to lack of cultural capital. I understood that students did not have access to college-going guidance and resources at their schools. I "uncovered the lie" by looking behind the mirror and knew that if I wanted to support their college aspirations, I had to network and access resources to support their transition to higher education.[9] As a *nepantlera*, I intended to create a bridge for students from under-resourced schools with college-going information.

I was also able to transpose these skills so that I could advocate for myself and seek out resources to help me along my pathway to the PhD and to the professoriate. My abilities to enact *la facultad* and serve as a *nepantlera* for students who aspired to be the first in their family to earn a college degree were strengthened once I read Anzaldúa's work. I was able to see that students needed more than information; they needed structural shifts to navigate higher education pathways. Now, as faculty, I continue on my journey of *conocimiento* by resisting educational inequities through my research, teaching, and service so that I can contribute to building the bridges that future generations of Chicana/o/x students can use as pathways toward success in higher education.

Overview of Book Chapters

The case studies in this volume provide a critical examination of the sources and types of inequity that continue to plague disenfranchised populations, as well as the value of the case study method for illuminating the same. In so doing, we go beyond presenting critical case studies of social inequality and education and (1) use Anzaldúan theories to take a look at the intersectional experiences of Chicana/o/x students at both two-year and four-year colleges, (2) connect the lingering history of coloniality with contemporary schooling experiences, (3) illuminate Chicana/o/x students developing pathways toward higher education for future generations, and (4) pave the way for educational leaders to acknowledge and foster assets such as la facultad and the abilities of students to develop community partnerships as a form of engagement. Thus, we engage asset-based and interdisciplinary perspectives to highlight the various strategies that Chicana/o/x students use to foster hope, resistance, and success in the education system. The book continues with seven chapters and a methodological appendix. The book is separated into three sections.

Section I, "Multiple Systems of Oppression along the Educational Borderlands," is comprised of chapters 1 and 2. In chapter 1, we provide a brief overview of postsecondary outcomes of Chicana/o/x students, propose the framework of education borderlands, and establish the conceptual *Framework of Atravesada/o/xs Nepantleando (FAN)*. To do so, we explain that critical race theory in education serves as an epistemological foundation of the book, which allows us to envision and develop the context of education borderlands for Chicana/o/x students. The chapter uses coloniality, deservingness, and borderlands to contextualize and explain the dehumanizing and marginalizing education policies and practices that Chicana/o/x students have to navigate. We contend that these policies frame Chicana/o/x students as atravesados, transgressors who were not meant to belong in the US education system but who eventually enact la facultad to maintain hope, resist inequality, and reach success—we coin this process within FAN as the *Facultad de los Atravesada/o/xs*. Chapter 2 then explains the notion of la facultad to conceptualize and illustrate that first-generation Chicana/o/x students can understand the inequalities fostered by education borderlands.

The second section of the book, "The Chicana/o/x Dream in the Community College Borderlands," comprises chapters 3 and 4. We use interviews and *testimonios* to transition to the second section of the book by establishing that within the education borderlands, Chicana/o/x students maintain hope, resort to resistance, and redefine success as they move from being atravesadas to nepantleras who navigate higher education. Chapter 3 focuses on the intersectionality of the prison industrial complex, the community college, and student-parenting. Chapter 4 shares the experiences of Chicana/o/x community college students who have a disability and who major in STEM fields. The chapters exemplify that students manage to maintain hope, despite being pushed away from education, and that they use their hope and pursue educational resources as a form of resistance with the intention to support their families and become an example for future generations. The section challenges the traditional understanding of the community college and reframes the sector as one that can help bridge the aspirations of Chicana/o/x students with academic success.

In the third section, "The Chicana/o/x Dream in the Four-Year University Borderlands"—chapters 5 and 6—we continue to be guided by intersectional identities of Chicana/o/x students in a four-year university.

Drawing on six *testimonios*, we show that the multiplicative forms of marginalization to which Chicana/o/x college students are subject inform their academic trajectory and empowerment. This section highlights that Chicana/o/x students also represent nepantleras in four-year universities as they navigate hostile education contexts and build bridges between higher education and their communities. Both chapters in this section highlight contemporary experiences of three Chicana and three Chicano students who identify as undocumented, in mixed-status immigration families, queer, and/or as having disabilities.

In the concluding chapter 7, we provide a broader discussion of what we believe the findings of our book suggest for preK–12 and higher education. In so doing, we contextualize our analysis and empirical results within the current higher education climate, given the developments by the Trump administration and the simultaneous rise in white supremacist hate groups and diversity initiatives in higher education. As such, we conclude by recommending specific practices, pedagogical approaches, and policies that address experiences relevant to the intersectional identities students embraced and discussed throughout the book.

As Gloria Anzaldúa (2002) echoes: "We are ready for change. Let us link hands and hearts together find a path through the dark woods step through the doorways between worlds leaving *huellas* (footprints) for others to follow . . . *si se puede* (yes we can)."[10] We hope this book contributes to the change needed to enact hope, resistance, and educational success for social justice—hence, *The Chicana/o/x Dream*.

Multiple Systems of Oppression Along the Educational Borderlands

Chapter 1

The Framework of *Atravesada/o/xs Nepantleando*

Theory produces effects that change people and the way they perceive the world. Thus we need *teorías* that will enable us to interpret what happens in the world, that will explain how and why we relate to certain people in specific ways, that will reflect what goes on between inner, outer and peripheral "I"s within a person and between the personal "Is" and the collective "we" of our ethnic communities. *Necesitamos teorías* that will rewrite history using race, class, gender and ethnicity as categories of analysis, theories that cross borders, that blur boundaries.[1]

PREVIOUS SCHOLARS have established that traditional higher education theories often fail to consider community college settings, do not account for systems of power that shape the experiences of students with intersectional identities, and invalidate social contexts.[2] In other words, the field of higher education does not centralize power relations that Chicana/o/x students navigate in the ever-present colonial contexts of education.[3] We take to heart and reiterate Anzaldúa's call for theories to align with the experiences of marginalized individuals who navigate intersectional systems of oppression. We therefore account for the intersectionality of systems of oppression that Chicana/o/x students navigate throughout their higher education pathways.

Educational institutions are presumed to employ seemingly race-, gender-, and class-neutral sociopolitical discourses in their curricula in cultivating knowledge in today's youths. However, studies have shown that the contemporary American educational system is built upon coloniality and does not capture adequately or even accommodate the histories and lived experiences of minoritized groups.[4] As such, since the late eighteenth century, the histories, cultures, and languages of Chicana/o/x students have been oppressed and erased from the US public educational system.[5] Yet coloniality and marginality do not affect members of the Chicana/o/x community in the same manner. Intersectionality scholars have previously argued for the multiplicative nature of social marginalization.[6] More specifically, multiple forms of inequality, along various axes of the social world, affect individuals' experiences and perceptions of the world around them.[7]

We present an overview of Chicana/o/x educational experiences and how their experiences vary due to different forms of marginality through an intersectional approach. Utilizing *testimonios*—first-person narratives of the sociopolitical inequality, oppression, and marginalities people experience—and in-depth interviews, we center the voices of Chicana/o/x first-generation college students in our analysis.[8] In so doing, we aim to reveal the ways in which these individuals enact *la facultad*, the ability to see beyond surface phenomena into the meaning of deeper realities—as a strategy to persist when faced with adversities and proactively begin to assert their belongingness in the educational system.[9]

Intersectional Overview of Chicana/o/x Schooling

Chicana/o/x youths make up the largest share of the young US Latinx population: about two-thirds of Latinx millennials are of Mexican origin, and nearly 70 percent of US Latinx younger than eighteen years of age come from a Mexican background.[10] With the median age of twenty-six among Mexican Americans (compared to thirty-seven for all US population and twenty-eight for US Latinx), many Chicana/o/x students are currently enrolled in primary, secondary, and postsecondary educational institutions. Despite their overrepresentation among US Latinx, only about 10 percent of Chicanas/os/x ages twenty-five and older have at least a bachelor's degree, compared to 14 percent among all US Latinx and 30 percent of the entire US population.[11] Even though studies have found similar levels of educational aspirations among Chicana/o/x students, compared with ethnoracial minorities, their unequal schooling opportunities compared to Asian Americans and white students are well documented in the scholarship.[12] Various social structural factors complicate Chicana/o/x students' educational experiences and affect their social outcomes. Even though we acknowledge a multitude of intersecting institutional obstacles, we continue with an asset-based perspective that centers the various strengths present in Chicana/o/x homes and communities.

Chicana feminists have written extensively on Latina students and posit they are holders and creators of knowledge because they engage in formal (academic) and informal (home/community) knowledge.[13] Delgado Bernal proposes the concept of *pedagogies of the home* and places cultural knowledge at the forefront to understand lessons from local communities and homes spaces.[14] Chicana college students use pedagogical formations such as the communication practices and learning that occur in the home as a tool for survival and resistance to multiple axes of domination.[15] Due to their ethnoracial minoritized status and gender, Girls of Color are often put in vocational tracks and/or directed toward feminized professions such as clerical positions, nursing, and teaching.[16] However, the teaching and learning that occurs in homes and communities allows Latinas to draw upon their cultures to resist sites of oppression based on gender, race, class, and sexual orientation.[17] Indeed, we view Chicanas' *testimonios* as a source of knowledge in refining what we know regarding the experiences of Chicana first-generation college students.

In alignment with a Chicana feminist agenda, which posits that strides toward social justice require the inclusion of everyone, we believe that the inclusion of male Latino/Chicano students will provide a more comprehensive representation that informs the ways in which Latino/Chicano students achieve and represent the Chicana/o/x dream of hope, resistance, and school success. Historically, urban youth—specifically, Black, Chicano/x, and Latino/x male students—have been depicted as deviant and prone to criminal behavior.[18] Katz, for instance, argues that schools contribute to the criminalization of Latinos.[19] Men of Color attending public schools are subject to policing by school personnel.[20] Some scholars attribute behavioral problems to being rooted in cultural gender socialization of Chicano/Latino boys through machismo, characterized by exaggerated male characteristics and rejection of any potentially feminine behaviors, which aligns with patriarchal standards.[21] Hurtado and Sinha reveal that Latino college students come to acquire a framework that exceeds machismo and how their intersectional identities—race, sexuality, ethnicity, and gender—impact the way they formulate their views on inequality and feminism.[22] That is, through exposure in college (i.e., ethic study courses, women's studies courses) and seeing women in their lives experience inequality, college men can shift their conceptualizations of feminism to transcend toxic machismo. However, machismo is part of the larger umbrella of patriarchy that the US has used to marginalize women; thus, Latin/a/o/x students have overlapping influences of machismo and patriarchy.

In addition to expectations around gender, Chicana/o/x students also grapple with immigration status and racist nativism. Numerous studies have found that undocumented status among Chicana/o/x parents can lead to their children's discursive ostracization in American society as "anchor babies." Chavez argues that the labeling of anchor babies entails that US-born children of undocumented parents, who are still birthright citizens, are not "real" citizens but part of an alleged conspiracy to take advantage of the United States.[23] This framing not only leads US-born citizens to become targets of anti-immigrant discourses and policies, but also constructs a binary of deserving and undeserving citizens.[24] Such framing of "anchor babies" both has adverse psychological effects on US-born Chicana/o/x youths and affects how mixed-status families (families with both documented and undocumented members) see inequalities and opportunities for their children and navigate through the larger society.[25]

Furthermore, students' own documentation status influences their educational and career trajectories due to blocked opportunities for social mobility.[26] Governmental programs and policies such as Deferred Action for Childhood Arrivals (DACA) and the California DREAM Act address document-status-related sociolegal barriers, adversities, and stress for undocumented youth who immigrated to the US as young children. However, these programs do not provide paths to citizenship and block social stability and mobility for the majority of undocumented individuals.[27]

Sexual minority status similarly leads Chicana/o/x students to experience social and educational marginalization. In general, heterosexual gender norms are policed and reinforced in school settings, and queer students often encounter hostile school and social environments.[28] At home, the enactment of nonheterosexual identities and behaviors are often policed; ethnoracially specific cultural norms and socialization regarding gender, sexuality, and family roles often hinder Latina/o/x sexual minorities from disclosing their sexual identity and/or orientation.[29] Even though ethnoracial minoritized student organizations provide queer-friendly environments and the need to acknowledge the cultural capital of Queer Students of Color has been identified as important, such support and resources are not available to all Queer Students of Color.[30]

Likewise, Students of Color with disabilities have unequal access to quality education that fosters their academic success. Historically, African American and Latina/o/x children were often "dumped" into special education classrooms, referred to as mental retardation programs, due to issues related to Spanish language dominance and lower IQ scores, both of which were due to racist exams manipulating familial socioeconomic and immigrant status.[31] More recently, Dávila found that Latina/o/x students with disabilities experience disability-specific microaggressions of low expectations, disregard, and bullying that leaves students disengaged and/or resistant to academic services.[32]

Although Chicana/o/x students face socioeconomic, political, and discursive obstacles in their educational experiences, some still successfully obtain a bachelor's degree and achieve upward social mobility. Scholars have identified immigrant optimism, trustful mentors and role models, and familial, institutional, and community support and engagement as the driving factors behind Chicana/o/x students' eventual success.[33] We build on the work of scholars who examine the experiences of Chicana/o/x and Latina/o/x students by using an Anzaldúan lens to offer clarity about the process by which Chicana/o/x students themselves make sense of their experiences.[34] We contribute to the literature by centering our analyses on the lived experiences of Chicana/o/x students to examine how they respond to and subvert systems of coloniality and oppression in the US educational system to achieve success.

The Epistemological Underpinnings of This Book

This chapter presents an interdisciplinary foundation that is beneficial when examining the experiences of Chicana/o/x students. Through the proposed concept of education borderlands, we account for the colonial roots of our nation and the resulting public education system by using coloniality, deservingness, and borderlands to contextualize the schooling experiences of Chicana/o/x students.[35] Although books read by current/ future educators and educational leaders likely do not acknowledge the history of the US education system and its (invisible) connections with current schooling conditions, this book is written in a manner that asks you, our readers, to reflect on your practices and self-assess what changes you need to make to ensure that you are not engaging in the marginalization of Chicana/o/x students. As such, we begin by explaining to all readers why and how the education system has been established and reproduced in ways that were not meant to benefit Chicana/o/x students.

Within such institutional contexts, we situate our student data within frameworks that we developed by building on Anzaldúan theories to explain that the participants understand they were marginalized both in the education system and US society writ large. As such, la facultad accounts for their ability to see the structures that produce inequalities. Finally, the student interview data helped us to develop the Framework of Atravesada/o/xs Nepantleando (FAN), which acknowledges the resistance efforts of Chicana/o/x students in developing bridges between higher education and their communities. The culminating Framework of Atravesada/o/xs Nepantleando presented in this chapter is representative of *The Chicana/o/x Dream*. First, we establish that inequities and marginalization persist in the education borderlands, which makes Chicana/o/x students feel like atravesadas/os/x who do not belong in the education system. Then, we highlight that, as atravesadas/os/x, Chicana/o/x students use their facultad to resist marginalization and transform into nepantleras by tapping into various institutional resources to navigate college. Finally, we assert that students redefine success to include ensuring that their communities also have access to higher education pathways.

Although we developed our frameworks after analyzing and coding the various sources of data, our researcher epistemologies were rooted in critical race theory and coloniality.[36] In so doing, we acknowledge that the experiences and insights of Chicana/o/x students can help inform how we improve the educational system for future generations—breaking down walls and, instead, creating bridges. Since the 1980s, theories developed by Gloria E. Anzaldúa have been instrumental to future researchers. Chicana feminist perspectives have informed the efforts of scholars to develop new theories that examine the educational experiences of Communities of Color.[37] We aim to challenge traditional education theories and frameworks that are developed without acknowledging the long-standing power relations developed through colonial structures in the US. Thus, we use critical race theory (CRT) in education as an epistemological lens to acknowledge that racialized inequities in the educational system are colonial, intentional, and ever present.[38]

Education Borderlands

Building on Acevedo-Gil, we define education borderlands as the nexus of deficit and marginalizing practices, policies, and ideologies present in the education system that Chicana/o/x students confront (see figure 1.1).[39] With education borderlands, we connect history with present time and begin with the premise that US institutions were founded on coloniality.[40] Mexicans and Mexican Americans were disenfranchised since the foundation of the US, and schools served as another infrastructure to reinforce marginalized positions in society.[41] Deservingness was one approach used in US schooling to denote that Chicana/o/x students do not deserve access to a quality education.[42] It is in this context of Chicana/o/x students representing the "other" within schooling systems that we conceptualize education institutions as borderlands, where multiple cultures collide and Chicana/o/x students are deemed as unworthy *atravesados*

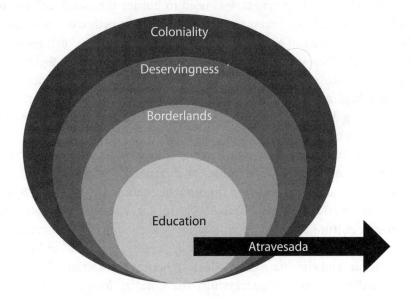

FIGURE 1.1   Education borderlands othering Chicana/o/x students as atravesadas/os/x

(transgressors).[43] Next, we present education borderlands to provide an in-depth overview of the process of othering in the education borderlands.

Coloniality as the Foundation of Education Borderlands

We acknowledge that the term *coloniality* is not used often when referring to the schooling system. Nevertheless, we stand on the shoulders of various individuals who highlight the need to acknowledge the marginalizing contexts so as to understand the experiences of Chicana/o/x students in order to better support their educational success. In framing schooling institutions as education borderlands founded on coloniality, we aim to contextualize the trajectories of Chicana/o/x students along their preK–20 trajectories as they maintain aspirations, resist the marginalizing process, and pursue educational success. Patel noted that coloniality in the US "involves settlers coming from other lands and engaging in intertwined projects of erasure of Indigeneity and anti-Blackness to preserve property rights for whites."[44] The public education system in the US was founded to reinforce such colonial relations and marginalize the Mexican ancestors of Chicana/o/x students.[45]

The US schooling system was used to bolster the state's abilities to "other" Chicana/o/x communities. Public officials believed that schools "were instruments of assimilation," which motivated the "inclusion" of Mexican children in public schooling systems.[46] Four key strategies were used to racialize and other individuals of Mexican descent through the public schooling system.[47] First, by the late 1800s, Catholic church officials were removed from the education sector and white individuals controlled the state, local, and county-elected positions in California, Texas, and New Mexico, thereby controlling public education legislation.[48] Second, as a response to increasing numbers of children of Mexican descent, the Spanish language was removed from public schools and speaking Spanish would warrant physical abuse.[49] Third, "school officials subtracted Mexican culture from the public school curriculum"; the curriculum was Anglocentric, presented a "distorted, stereotypical view" of Mexican Americans, and eliminated any "Mexican heritage" materials.[50]

Finally, in order to successfully marginalize Mexican communities, elected officials established a segregated society and schooling system through various covenants and legislations.[51] In order to segregate

Mexican families, they were framed in a racist perspective as a culturally inferior group. With Mexican individuals representing 90 percent of the agricultural workforce, US farmers and white citizenry benefited economically from marginalizing the communities and aimed to reproduce a cheap labor force. Mexican American children were part of the racist IQ movement, which was used to justify their exclusion from traditional public schools. By claiming that Mexican students maintained inherently inferior intelligence levels, they were segregated to schools that aimed to "cleanse them of cultural defects," Americanize students, and provide a limited vocational education, often through physically and emotionally abusive practices.[52]

Such a brief historical overview allows for the connection between colonial structures and the education system, which were used to maintain an inferior racial caste system. Through the lens of deservingness and borderlands, next, we will show that Chicana/o/x students continue to encounter these four strategies in their schooling.

Deservingness

Patel argues that *deservingness* continues to be used with the aim to reinforce coloniality because "the relationship of person to state is the foundational purpose of the trope of deservingness, who deserves to be included under the state, and who . . . must be stateless."[53] In other words, deservingness is used by the state to legitimize existence and define who belongs and who does not belong in the US Deservingness justifies who does and does not deserve to benefit from a quality education.[54] As such, stereotypes, laws, and policies represent arsenal weapons used to define and reinforce exclusion. Patel argued that understanding the application of deservingness among various populations would serve as a strategy to resist continued coloniality.[55] To that end, we use deservingness to contextualize the contemporary conditions present in both the preK–12 and higher education systems.

Borderlands

The notion of *borderlands* is founded on structures of colonization and deservingness. Similar to Patel, who noted the "long-standing" structures of coloniality and deservingness, Anzaldúa defined borderlands as a "residue" of colonization.[56] Anzaldúa theorized that borderlands are both physical and psychological: "Borders are set up to define the places that, are safe and unsafe, to distinguish us from them . . . A borderland is a vague and undetermined place created by the emotional residue of an unnatural boundary."[57] In other words, borderlands are present in spaces where colonization once existed and multiple cultures (or worlds) collide with one another.

The four colonial mechanisms just mentioned, which were used to establish who deserved access to a quality education in the US education system, remain in place and represent the education borderlands. First, the majority of teachers and educational leaders in preK–12 and faculty in higher education are white. Taking into consideration that over 80 percent of teachers in preK–12 schools identify as white women, whose subject positions tend to create relations of pastoral care and beneficence rather than power disruption, we contend that lack of access to a teaching force that is representative of student backgrounds becomes a colonial project.[58] Overall, preK–12 schooling structures and teachers contribute to internalized racism and self-doubt among Chicana/o/x students.[59] Furthermore, undocumented students are told blatantly by local, state, and national legislative actions (and lack of action) that they do not belong in preK–12 education and postsecondary education.[60]

Second, until recent years, bilingual education was often nonexistent, and states have attempted to outlaw it in preK–12 schools; in California, it was through Proposition 227. A recent movement of dual-language immersion programs is also problematic, particularly because of the way that "uncritical implementation of two-way immersion can serve as a double-edged sword that commodifies Latin@s' linguistic resources."[61] Third, Chicana/o/x culture and history continue to be nonexistent in the preK–12 curriculum, and racialized curricular experiences contribute to internalized racism.[62] Furthermore, legislators and individuals in power continue to prevent the curriculum from reflecting Mexican history and culture. For instance, Arizona passed HB 2281 as a racist (and unlawful) attempt to eliminate the teaching of Mexican American studies. In 2018, the California governor overturned AB 2772, which aimed to establish a pilot program that required students to enroll in a semester-long ethnic studies course. Time and again, the policies and practices enacted in the public education system are designed to exclude Chicana/o/x students from belonging.

Finally, schools are racially segregated in the present time, even more than before *de jure* segregation was overturned with *Brown v. Board of Education*.[63] Within the segregated majority Chicana/o/x or Latina/o/x schools, students likely do not have adequate resources to learn.[64] As a result, the academic outcomes of Chicana/o/x students are no surprise; only about 23 percent of Latina/o/x students have an associate degree or higher.[65]

Given the colonial foundation of preK–12 and higher education structures and its lingering mechanisms, we use borderlands theory to contextualize the experiences of Chicana/o/x students along the higher education pipeline.[66] In doing so, we build on the work of previous scholars who have found the concept of borderlands useful when examining the experiences of Chicana/o/x and Latina/o/x students in both preK–12 and higher education contexts.[67] These studies highlight that education structures represent spaces where Chicana/o/x and Latina/o/x students have to navigate hostile contexts.[68]

Chicana/o/x Students as Atravesadas/os/xs in the Education Borderlands

In line with deservingness,[69] Anzaldúa explained that within the borderlands, "the prohibited and forbidden are its inhabitants. *Los atravesados* live here. . .those who cross over, pass' over, or go through the confines of the 'normal.'"[70] She labeled individuals who did not belong in society as *atravesados*, who lived within the borderlands (both psychologically and physically); they were individuals defined as not belonging within the US. Anzaldúa's (1987) theorizing is in line with Patel, regarding statelessness, belonging, and deservingness.[71] We therefore frame Chicana/o/x students as *atravesadas/os/xs* who navigate colonial schooling structures, which were not established for their academic success. In other words, this book is rooted in the notion that US educational institutions were not established to provide Chicana/o/x students with access to knowledge production, intersubjective relations, and labor. The nexus of this context is established in the education system through an unwillingness to engage in processes required to prepare Chicana/o/x to enter positions of power where they are knowledge producers.

Represented by the black arrow in figure 1.1, we illustrate that the education borderlands ostracize Chicana/o/x students as *atravesadas/os/x*, or transgressors, who are pushed out of the education system by framing them as individuals who do not belong. We argue that within the educational borderlands, Chicana/o/x students represent atravesadas/os/xs because they experience a subjugating educational system, one that reminds them they do not belong and do not deserve an education. Numerous scholars have established that Chicana/o/x and Latina/o/x students experience inequities and marginalization in preK–12 and higher education contexts.[72] Such a context aligns with previous research, which documented that majority Latina/o/x schools are more likely than majority white schools to be overcrowded and lack qualified teachers.[73] Majority Latina/o/x schools also maintain "severe shortages of college preparation teachers and advanced placement classes."[74] A lack of resources then contributes to limited access to college preparation curricula and college information for Latina/o/x students.[75]

Moreover, high school counselors often have low expectations, underestimate the academic potential, and attempt to limit the educational aspirations of Latina/o/x students.[76] Latina/o/x students also experience a criminalizing and policed high school context, which reinforces the notion of educational borderlands.[77] Through underfunding, policing, and academic underpreparation, Chicana/o/x students are positioned within the education borderlands as *atravesadas*.

La Facultad de los Atravesada/o/xs

Nevertheless, Anzaldúa also establishes that, as *atravesados*, Chicana/o/x individuals have access to la facultad.[78] In figure 1.2, we propose that while the education borderlands prepare students to view the world from a deficit Eurocentric perspective, their experiences with living on the margins of society and navigating the physical and psychological borderlands allows them to enact la facultad and see the underlying US structures of inequality. Anzaldúa explained that atravesados live on the margins of society and navigate the physical and psychological borderlands.[79] She argued, "There is a rebel in me—the Shadow-Beast. It is a part of me that refuses to take orders from outside authorities. It refuses to take orders from my conscious will, it threatens the sovereignty of my rulership."[80] Anzaldúa

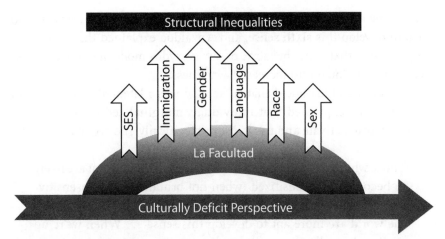

FIGURE 1.2   *La facultad de los atravesada/o/xs*

argued that as a queer Chicana, the Shadow-Beast fueled her to resist the marginalization process.[81] This framework is rooted in the findings we present in chapter 2, in which the student participants share their experiences with la facultad and highlight that it is interconnected with hope. In particular, the student experiences establish that while they are able to identify various inequities through la facultad, they are able to sustain their hope for a better future through education.

Anzaldua (1987) explained that as atravesados, individuals can enact la facultad. She defined la facultad as

> the capacity to see in surface phenomena the meaning of deeper realities, to see the deep structure below the surface. It is an instant "sensing," a quick perception arrived at without conscious reasoning. It is an acute awareness mediated by the part of the psyche that does not speak, that communicates in images and symbols which are the faces of feelings, that is, behind which feelings reside/hide. The one possessing this sensitivity is excruciatingly alive to the world.[82]

La facultad entails the ability to beyond the superficial; it allows for individuals to see structures below surfaces; it is a sixth sense of awareness.[83] Those who are on the margins of society develop la facultad, especially when they are feeling oppressed or experience pain.[84] Such fear can also help to develop this sixth sense, and Anzaldúa explained that "confronting anything that tears the fabric of our everyday mode of consciousness" sends an individual into increased awareness.[85]

While Anzaldúa noted that la facultad was a latent ability present in everyone, she explained that individuals marginalized in society were more likely to activate and use it. More specifically, she argued:

> Those who are pushed out of the tribe for being different are likely to become more sensitized (when not brutalized into insensitivity). Those who do not feel psychologically or physically safe in the world are more apt to develop this sense . . . When we're up against the wall, when we have all sorts of oppressions coming at us, we are forced to develop this faculty so that we'll know when the next person is going to slap us or lock us away . . . It's a kind of survival tactic that people, caught between the worlds, unknowingly cultivate.[86]

In other words, when individuals are in spaces where they are othered and under pressure, they can enact la facultad as an ability to survive within these hostile environments.[87]

This book builds on a small number of existing studies that begin to examine the role of la facultad in the educational trajectories of Chicana/o/x students. In particular, Acevedo-Gil bridged the college choices experiences of Chicana/o/x students with their transition to college by finding that they enacted la facultad to anticipate postsecondary obstacles.[88] This process entails Latina/o/x students anticipating that they will experience postsecondary obstacles related to their immigration status, first-generation status, low-income background, and/or academic preparation, which the students then experienced at some level once in college.[89] Most recently, Muñoz intersected la facultad with cultural citizenship to exemplify that "politicized Latina/o/x undocumented students" navigate various spaces as they develop an understanding of their legality and "hone their critical legal consciousness."[90]

In her later work, Anzaldúa noted the ability to navigate coloniality by enacting la facultad. In other words, enacting la facultad can facilitate the process of developing skills, which is why we contend that enacting la facultad as a form of knowledge within spaces of *nepantla* connects with other toolsets used by Latina/o/x students to access and navigate higher education, such as epistemology of a brown body, pedagogies of the home, funds of knowledge, and community cultural wealth.[91] All of these represent various forms of knowledge rooted in the intersectional experiences and historical knowledges of Latina/o/x families and communities.

Because the framework of community cultural wealth includes many of the forms of knowledge and has been cited widely since its publication, we focus our discussion on the connection between la facultad and community cultural wealth, which represents the various forms of knowledge that Communities of Color employ to navigate schools and other social systems.[92] Yosso and Solórzano acknowledged that a CRT framework served as an asset-based lens to reveal insights that individuals with a deficit lens could not see.[93] They explained: "We assert that CRT helps researchers, teachers, and policy makers 'see' the cultural wealth (as opposed to deficits) in marginalized communities."[94] We contend that their explanation aligns with la facultad as the ability to "see beneath the surface" of deficit interpretations and definitions of Communities of Color to understand that "cultural wealth is found in the histories and lives of Communities of Color and has gone unrecognized and/or unacknowledged."[95] This process is represented by the hope, resistance, and success of Chicana/o/x students highlighted in this book.

Although community cultural wealth originally entailed sixteen forms of capital, Yosso narrowed it down to six—but it is important to note that the six forms of capital are not "mutually exclusive or static"; instead, they inform one another and overlap.[96] Yosso defined familial capital as the cultural knowledge that is nurtured within and between *familia* and that carries a sense of community history, memory, and cultural intuition.[97] Memory and cultural intuition particularly align with la facultad as a form of knowledge that may not be explained but is used to guide both researchers and students in the preK–20 educational pipeline.[98]

Resistant capital includes the skills that individuals develop when challenging inequality. Students develop these skillsets develop because they resist subordination.[99] When considering that la facultad also develops in order to survive and thrive in marginalizing contexts, there is an alignment with resistant capital. Navigational capital refers to skills that are used to maneuver social institutions that were "not created with communities of color in mind."[100] Cuellar and her colleagues explain that navigational capital serves to recognize "that students operate in liminal spaces within educational contexts and adapt to these new cultures."[101] Although they do not use an Anzaldúan lens, the explanation represents a clear connection with using la facultad to navigate liminal and overlapping cultures present in the borderlands through nepantla. Therefore, we conceptualize that Chicana/o/x students engage with their facultad to navigate the marginalizing contexts within education borderlands.

As mentioned previously, Students of Color are holders and creators of knowledge; their knowledge informs the ways in which they respond to and resist against multiple axes of domination.[102] Chicana/o/x student experiences represent a source of knowledge to refine current understandings of how inequality impacts Chicana/o/x first-generation college students in the US. We take an intersectional approach in this framework to highlight that Chicana/o/x students understand that various factors of inequality are not additive, but multiplicative—which in turn shapes their perceived chances of succeeding despite existing social inequalities.[103]

The Framework of *Atravesada/o/xs Nepantleando*

Our results suggest that Chicana/o/x college students understand and define an inequality framework. Rooted in Chicana/o/x student experiences, we propose the Framework of Atravesada/o/xs Nepantleando (FAN). Through FAN, we explain that intersecting identities allow students to see various structural inequities and critique institutional processes that reproduce marginalization. The bottom arrow in figure 1.2, labeled Culturally Deficit Perspective, acknowledges the colonial roots of education that reproduce a deficit perception of Chicana/o/x students and communities. The concept of pedagogies of the home, as Delgado Bernal proposes, places cultural knowledge at the forefront to understand lessons from local communities and homes spaces.[104] That process is represented by La Facultad in figure 1.2, which serves as a convex lens that Chicana/o/x students use to see that institutions produce various inequities. In other words, la facultad informs the development of a student's critical consciousness. The student experiences help to identify that knowledge develops from various marginalization experiences, which highlights the importance of us moving beyond understanding inequalities to challenging them. Thus, we continue by explaining that the student interview data resulted in the Framework of Atravesada/o/xs Nepantleando.

Anzaldúa clarifies that "those who survive are apt to display la facultad and may choose to function as nepantleras."[105] Thus, the interview and testimonio findings presented in chapters 2 through 6 allow us to dig deeper into FAN (see figure 1.3). In the chapters, we denote that after enacting la facultad, atravesadas may navigate the education system as nepantleras. This process highlights that Chicana/o/x students who are deemed "unworthy" transgressors/atravesadas by policies, practices, and ideologies use la facultad to navigate the education system as nepantleras. In this process, la facultad facilitates the transformation of the hope maintained as atravesados to resist as nepantleras and successfully navigate systems of higher education.

Before defining nepantleras, it is important to understand the notion of nepantla. *Nepantla* is a Nahuatl word representing the in-between space of multiple and overlapping worlds, which resembles the space of borderlands.[106] Anzaldúa theorized that "living between cultures results in 'seeing' double, first from the perspective of one culture, then from the perspective of another. Seeing from two or more perspectives simultaneously renders those cultures as transparent."[107] Thus, when in nepantla, a nepantlera has the ability to see multiple cultures in their overlapping,

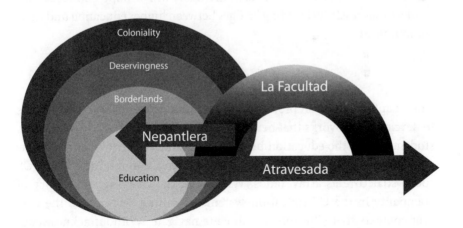

FIGURE 1.3   Framework of Atravesada/o/xs Nepantleando: la facultad facilitating the process for atravesadas/os/xs to navigate the education system as nepantleras/os/xs

complementing, or conflicting relationships. Nepantleras "are threshold people: they move within and among multiple often conflicting, worlds."[108] Mignolo reminds readers that "nepantla is not a happy place in the middle."[109] Nepantleras are susceptible to wounds, including isolation and rejection from their conflicting worlds.[110] Nevertheless, a nepantlera aims to transform perspectives and possibilities. In being able to see multiple perspectives and identify with multiple cultures, nepantleras also aim to build bridges between these worlds.

We build on previous studies by proposing the FAN based on the student narratives presented in this book. We know that first-generation Chicana/o/x college students navigate multiple worlds when adjusting to college, including family, peers, work, and college.[111] During this time of negotiating multiple worlds and demands, students experience nepantla as a liminal space as they successfully navigate the multiple and colliding cultures present in higher education.[112] We also know that, through painstaking work, Chicana/o/x families develop metaphorical bridges between communities by navigating liminal spaces.[113] The student testimonios in chapters 3 through 6 illustrate the lived experiences of Chicana/o/x students as they navigate higher education with the aim to benefit their communities. In those chapters, we use the Framework of Atravesada/o/xs Nepantleando to exemplify that Chicana/o/x students navigate higher education systems successfully as individuals whose hope and resistance results in successfully building bridges between higher education and their communities.

Chapter Summary

This chapter is built on previous studies guided by our research findings to develop frameworks that better explain the experiences of Chicana/o/x students. First, the education borderlands framework provides a foundation to contextualize the position of Chicana/o/x communities in the US social structure as atravesados. Without acknowledging the history of coloniality in the US education system, we cannot understand the current contexts that Chicana/o/x students navigate. Without acknowledging the marginalizing structures, we cannot understand why and how a Chicana/o/x student succeeds in transitioning from an atravesado—one who has not belonged in education—to a nepantlera—one who can navigate multiple cultures and systems, even if in future moments, they feel like they do not belong. With the Framework of Atravesadas/os/xs Nepantleando, we assert that by experiencing inequities, la facultad allows los atravesados to see the structures present in US society that aim to reproduce the marginalization of Chicana/o/x communities.

Chapter 2 begins with the experiences of Chicana/o/x students to show that they consider and think about the marginalizing contexts that they navigate. As we attempt to transform schooling structures, the information presented in chapter 2 is important to consider because the education system is interconnected with other social structures. Thus, the student survey data in chapter 2 serves to detail that first-generation Chicana/o/x college students used la facultad to move from a deficit understanding of cultural-based stereotypes toward seeing and operationalizing structures of inequality. Finally, data from hundreds of student interviews and testimonios served to conceptualize the Framework of Atravesada/o/xs Nepantleando as a process that entails atravesados using la facultad to navigate institutions as nepantleras who accessed institutional resources with the intent to support their communities.

The culminating Framework of Atravesada/o/xs Nepantleando presented in this chapter is representative of *The Chicana/o/x Dream*. We remind the reader that inequities and marginalization persist, but we concentrate on highlighting that, as atravesadas/os/x, Chicana/o/x students use their facultad to resist marginalization and transform into nepantleras by tapping into various institutional resources to navigate college, while successfully ensuring that their communities also have access to higher education pathways. We use the framework and student voices ultimately to recommend specific policies, practices, and pedagogical approaches that address the experiences relevant to the intersectional identities students embraced and discussed throughout the book.

Chapter 2

(with Socorro E. Cambero)

Engaging la Facultad to Explain Marginalizing Processes

It would be Asian, not because of more opportunities, but they look for it more. You see, it's harder for Asians to get into universities, but they put effort into it. Hispanics, and African Americans, it's not as frequent. Asians themselves have the advantage because they are hardworking. Stereotypes [are] true. It's because they put effort, that's why the stereotype [exists].

—Diego, Chicano, age twenty-one

To me inequality in America means not being able to feel comfortable in your own skin, in other words not being able to fully express your gender, sexuality or how you identify yourself because of what society expects from you. Inequality means not being treated the same because you are a female instead of male or vice versa. However, opportunity in America means having access to higher education regardless of your sex, gender, ethnicity or legal status within the country. Opportunity means, being able to have access to free health care, free education, and free social services.

—Alejandra, Chicana, age twenty

AS PRESENTED IN CHAPTER ONE, the Framework of Atravesadas/os/x Nepantleando entails Chicana/o/x students navigating higher education successfully with the intent of building bridges between their communities and higher education. Before navigating higher education as atravesadas/os/x nepantleando, the process includes Chicana/o/x students being framed as atravesadas/os/x, tapping into their facultad, and

37

accessing resources. In this chapter, we draw on data from interviews with Chicana/o/x first-generation college students to exemplify that, as atravesada/o/xs, Chicana/o/x individuals have access to la facultad—what we call the Facultad de los Atravesada/o/xs.

The data derives from fifty-four Chicana/o/x students from a California Hispanic-Serving Institution (HSI) that has a Carnegie Classification as a public four-year university with very high research activity. On the one hand, the Facultad de los Atravesada/o/xs accounts for both Chicanos and Chicanas using cultural explications, such as stereotypes, a hard-work ethic, and ethnic values as part of the inequality and opportunity puzzle and thus further obfuscating the structure and culture binary. Diego, for instance, states, "Asians . . . are hardworking. Stereotypes [are] true. It's because they put effort, that's why the stereotype [exists]." On the other hand, we highlight that Chicana/o/x students use la facultad to identify and operationalize structural factors, such as racism, sexism, and the lack of economic opportunities, perpetuating social inequalities. As evidenced by Alejandra's statement at the start of the chapter, once students can access la facultad, they deploy more nuanced and intersectional understandings of these material factors of inequalities. We therefore explore and complicate the two opposite ends of the spectrum throughout this chapter.

As indicated in our education borderlands framework, the education system intersects with other institutions to (re)produce a negative and deficit narrative of Chicana/o/x communities. It is within such oppressive contexts that students enact their facultad. As Anzaldúa elaborated, "Personal and collective setbacks, obstacles, and oppressions which the dominant culture puts on mestizas/Chicanas and turn them around into facultades, into positive aspects, into skills, into learning how to cope with stress and oppression."[1] In other words la facultad serves as a skill to navigate hostile institutions, such as higher education.

We highlight that ethnorace and gender shape students' understanding and explanation of marginalization in the borderlands. When students used cultural explanations, they referred to ideologies, values, norms, and beliefs of ethnoracial communities that often attribute inequality to stereotypes. Nevertheless, the majority of students used structural explanations of inequality as a matter of political economy, such as how social, political, and economic capital are organized and stratified within the

United States. Individuals' social locations, such as race, class, and gender, often play a major role in shaping people's life outcomes and people's positions in explaining social stratifications. Chicana/o/x respondents shed light on the ways inequality in the United States manifests as a product of structural factors, such as unequal power distribution, racism, income inequality, lack of institutional resources. Next, we provide examples of both cultural and structural explanations.

Narratives and Perceptions of (In)equality and Opportunities

Chicana/o/x students face various sociocultural obstacles in their educational experiences that often complicate their actual socioeconomic outlooks and trajectories. In particular, socioeconomic status, gender, and immigration status of Chicana/o/x youths often dictate the ways in which they understand their positions in the larger social structure, the opportunity structures, and their perceptions of the American dream.[2] At the same time, Chicana/o/x students likely experience internalized racism due to racialized experiences that occur in preK–12 curriculum and interactions with teachers.[3] Let's now turn to the perspectives of Chicana/o/x college students in the higher education borderlands.

Chicana/o/x students in this study, as figure 2.1 shows, consider various contributing factors of US inequality, ranging from cultural to structural factors. Nuanced gendered differences abound in how these factors contribute to larger social inequality, as also shown in figure 2.1. The most prominent contributing factors to inequality identified by both Chicanas and Chicanos were structural: racism and socioeconomic status (SES; 53 percent each among Chicanas, 46 percent each among Chicanos), followed by educational opportunities or (32 percent among Chicanas, 30 percent among Chicanos). Unsurprisingly, Chicanas were more acutely aware of gender inequalities than Chicanos: it was the third most frequently mentioned factor of inequality among Chicanas at 28 percent. On the other hand, stereotypes (26 percent) was the third most prominent contributing factor to social inequality among Chicanos. Overall, both Chicanos and Chicanas were acutely aware of the structural factors as perpetuating social inequalities in the contemporary American society. Yet they were

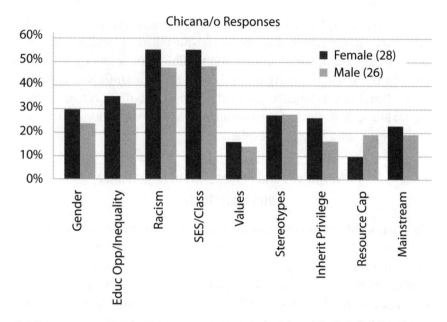

FIGURE 2.1   Perceptions of existing inequalities by Chicana/o students

also cognizant of the cultural dimensions of inequality, such as stereotypes, values, and those characteristics considered out of the mainstream, such as immigrant status, skin color, and language skills.

Our interview findings further illuminated these conceptualizations among Chicana/o/x respondents, informed by their own structural and cultural experiences of social inequalities. Intersectionality scholars have repeatedly argued and found that multiple forms of inequality simultaneously affect individuals' experiences and perceptions.[4] Likewise, Chicana/o/x students occupy a unique position in the society, as their social marginalization is multiplicative. They are subjugated and discriminated against in the larger American society as ethnoracial minoritized people and immigrants or children of immigrants; additional subjugation as women, sexual minorities, and coming from a disadvantaged social background may also burden many of them. However, these different forms of subjugation do not apply to Chicana/o/x individuals uniformly. As Patricia Hill Collins has argued in her conceptualization of the matrix of domination, systems of oppression exist and intersect, influencing the penalties and privileges that individuals experience based on their identities.[5]

Toward *La Facultad de los Atravesada/o/xs*

As shown in McCabe's, Conchas's, and other seminal scholars' work on education and social inequality, these experiences of Chicana/o/x youths are seldom reflected upon at the institutional level, and Chicana/o/x students often express frustration in feeling marginalized, unwelcomed, and tokenized.[6] However, we find that Chicana/o/x students do not simply accept these experiences of marginalization; rather, they turn these experiences into knowledge. Feminist standpoint theorists have argued for the importance of considering one's standpoint in the society as a starting point for enquiry.[7] From this perspective, Chicana/o/x individuals are not only occupants of a standpoint, but also knowing subjects in their own rights, rather than objects known by others.

Based on the data, we name the process of critical consciousness among the students as the *Facultad de los Atravesada/o/xs*, informed by Chicana feminist theoretical paradigms. As mentioned previously, Students of Color are holders and creators of knowledge, and their knowledge informs the ways in which they respond to and resist against multiple áxes of domination.[8] We view Chicana/o/x students' responses as a source of knowledge in refining current understandings of how inequality impacts Chicana/o/x first-generation college students in America. Therefore, we take an intersectional approach to propose that Chicana/o/x students understand that various factors of inequality are not necessarily additive, but multiplicative; such multiplicative understandings in turn shape the ways in which they perceive their chances of succeeding despite existing social inequalities.[9] We suggest that the *Facultad de los Atravesada/o/xs* process best captures how the respondents describe inequality in the United States vis-à-vis culture and structure.

Our descriptive data suggests that they view inequality in the United States as a product of unequal power distribution, racism, income inequality, lack of resources and opportunity, and stereotyping. However, a deeper analysis into the interview data provides nuance and suggests that their perceptions of inequality differ by gender. Drawing on Anzaldúa's work on mestiza consciousness and Delgado Bernal's work on pedagogies of the home, we show that Chicanas' social critiques and conceptualizations of inequality—racism, educational inequality, and income inequality—draw upon the lessons they learn in the family, associated with the Spanish language, income inequality, racism, and job inequality that belittle Chicana/o/x families.[10] As Hurtado claims, one must analyze multiple strategies within the context of intersecting realities in order to understand Chicana/o/x resistance.[11] In so doing, the *Facultad de los Atravesada/o/xs* process is used to best understand how inequality is conceptualized across first-generation Chicana/o/x college student respondents, and it informs contemporary Chicana/o/x resistance toward ideologies depicting the Chicana/o/x community through a deficit lens that link both representation and social structure.

Chicana feminists have written extensively on and contend Students of Color, particularly Chicana students, as holders and creators of knowledge; they engage in formal (academic) and informal (home/community) knowledge.[12] Building on a Chicana feminist perspective, we frame the knowledge that develops from marginalization as la facultad. Let's now listen to their own words, in their own voices.

Ahistorical and Stereotype Perspectives

Even though Chicana/o/x students unanimously perceived social inequalities to be rooted in structural factors, their explanations for overcoming such structural inequalities fluctuated between cultural and structural explanations. Some relied on one-dimensional cultural explanations that reify individualistic and meritocratic *model minority* typology in explaining Asian Americans' success in the United States. In these respondents' eyes, white privilege was not simply a product of racism or classism, but a combination of economic privileges and historically accumulated social networks and capital. Danny's response best captures this assessment:

> White people get more opportunities. They start off with more opportunities than immigrants because most immigrants come in not knowing much English, and then have to start at the bottom and work their way up. So future generations of immigrants have more opportunities than older generations, but obviously the Caucasians have already been here for the hundreds of years that America has existed. They've had the opportunities from the start, so they're ahead of the game.

As shown, some Chicana/o/x respondents attributed white Americans' success to a result of accumulated privileges at the expenses of low-income minoritized groups and immigrants. However, these responses lack a historical understanding of meritocracy because, by attributing access to opportunities for whites to being in the US for "hundreds of years," the participants fail to credit the history of Mexicans in the US and attribute the lack of access to opportunities to colonial structures.

Moreover, when some Chicana/o/x students make sense of the success of minoritized people, especially the success of Asian Americans, they often rely heavily on the model minority imagery, citing Asians Americans' cultural inclinations toward individuals' hard work and values in education. When asked who they think is doing well in the American society, Jamie stated, "Asians because their culture has taught them that their education is everything in life and should always come first." Similarly, Ivonne states, "I consider Asian Americans to be superior in this society because they are smart about everything they do. They know how to better themselves and know how to manage their money. And they crave to be better and be the best at what they do." Respondents like Jamie and Ivonne credited the success of Asians Americans to the Asian cultural values of emphasizing education, continued motivation, and delayed gratification. Again, through these statements, students reproduced deficit cultural stereotypes.

On top of this cultural value on education, Chicana/o/x respondents also perceive Asian Americans as exceptionally hard working. This sentiment was best captured in Diego's response: "It would be Asian, not because of more opportunities, but they look for it more. You see, it's harder for Asians to get into universities, but they put effort into it. Hispanics, and African Americans, it's not as frequent. Asians themselves have the advantage because they are hardworking. Stereotypes [are] true. It's because they put effort, that's why the stereotype." Diego's response not only reflects the prevalence and stickiness of the model minority imagery in explaining Asian Americans' success, but also resonates with the *culture of poverty* thesis that pathologizes and justifies the social subjugation and disadvantages of minoritized people as a product of their own doing.[13] By justifying racial stereotypes as "true," Diego dismissed the structural conditions that shape many Black and Latina/o/x Americans' socioeconomic precariousness and consequent inability to pursue any form of social mobility. Further, implicit in such a statement is that Asian Americans, much like Latina/o/x and African Americans, may be disadvantaged as immigrants and through racialization, but they persevere by looking for and obtaining limited opportunities through individual work ethics.

Interestingly, Chicanos simultaneously invoked meritocratic and individual ideals of opportunity and success, insinuating that opportunity is available for all and upward mobility is possible, so long as one works hard for it. Christian's statement acutely captures such a standpoint:

> Opportunity to me is something that could come at any moment, it is something that I see as the gateway. Meaning that one opportunity could lead to another. The good American dream at its finest is built on opportunities. Good old inequality is a difference. Such as wealthy individuals versus working class. Some have money and some don't. Inequality sets are social classes. It is a main case in our society. But with opportunities, you can work your way up. Without inequality, you can't have opportunities.

For respondents like Christian, social inequality was simply a byproduct of how the American opportunity structure is reinforced: the idea of "opportunities" is possible because of social inequality. Even though the majority of Chicanos acknowledge social inequality as divisive and deeply rooted in unequal class structure, the vague idea of "opportunity" is a pursuable goal regardless of one's status. Implicit in such an argument is the idea that the American Dream may be available for everyone, but only attainable so long as one is willing to work for it, further reinforcing the myth of American meritocracy and individualism in achieving success.

Defining Inequality

In juxtaposition to reifying the myth of meritocracy, the majority of respondents saw that the factors of inequality—such as socioeconomic differences, racism, and sexism—all buttress white privilege and that white Americans benefit from accumulated privileges. The most prominent theme in Chicana/o/x students' responses was the centrality of class in explaining inequality. More specifically, respondents emphasized the relationship between economic capital and access to opportunities, especially through education. According to the respondents, those with vast economic capital were likely to have access to other forms of capital, and these capitals interact concurrently and influence the opportunity one has.

Jorge perceived social inequality to impact minoritized individuals the most: "Well, inequality is usually the minorities are the ones who face it. It's not the rich people, who are well off that deal [with] it. Because America is divided in different classes, the lower class, usually the minorities, have a much harder time to access opportunities to succeed." Jorge described social inequality as a "minority problem" that rich people do not have to worry about and said that the lower socioeconomic status of minoritized people hinders them from accessing available opportunities to achieve social mobility. As evidenced in these responses, Chicana/o/x respondents can exhibit critical understandings of the relationship between their ethnoracial minoritized status and the larger socioeconomic structure that affords some individuals access to opportunities at the expenses of the hindered upward social mobility of others. Yet again, distinctive gendered conceptualizations were observed in the ways in which social inequality adversely affects minoritized individuals.

Chicanas, on the other hand, expressed a more nuanced and intersectional understanding of how structural inequalities are complicated and compounded not only by class positions, but also by other forms of marginalization. They typically resisted meritocratic and individualist ideals of upward mobility. For instance, Vanessa described inequality as complicated because various factors contribute to inequality. She stressed that inequality primarily affects minoritized people, pinpointing how socioeconomic status and ethnicity intersect to impact the opportunity a student has: "Inequality in the US is complicated and affects a lot of people but especially minorities . . . For example, most of my people [Mexican Americans] don't have aunts and uncles that are lawyers and doctors to help us gain access to a career path that can lead to higher SES [socioeconomic status]. It's a lot harder to 'make it' just relying on the people you know to help you get your career on track." Vanessa's response highlights that education level among family members is an important factor for the opportunities one has in America but candidly states that minoritized groups have historically been affected by occupational inequality.

Similarly, Alejandra described inequality and opportunity as anti-thetical, contingent on various factors:

> To me inequality in America means not being able to feel comfort-able in your own skin, in other words not being able to fully express your gender, sexuality, or how you identify yourself because of what society expects from you . . . However, opportunity in Amer-ica means having access to higher education regardless of your sex, gender, ethnicity, or legal status within the country. Opportu-nity means being able to have access to free health care, free edu-cation, and free social services.

Whereas most of the males saw inequality and opportunity to be different sides of the same coin, Alejandra's perceptions directly challenged those of the men and are, furthermore, antithetical. She illuminates that a mestiza experiences the world by straddling various opposing power structures that embody a normative identity, which grants a person opportunity, whereas embodying a deviant identity will engender inequality.[14] More importantly, Alejandra employed a critical race perspective because she saw the intersection of race and class to examine opportunity and inequal-ity in America. In other words, if one embodies an identity deviating from normativity—being a woman, a Person of Color, nonheterosexual, or an immigrant—they are systemically marginalized when trying to access social services, health care, and education. As Alejandra emanates, oppor-tunity and inequality are dichotomies; opportunity is power; inequality is a ramification of lacking power.

Further, Arianna saw the intricate and intersectional power relations embedded in contemporary American society: "I think inequality is still present in race and gender. I think everyone is offered the same opportuni-ties, yet white males still obtain better job positions and wages." Chicana respondents, like Alejandra and Arianna, not only invoked intersectional understandings and relationships among social inequality and oppor-tunities in the United States, but they were also more likely to rebuke meritocratic or individual ideals and suggest that other factors also simul-taneously perpetuate inequality in America. Chicana respondents did not deny that opportunities exist in the contemporary American society; rather, they critically acknowledged that these opportunities were only available for a small segment of privileged individuals, such as white men, while further systematically marginalizing certain identities as inferior to those deemed normative.

Abilities to See Inequality and Unequal Opportunities

Many respondents in this study connected their experiences and perceptions of social inequality in the United States to their immigrant and/or ethnoracial minoritized backgrounds. In so doing, Chicana/o/x students often equated immigrant background or ethnoracial minoritized status with low socioeconomic status and with an impediment to achieving social mobility. Implicit in such understanding is the conceptualization of inequality as rooted in the exploitation and marginalization of People of Color.

Zulema explained that not only are minoritized individuals more directly affected by social inequality in the United States, but inequality also persists as a result of more privileged people's willful ignorance toward a myriad of social issues that do not affect them:

> Inequality in the United States is complicated and affects a lot of people, but especially minorities. The people who face it are more aware of the extent of it as a major issue because they see every day how it affects their life and future. People who are higher SES [socioeconomic status] or nonminority don't really see it as an urgent issue because they don't face inequality in their everyday lives and don't feel that it poses a real barrier for them.

Zulema's response elucidates the hidden privilege of white and/or socioeconomically advantaged individuals in contemporary American society: they have the luxury to ignore the ramifications of social inequality because they do not have to experience them. Instead of trying to understand the effects of these social problems and tackling them as a society, more privileged individuals either turn a blind eye to these issues or rely on their preconceived notions to justify persisting inequality as a result of disadvantaged individuals' own doings.

Even though many Chicana/o/x students referred to their immigrant family background to explain their own experiences of social inequality in the United States, the ways in which they discussed their immigrant backgrounds differed by gender. More specifically, Chicanos stated their backgrounds rather matter-of-factly and in relation to their lower socioeconomic status, whereas Chicanas portrayed vividly that their own immigrant parents or Mexican immigrants in general are marginalized and exploited, critically analyzing how inequality traps many immigrant families in poverty. Jesus related his experiences of inequality to his parents' previous undocumented status:

> In America, inequality is very common, especially in my experience. I am a son of two former illegal Mexican immigrants and grew up belonging to the lower economic class. I have experienced inequality for a majority of my life and witnessed it in my hometown. Opportunity in America is definitely there, since I believe I have the opportunity to move the economic classes. The problem is that inequality limits one's own opportunities because of the resources available to each individual. I have nowhere [near] the same resources as a middle-class individual in order to match their spectrum of opportunities.

For Jesus, his parents' previous undocumented status contributed to his family's low socioeconomic status and his difficult upbringing. Although he was aware of unequal distribution of resources, he believed it was a matter of a "spectrum of opportunities" and that he could achieve upward social mobility through whatever opportunities became available for him. Jesus's response was typical of many Chicano respondents; they perceived the socioeconomic disadvantages they experienced and/or witnessed as stemming from their minority backgrounds as children of poor immigrants and/or minoritized people. Yet they did not go into details of the hardships their immigrant parents experienced, nor did they show any suspicion of the premise of "opportunities for all." Rather, they believed that even the most disadvantaged people could access opportunities, however limited they may be, and that upward mobility is possible. Again, they invoked both individualistic and meritocratic attitudes in explaining social inequality and opportunities they had access to with an immigrant background in the United States.

Defining Structures That Reproduce Social Inequality

The next largest contributing factor for inequality after racism (46 percent), SES/class (46 percent), and educational opportunities (31 percent) among Chicana/o/x respondents was stereotypes (26 percent). Many of the respondents referenced stereotypes that criminalize Chicana/o/x individuals but benefit white people. Rafael, for instance, reflected on white people benefiting from the barriers minority groups encounter as a result of unequal treatment: "Inequality is barriers placed upon certain groups of people that other groups won't have to face, from stereotyping, unequal police treatment, unequal sentences, discrimination, racism. Whites are most successful; they don't have barriers to jump, often stereotyped in a good way. White privilege and institutions are set up for them to succeed." Rafael discussed that white people unconsciously benefit from the negative stereotyping impacting minoritized groups, such as racial profiling, racism, and discrimination. Enrique also conveyed a similar sentiment, stating, "Those of white descent are the superior ones. There is not any stereotyping or racial profiling which makes for better opportunities." The respondents stated that white people benefit from a system of stereotypes that deems white people as "dominant" or the "superior race." As such, white people benefit directly from positive stereotypes depicting them as fit for opportunities, marginalizing Chicana/o/x communities and perpetuating negative stereotypes. In other words, negative stereotypes contribute to society's understanding of Chicana/o/x people as atravesados who are undeserving and incapable of being in positions of power.

Interestingly, a specific theme that emerged *only* from Chicanas' responses was that society associates Spanish language in the US with inferiority in mainstream society. Many Chicana respondents shared that Spanish is not regarded as highly as English in America and frequently connected this sentiment with American schools. As we mentioned in chapter one, the education borderlands framework takes into account that through coloniality, Spanish in schools has historically been subject to scrutiny in the United States. Considering that fluent bilingual Latina/o/x students often prefer to speak Spanish in households, Spanish is central to the Chicana/o/x cultural identity.[15] While the deficit framing of speaking Spanish is meant to marginalize students, Chicana participants enacted their facultad to see beneath the structures of marginalization and reframe speaking Spanish as an asset.

As Rosa asserted, discrimination against and marginalization of the Spanish language in the larger society unfairly labels Latina/o/x students as inferior, undermining their capabilities, while highlighting and centralizing their "weaknesses." She stated, "White people are given more opportunities in terms of educational resources, acceptance and primary language, providing them with an advantage. Latinos for example in elementary and even up to high school are required to take tests that test their ability to speak and understand the English language, our capabilities are based off tests that limit us." Rosa's response discloses that social acceptance, education, and language intersect and perpetuate inequalities in the classroom. In other words, if students are viewed as non-native English speakers, they are systematically marginalized from higher education because of their unfamiliarity with the English language; language becomes another form of defining Chicana/o/x students as atravesados who do not belong in education. Valenzuela noted that students enrolled in English as a second language classes were labeled as having "limited English," rather than being labeled as "Spanish dominant."[16] Such a narrative places the blame on one's language and fails to provide a space where students can capitalize their strengths. Moreover, it is rooted in the four colonial strategies to marginalize Chicana/o/x communities and divulges the patent racist structures that deem Chicana/o/x culture—and perhaps the larger Latina/o/x culture—as inferior to American culture.

Rosa also complicated the traditional education system through a mestiza viewpoint. She asserted that the traditional education system not only reduces students to simple recipients of knowledge, but further reproduces social inequality via the testing platform and the language barrier. Spanish-dominant students are particularly vulnerable to such added marginalizing mechanisms in educational institutions. First, the language barrier impedes Spanish-dominant students' abilities to understand the test content. Second, meritocratic logic assumes testing is an adequate form to measure academic potential but negates the lifelong harmful implications of high-stakes tests.[17] Thus, Rosa's response heeds the additional barriers that Spanish-dominant youth experience when their academic performance is tested, which reinforces deficit discourses deeming Chicana/o/x students academically incompetent.

Chicana respondents, like Janet, use their facultad to subvert such mainstream assertions and present a paradigm shift that recognizes Spanish as an asset and strength, rather than a barrier: "People who aren't from America aren't given the same opportunities that Americans who were born here have. Immigrants from Mexico aren't given the same opportunities as Americans because they might have bad English, but it doesn't always mean that they can't perform the task the same, or maybe even better than an American." Janet stated that immigrants from Mexico do not have the same opportunities due to Spanish being perceived by others as a barrier and inhibition to completing tasks, poignantly stating that immigrants' native language is devalued in the workforce. Janet's response is also exemplary of Chicanas rejecting and challenging the idea of American meritocracy: although upward mobility is imagined to be achievable by everybody, so long as one works hard, this is not the case for those who experience language barriers.

Janet also candidly stated that Spanish speakers are just as capable of completing the tasks English speakers can. Like many other Chicana respondents, Janet's use of la facultad was evident because she grappled with contradicting power dynamics by bringing attention to a paradox: the language many Mexican people carry, which is viewed as inferior, is not an obstacle but an asset. By paying particular attention to the process of English perpetuating inequality in America, it becomes evident that Chicanas are aware that the Spanish language is viewed as a deficit by society, but they engage with la facultad to embark in conversations challenging the discourse. Their critiques are a form of resistance as they enact their facultad to reflect on opposing power dynamics and straddle different worlds: one where Latina/o/x culture is embraced through practices such as language, and a second world where the Spanish language is devalued.

Chicana students exhibited more nuanced understandings of social inequality in relation to their immigrant family backgrounds. As Lopez finds, daughters in immigrant families are more likely to have a dual frame of reference for and deeper understanding of parental sacrifice and struggles.[18] This is exactly what Chicana respondents referred to in their conceptualization of social inequalities, as shown in Amelia's response:

> Most Mexican immigrants come to the US with very little resources in order to provide a better future for their family. They

usually need to take odd jobs and jobs that take advantage of the
fact that they're undocumented. They use that as leverage against
them if they want higher pay or want to complain. [Immigrants]
aren't given the same opportunities to grow that citizens have.
They're unable to pay for their children's tuition.

In her response, Amelia made the connection between economic capital and educational opportunities. She also drew from particular vul-
nerabilities immigrants that face in their attempts to provide a "better
future for their family." Like Amelia, many Chicana respondents invoked
the immigrant narratives—recognizing the difficulties immigrant families endure to support and provide for their children—and connected
their parents' immigrant struggles to hardship in their pursuit of success
through education.

Moreover, Amelia's response exemplifies how many Chicanas understand labor exploitation of immigrants in relation to their own experiences.
Amelia asserts that immigrants are trapped in a powerless position because
employers will use their citizenship status as leverage. Muñoz-Laboy and
colleagues found that Mexican migrant workers in the United States live in
social environments characterized by extreme poverty, which is associated
with lack of legal rights and limited access to health care services.[19] In other
words, immigrants come to the United States believing that America will
offer greater opportunities, but realize opportunity is not available because
they are devalued and exploited due to citizenship status.

Furthermore, Chicana student responses regarding labor exploitation
and immigration reflect their own racial and gendered upbringings. As
Amelia mentioned, parents immigrate to the US believing more opportunity will be available for them and their children, but their immigration status places them in vulnerable positions because employers exploit
and devalue their labor. Consequently, immigrants are unable to provide
children—members of the family associated with mothers—with the education the American dream suggests. In addition, Chicanas respondents'
concerns regarding labor and family demonstrate that women are integral
to the family; they work in the private sphere and in the public sphere.
Thus, they view mothers as figures that are resisting patriarchal structures that devalue women's labor, developing the dual frame of reference
by which they evaluate, understand, and respond to social inequality from

their own unique perspectives as daughters of marginalized and exploited immigrants.

Chapter Summary

Through the process of the *Facultad de los Atravesada/o/xs*, we find that Chicana/o/x students have diverse conceptualizations of inequality and opportunity in the United States. They not only exhibit critical and engaged understandings of social inequality in the United States, but also are aware of their own marginalized positionalities in the society. We find that gender further complicates such formulation. Even though all respondents are critically aware of the limitations that the lack of economic capital poses in acquiring necessary educational resources and social capital and networks, Chicanas exhibit much more critical, nuanced, and intersectional understandings of inequality, informed by their *mestiza* consciousness. In doing so, Chicanas critically interwove issues of cultural and linguistic dominance, exploitation of immigrant labor, and immigrant parents' struggles and sacrifices to their conceptualization of inequality.

We also find that Chicana/o/x students perceive white Americans to be direct beneficiaries of unequal opportunity structures in the United States, while Asian Americans are culturally predisposed to overcome such adversities through their ethnic values and hard-work ethic. A few Chicana/o/x respondents also cited Latina/o/x values on hard work as a driver of the group's success. These perceptions reflect Chicana/o/x youths' adherence to the individualist and meritocratic American dream, in which immigrants and minoritized people could overcome structural disadvantages through continuous hard work and emphasizing the "right" values. Surprisingly, no gender differences are observed in such perceptions. This chapter highlights that the economic precariousness of immigrant families, coupled with the marginalization that Chicana/o/x youth experience as socioeconomically disadvantaged ethnoracial (and sometimes linguistic) minoritized people, leads them to deploy nuanced understandings of inequality.

The student voices illustrate that despite the unequal opportunity structures in the United States, many Chicana/o/x youths still believe in the American dream and actively pursue it. In this sense, Chicana/o/x youths are learning to become a part of the two worlds they belong to—the American one and the Mexican (immigrant) one. As Anzaldua contended, these students occupy the borderlands, where they are culturally and physically neither fully Mexican nor American, a place "created by the emotional residue of an unnatural boundary."[20] As a result, they occupy a unique position in the larger American society, where they have to defend their belongingness, their cultural and ethnic identities, and the legitimacy of their stories. Yet they understand, navigate through, and resist against their marginalities, empowered by the cultural knowledge they have accumulated from pedagogies of the home.[21] In so doing, their pursuit of opportunities and success in the presence of various structural and cultural inequalities that undermine their identity, potential, and "otherness" becomes an act of resistance itself. In the following section, we focus on the community college sector specifically as a representation of education borderlands that Chicana/o/x participants navigated by using la facultad and accessing institutional resources.

The Chicana/o/x Dream in the Community College Borderlands

Chapter 3

Navigating the Community College as Student-Parents

The world is not a safe place to live in. We shiver in separate cells
in enclosed cities, shoulders hunched, barely keeping the panic
below the surface of the skin, daily drinking shock along with our
morning coffee, fearing the torches being set to our buildings,
the attacks in the streets . . . Blocked, immobilized, we can't move
forward, can't move backwards. That writhing serpent movement,
the very movement of life, swifter than lightning, frozen. We do not
engage fully. We do not make full use of our faculties. We abnegate.
And there in front of us is the crossroads and choice: to feel a victim
where someone else is in control and therefore responsible and to
blame (being a victim and transferring the blame on culture, mother,
father, ex-lover, friend, absolves me of responsibility), or to feel
strong, and, for the most part, in control.[1]

W E CONCEPTUALIZE that enrolling in the community college sector perpetuates the educational borderlands experienced by Chicana/o/x
students in the preK–12 sector. Latina/o/x students are more likely than
their peers to enroll in community college, but the sector is often under-
funded and under-resourced.[2] For instance, the California Community
Colleges (CCC) system enrolls 25 percent of all community college students nationwide, and 43 percent of CCC students identify as Latina/o/x.
Financial divestment in the community college sector represents a clear
indication of the state devaluing the education of community college students.[3] Within the CCC system, over 80 percent of Latina/o/x students
leave without earning a certificate, degree, or transfer; for the majority of
Latina/o/x students, the community college sector can represent their exit
point in the educational pipeline.[4]

Community college practices and policies reinforce the K-12 sentiment that Chicana/o/x students do not belong in higher education. For instance, until the recent shift with AB 705, the majority of Latina/o/x students were placed into developmental education courses, which represented a key obstacle preventing completion.[5] Being placed within a broken educational system that does not foster completion sends a message that students do not belong in higher education. Community college Latina/o/x students also experience academic invalidations, which represent direct and indirect messages from institutional agents that they do not belong in college.[6] From the assessment practices utilized in higher education placing students below college-level courses, to instructors demeaning a student in front of the class by implying that she should know the answer to her own question, students encounter academic invalidations. Combined, policies and practices forge educational borderlands for community college students that establish a context for students to feel like they do not belong in college.

In this chapter, we share the lived experiences of two Chicana/o/x students who are student-parents and who have been affected by the prison industrial complex. We highlight that despite the institutional obstacles that students face due to intersectionality, they maintain the hope of pursuing a college degree, engage with various resources, and resist marginalization processes. The two student narratives exemplify that Chicana/o/x students reframe success to include the possibility of serving as nepantleras/os/x who support peers and family members with their future higher education goals. In particular, as student-parents, success was also represented by being able to foster a loving home for their children.

Chicana/o/x Students in the School-Prison Nexus

Various studies have focused on the school-to-prison pipeline and its influence on Latino males exiting the education pipeline.[7] The school-to-prison-pipeline metaphor highlights our notion of education borderlands and Chicana/o/x students receiving messages that they do not belong in the education system. Nevertheless, the metaphor has been challenged because it focuses narrowly on disciplinary practices and policies, and, though "both institutions operate as one in the same under the same set of rules,"[8] we acknowledge the broader interconnections found within the matrix of domination or matrices of power.[9] In particular, the prison industrial complex impacts the lives of Chicana/o/x communities because about 17 percent of Latino males will be incarcerated during their lifetimes.[10] As far as being committed to juvenile detention facilities, Latino youth are 65 percent more likely than white young men to be detained.

About six hundred thousand prisoners are released every year across the United States.[11] Upon release, formerly incarcerated individuals will likely face discriminating hiring practices that result in lower wages, unemployment, and reluctance in hiring because of their criminal records.[12] Thus, it is not surprising that about 68 percent of previously incarcerated individuals will be rearrested within three years of release and 77 percent will be arrested again within five years of being released.[13]

To address recidivism rates, the Second Chance Act of 2007 established a focus on improving the schooling provided in prisons, jails, and juvenile residential facilities.[14] Participating in education programs while incarcerated decreases the likelihood of recidivism when compared to individuals who do not participate in schooling.[15] Various four-year colleges and community colleges across the nation have developed partnerships with juvenile and adult incarceration facilities.[16]

However, the prison industrial complex has implications for more than the individual who is incarcerated; their children are also affected by incarceration. Because the US has the highest incarceration rate in the world, one in forty-three children has an imprisoned parent.[17] While some studies find that the academic outcomes of students with incarcerated mothers did not vary from their peers, other studies find that children with incarcerated fathers are more likely to perform poorly academically.[18] Of course, contact with the incarcerated parent can be a mitigating factor; for instance, children who have weekly contact with their incarcerated mother are four times less likely to be suspended or stop out from school, but visiting policies limit that possibility.[19] Students with incarcerated parents experience a reduced connection to schooling and are less likely to pursue higher education.[20] Unfortunately, regardless of parental incarceration status, "school characteristics promote (or prevent) [academic] success equally across individuals with and without a parental incarceration history."[21] With this in mind, the first narrative in this chapter is focused on Javier, a twenty-four-year-old student-parent in the community college who has been in and out of the incarceration system since he was thirteen years old. In the second narrative, we highlight the experience of a Chicana student-mother whose father was incarcerated.

Chicana/o/x Student-Parents in Community Colleges

Student-parents represent another population of interest to understand the complex experiences of Chicana/o/x students. When it comes to knowing the statistics and experiences of student-parents, there is a dearth in the literature, particularly for students who are fathers. The limited research available notes that over 11 percent of all undergraduate students identify as single mothers, and 44 percent of them attend community college.[22] Single mothers make up 21 percent of all community college students.[23] Of those who are single mothers attending community college, about 40 percent are on the verge of stopping out because they have to care for their children.[24] More specifically, 19 percent of Latina college students are single mothers.[25] On average, Latina single mothers in community colleges have about $4,697 of unmet financial need, which is $908 more than their white counterparts.[26] While promising institutional support systems include affordable child care, faculty mentoring, peer support, and spaces on campus that welcome children, access to such resources is rather limited.[27] Ahead, we share two stories that intersect the prison industrial complex with student-parents navigating the community college sector to highlight *nepantleando* as part of their future success.

Atravesadas/os/xs Nepantleando
Javier, Previously Incarcerated Student-Father
Nepantleando in Community College

At the time of his interview, Javier was a father of two children and attending Skills College in Southern California. Javier grew up in South Central Los Angeles and had been in and out of incarceration since he was thirteen years old: "I started getting into trouble and started going to juvenile detentions and until now . . . It started when I was thirteen, fourteen, fifteen; I was incarcerated, but I would come in and out, in and out." However, he always enjoyed school: "Maybe because I was always in group homes and placements and camps so, when I used to go to school, it was like being free. It was just like being around people. Just socializing and it's different, it's different. I did used to like to learn, I did."

By seventeen years old, Javier had graduated high school but with no college guidance in place, he resorted to crime:

> I graduated in placement, in placement and I got out. They termi-
> nated my probation. I had my high school diploma at seventeen. I
> got out and I wanted to go to school, but I got a security job. I got
> me a security job and I was making money like that security and
> then while I had my diploma and I don't know, the work finished
> and I don't know, I didn't go to school. I didn't go, I don't know
> why. But I wanted to go to college and I started robbing.

Although schooling had become a haven for Javier and he aspired to earn a college degree, lack of access to a college counselor and being unemployed influenced his decision to earn money through criminal activity.

In the juvenile detention center, he began to receive college guidance: "I went to camp because I was still underage. I was still seventeen, so they still, so they sent me to camp and I was already a graduate, and so, the only thing I was doing there is they were using me for like as a janitor, maintenance, take care of the camp, water the plants and I was the oldest one there . . . They started taking me to colleges. Like to outings to little trips to check out colleges and yeah, that's how it happened." As an inmate in the juvenile detention center, Javier was framed as an *atravesado* who was not allowed to belong in society, but his age and high school diploma allowed him to gain leadership experiences. This culminated in the detention center staff encouraging him to pursue a vocational degree in the local community colleges.

Even though Javier loved to learn, the staff only offered a vocational degree; the idea of transferring to a four-year college was never presented to him as a possible option. At that time, he aspired to become a parole officer and support youth like himself: "Then it's like checking out Limón College and then that's how it happened; I made up my mind that I don't want to—I wanted to take criminal justice back then . . . To become a PO, a probation officer . . . But since I got out and I got these two strikes, I can't do that no more. So, that's when I was like my second choice was like welding." Even though Javier was presented with college as a vocational option, his dream was to become a parole officer because he hoped to be an influential support for youth like himself who wanted guidance:

> I was in the system for a long time and I've been, I've seen a lot of POs and I would be perfect. I would be like, I know how to talk to them, how to handle them, how to school them and teach them and you know, all of it. I had some cool probation officers in there that made me change, made me think different . . . They understood, some of them understood like I'm not, I used to cause trouble, and get in trouble . . . I guess I needed attention or something, I guess so. I guess they understood because before someone would just be loud, "Go to the box, go to the hole," and I would go to the hole every time . . . This other (one) would be like "Don't even worry about it" . . . trying to teach me a lesson but not as tough.

Javier had plenty of experiences with officers who punished and further criminalized youth in the juvenile detention center. By being sent "to the hole," he was reminded constantly that he was an atravesado. Instead, one officer understood that, as a teenager, Javier needed attention and guidance, not to be further criminalized. He inspired Javier to want to be a parole officer and support other criminalized youth. In such a role, Javier would have been able to support youth as a nepantlero because he would have been able to provide guidance and mentorship for them to return to a college pathway.

However, that career pathway was never presented as an option to him. He only had access to other vocational programs:

> It was in [Juvenile Detention Center] in Los Angeles County . . . They had this other program for first responders, they had this one program landscaping, like preventing forest fires . . . I didn't know nothing about welding until these guys [from Los Angeles] came . . . They are like, "We want to start this program for youth to go to Skill College." . . . So they got a lot of people from this area to participate in this one program, you know, with high school diplomas.

Javier was able to access the program because he had earned his high school diploma while in the juvenile justice system. Although he was not interested in welding, given his options and the information presented, it seemed like the best opportunity at the time.

Javier began taking online classes while incarcerated and, when he was released, he contacted the program recruiters:

> When I got out, I got connected with them and they called me. I was still taking online classes and they put me in the college till spring and so I finished college and then I came to the welding classes and I guess, then I had a girlfriend and I had just got out, it's my baby's mama . . . They helped us out with money, with clothes, with food, you know, they—it was like a program. They took us out to Six Flags and they bought all my equipment for welding that I needed. They bought my boots, my helmet, my gloves—everything.

The program was an essential support for Javier to (re)establish and begin his life outside of the prison industrial complex. The program aimed to support students on various levels: the individuals did not simply enroll students in a welding program, they provided financial and social support.

At the same time, it was an intense program that required complete commitment from each individual:

> I used to come here at seven and get out at eleven . . . Take two hours of online classes . . . Then, I get out like around three so we were already aback in the program like around three thirty and to work more on our online classes and homework and we leave like around five and it gives my girl, she wanted more time for her, because she used to get out of school at twelve and I didn't come home till like six thirty and the bus and everything. I guess she got to me and I was young and I quit everything and I started doing it, what I used to do and I guess that's what happened . . . and I got into welding in two weeks, but I left. They bought all my equipment and everything . . . I was eighteen.

Javier was involved in college and program requirements almost twelve hours each day. Without being able to drive, the commitment was not allowing him to balance his responsibilities at home. While the program may have attempted to support students on a personal, social, and academic level, it did not account for ensuring that students were prepared to transition back to their families, particularly those who were student-parents. The commitment proved to be too much for Javier and his girlfriend, and he was forced to stop out of college.

Family Members and Educators Supporting Javier's College Aspirations

By the age of twenty-four, he had been out of prison for about a year, with two strikes, and "couldn't get a lot of jobs." But as a father of two daughters, he had a different mentality than years before and he was committed to earning a college degree: "It's the longest I have ever been not in. I'm different now from before. I got a family now. I got two little girls . . . My kids changed me, turned me humble, turned my whole thinking, everything, my heart everything . . . She was pregnant when I got incarcerated, so when I got out, my girl was two years old and this was new to us . . . This time it's different. She thinks different. I think different." With two strikes on his record and two kids, Javier was motivated to remain committed to earning a degree and not returning to prison. His girlfriend was supportive, and they both understood the benefit of him pursuing college.

Javier explained that his uncle and cousins served as role models to help him believe that his aspiration of earning a college degree for the benefit of his family was realistic:

> My uncle, he's a plumber . . . When I see him finish his classes and start working for LAX [Los Angeles International Airport] as a plumber and started winning this money and living like good like going out to Florida and going to fancy little restaurants and taking out his wife and his kids and that's what influenced me a lot, a lot, a major part . . . As kids, my cousins, one of them started going too, he still goes here; he's taking plumbing classes . . . The other one is taking architect class and I kind of grew up with them when I was smaller, you know, and they had a lot to do with it too.

Although his family members were not pursuing welding, Javier was able to see that a community college degree would benefit his own immediate family. His uncle spoke with him with the intent to motivate him and activate his aspirations. Javier explained: "He told me to finish it to, 'Don't stop, it's going to pay off' because he's, you know, now he got his house and he said, 'Don't give up. Stay in, stay in, stay in it and do your work and trust me.' He's like, 'You know, it's going to pay off and (for) you, even more; plumbing, you know, it's good money. But welding where you going it's going to be a little more, way better.' So, that's influenced me a lot too." Javier's uncle reminded him that welding would likely be a better-paying profession, when compared with pluming. In Javier's explanation, it was evident that he was motivated by the possibility of owning a home and providing a stable future for his family.

Although he was unaware about welding as a career prior to the recruitment program, once in his coursework, Javier enjoyed welding. He shared:

> I like everything about it. The burning, the melting, the putting stuff together—everything about it . . . Only certain people can do it . . . It's a skill and you know, the appearance. My girl likes it too, "I'm with a welder." . . . The gas welding, that's what I learned and it was fun. It was fun and a lot of practice and a lot of practice, a lot of patience. A lot of focus, a lot of, you got to pay attention to it, it's a skill. It's a technique and if you are just doing it the way they are telling you and you are just doing it to get it done, it's not going to work. You really got to be into the skill, into everything so you can catch everything, every move, every angle, just catch everything and it's nice because you just catch it when it comes out just you are happy for yourself.

Being able to weld provided Javier with the opportunity to acknowledge his skills, which were validated by others as well. Welding became a validating experience, which he could accomplish proudly. In this validating context, Javier was no longer an atravesado; he felt that he belonged in the classroom and in the profession.

In addition to having family members as role models who contributed to his establishing college aspirations, Javier also had access to institutional resources. He had been supported by various programs, which, in the past, had resulted in him completing high school and pursuing college. He recalled one instructor in particular:

> Shawn influenced me a lot . . . The way he talks. He shows a lot of proof. You know, he doesn't just talk about it. He imitates a little bit of his life stories, you know. Like how much he was making and what he went through and how much he makes now and how his life is now and he's a good teacher too, you know. I thought he was just going to like leave us there and teach us, but no, he's actually, we want to learn and we tell him, and he sees it, he's gonna—he's there. No matter what, and I liked—he's more understanding and more like you can relate . . . I want to just be like him.

Shawn shared his experiences, and Javier could relate. Through that process, Javier found someone who was a role model and he hoped to be able to change his pathway from being incarcerated to earning a college degree, securing a career, and supporting his family.

Within the welding courses, Shawn helped to develop a collaborative community among the students. Javier recalled: "I come to classes in the mornings and he's listening to some music that I like too and during the class, he makes comments and remarks and examples that I can connect to that is in the same place, you know, that type of stuff and made me feel comfortable, you know, and not just like a student, like actually made me like loosen up and like laugh with the class." Javier was able to relate to and connect with the welding instructor, which, in turn, helped him connect with his classmates. As such, he was able to develop a community among his classmates: "I just made friends with like two, three . . . It's fun. It's like 'Look, like look, look, check this out.'" In the course, the instructor fostered a classroom environment where Javier and his peers were able to support and validate one another through the learning process.

In fostering such an academic space, Javier was able to enact his abilities as a nepantlero by supporting his peers. He explained:

> I barely got into this today and I'm already getting it done good and there is some people that you know, it takes for them a little longer, but they still don't get it . . . I used to like to go and teach

them like, "This, do it like this," and other people used to do it to me too, like when I didn't get a trick on how to do it, then they help me out . . . We help each other out like both the tests, because we both used to like learn at the beginning like learn in class and know the same thing so we would read the question to each other, you know, and then we figure out the best question and . . . then we get it.

Javier highlighted his abilities to succeed academically and he looked forward to supporting his peers and ensuring that they also understood the material. As such, his abilities as a nepantlero were enacted by helping his peers with welding. The positive classroom experience validated that he could belong in higher education and meet his goals because he was able to teach others.

Javier also had access to other career and college programs. For example, because he was receiving welfare, he had access to a guidance program that aimed to support his completion of a degree. Such support included having access to funds to pay for childcare and welding materials. He also completed a program that focused on college preparation. He explained that the program would "teach you how to write notes and stuff like that, little basic stuff . . . It can be helpful. They gave me a little certificate, $150 certificate when I was done with that class, so it was cool." The program services aimed to ensure that students were receiving financial assistance and the academic support needed to complete. He also had access to counselors through the program and he acknowledged:

The (program) counselors, they do a lot . . . When they don't want to do their stuff, like they supposed to do it, (the program counselors) get on there and they call them and they do help a lot because they be breaking their head, and they just make it easier . . . They get on them. "What's the problem? Okay, let me check." They get it done and they make it better. Like they get something out of it. He always, I'm talking about Hillside, he always handles your problems, my problems.

Due to his low-income status, Javier was part of the program available to welfare recipients. Thus, he had institutional advocates who would ensure that other departments were supporting him adequately and he had access to a counselor who cared about his future. Considering the invalidating and dehumanizing experiences that he may have encountered when he was incarcerated, the community college vocational program became an environment where Javier could receive the support that should have been provided earlier on in his preK–12 education.

Encountering Ongoing Obstacles

However, a lack of housing resulted in experiencing personal obstacles that began to interfere with his abilities to complete the welding program. During his first semester, he had to move out of his girlfriend's parents' house. He explained the negative implications of not being able to live with family: "The financial aid, applied for it and I received it and I wasted it. It helped me to get by because that's when I wasn't with my girl and it helped me get by." He used his financial aid to cover living expenses, but he could not save any money to secure a home for him and his family: "When I moved in with my girl . . . My mind was in school and my family. When we separated, I was at my mom's house and I couldn't concentrate and I couldn't focus. I was still learning new stuff in the welding [program], but I couldn't focus too much on my books." As he stated earlier, his aim was to earn a college degree so that he could provide a stable home for his children. When he moved out from his girlfriend's parents' house, there was also a death in his girlfriend's family. He explained: "So much stuff happened there in between and, when she died, that's when I left too, so she went through a lot. We were all going through a lot." Once again, he found himself in nepantla facing contradictory expectations: he was attempting to engage with the programmatic support, but he also needed to support his family. Being away from his family influenced his abilities to concentrate on his academics, required that he spend his financial aid on housing, and interfered with his learning.

When Javier began to encounter such problems, his classmates and instructors noticed. He explained: "I stopped being ambitious. I was telling Shawn like, 'Come and teach me and show me,' like it went down after them problems . . . Then I was with a friend there that I always talked to at the beginning we always getting our welding done and we are advancing in our welding and then he seen it too and he's like, 'Man what's going on?' Like, 'Man, I'm going through some kind of divorce.'" In the short period of time that he was at the community college, he was able to develop supportive relationships with the instructor and his peers. Javier trusted them and talked about his personal concerns: "They used to always tell me, 'What's wrong? What's going on?' but I did always used to talk to them. When they started, I told them, 'Man this is what happened to me.' Like, 'Man, that's happening but keep coming to school, keep coming to school.' It's like, 'It ain't easy, man, it ain't easy going through this because I'm new to it. I'm new to this family thing and this kid stuff and this problem stuff . . . and school.'" Javier reflected on having to transition from being incarcerated to navigating the multiple responsibilities of being a full-time college student, partner, and parent. His peers and instructor were encouraging, but he needed more guidance to balance personal concerns with academic responsibilities, something that the programs did not address.

Javier was eligible to receive financial aid, but it took much longer than anticipated, which made his situation worse. He explained: "They could have hurried up with my financial aid, maybe it was that because I wasn't working. I wasn't doing nothing. All I was doing was going to school." Javier's financial concerns were intensified because he had to attend college without receiving financial aid reimbursement for a month. The lack of financial support and inability to work while he pursued the welding degree made him reconsider the decision to pursue college; the lack of money impacted other areas in his life and it was challenging for him to pursue college: "In every way—transportation—every way, it's needed because I don't really have nobody that can help me like that, you know? I got to do it myself . . . Nobody else going to, nobody else is going to do it." Javier was able to enact his facultad to understand that without either access to financial aid or being able to work, he could not afford to continue pursuing the program as a full-time student. His financial need was interconnected with having to ride the bus for over an hour each day. Not being able to afford a home for his family also added to the stress of not being present with his family.

Regardless, Javier's mother encouraged him to continue pursuing a college degree. He recalled: "She wanted me to keep going to school. [She would say,] 'Keep going to school, don't mess up. How is school? How you doing in school?'" Thus, his mother served as a source of support to maintain his hope and aspirations.

Continued Atravesado Status

Regardless of the obstacles he encountered, Javier continued to establish career aspirations in welding, but his status as a convicted felon followed him: "Get into the aerospace, but again, the aerospace [is] with NASA and I got two strikes and I guess if you go work with them, a lot of that stuff is going to be confidential and that's where I'm headed first, to the aerospace. If they don't, if it's a problem with strikes on my record, then pipe welder, but Shawn said he knows you got to be real good for the pipe welder so, I can do it." Javier aspired to pursue a career in aerospace engineering because he saw it as a challenge that he could meet but he knew that could be impossible if the companies did not hire previously incarcerated individuals. His hope and aspirations for the future became apparent every time he spoke about welding and his abilities to succeed. Evident in Javier's answer was that he hoped to work in an environment where he was challenged because he was confident in his welding abilities. His status as a permanent atravesado, due to his criminal record, was also evident as he reflected that "strikes are forever . . . Companies . . . that don't want to hire, don't hire you at all, not even the navy . . . Not even the army want to get you for felonies no more. I'm still going to try with the NASA." Despite knowing that NASA would likely conduct a background check and his criminal record might impede his ability to be hired, Javier's resistance was evident in his plan to still apply for a job there.

Despite understanding that a welding could provide a stable economic future and his commitment to pursue a college degree, Javier questioned whether he would be able to continue enrolling in the program: "I'm not sure about coming on spring. I'm going to come back, but maybe not spring because, well, we were staying, me and my girl were staying at her parent's house and I wanted to move out . . . She works, but it's not going to cover a new place and that's why she wants me to work and I guess when she gets her raises and it won't take long for me to come back to school." As a student-parent from a low-income background, Javier had to navigate multiple identities that often collided with one another. While in nepantla, Javier had to navigate prioritizing his parent identity by securing a job that he could qualify for, given his criminal record, over attending college full-time.

Javier's desire to persist in the welding program was evidence of his hope to become a nepantlero. Ultimately, he aimed to complete his program and earn his degree because he understood that a degree would result in multiple benefits for his family's future: "It was like, I have to get it done, for my kids and for my family . . . It's like I have to get this done. I want to get it . . . It would mean a lot in my life. It's an accomplishment and it's going to pay off later on . . . financially and my pride. I don't think anybody else cares, only my family." In his reflection on why he wanted and needed to earn the college degree, Javier shared that it had more than economic implications. Javier knew that it would matter to his immediate family, his extended family, and himself. Most apparent in his response was that he would be able to be proud of himself if he accomplished earning a college degree. A college degree in welding would serve to counter his criminal record so that he could continue enacting his abilities as a nepantlero in the future. Whether he worked as a welder for NASA or a pipe welder, earning a college degree would strengthen his abilities to foster opportunities for his children in the long term. Being a role model for himself and his family continued to fuel his motivation to pursue a college degree in welding.

Giselle, Nepantleando as a Student-Mother in Community College

Giselle was born in Los Angeles, California. Her mother worked in a jean factory and her father has been in prison most of her life. She is the middle child, with a sister who is about two years older than her and a younger brother. Although she aspired to pursue a college degree, she explained that in high school some teachers were not invested in students: "Sometimes there was no point of going to class because the teachers would be like, 'Oh, open your textbook and do your work.' They would not explain the work. It didn't really matter if you turned or didn't turn in your homework. Those were the bad teachers. They didn't really care. They would just find an excuse to kick you out of the class." In addition to teachers not being concerned with teaching students, she also began meeting friends who decided not to attend such classes and she "started ditching classes" during her first semester in ninth grade. Giselle's experience in high school demonstrates a context of education borderlands as unwelcoming and one where she learned that school was not a place where she mattered.

Fortunately, by her second semester, she was able to redirect her frustration into resistance by focusing on her schooling, and by tenth grade, she "had straight As." Giselle was motivated to pursue a college degree and advocated for herself. For instance, when Giselle was in tenth grade, her older sister was a senior and she attended a college field trip with the high school. Even though the field trip was only for twelfth-grade students, Giselle advocated for herself and the teacher was receptive:

> [The tour] was only for seniors but I wanted to go because my sister was gonna go . . . I was like, "I want to go." I signed up and the teacher that took the students, he really liked my sister so my sister was like, "Can she go?" He let me go, so he gave a field trip slip and I went . . . I really liked it. I went to a class and it seemed like the professors were really educated and they would teach you good. I liked it . . . It felt like that was the school for me.

The California State University (CSU) campus was the first college that Giselle had ever stepped foot on and she felt like she could belong there. Because the teacher was willing to let her visit during tenth grade, she established a goal to attend that CSU campus.

However, by eleventh grade, she was pregnant. When she found out, she became even more focused on her schooling. She explained: "I would take extra credit, everything I could, so I could have my grades and graduate from high school and come to a community college or a university. It really didn't matter to me but that was my thing." She began twelfth grade with a strong academic record but could no longer maintain her academic performance because she had her son a week before her senior year began.

She managed to miss only the first two weeks of school but explained that it was a challenge for her:

> It kind of put me behind because I actually felt depressed because I felt like I wasn't myself sometimes. I tried to be someone I wasn't and it was hard because I felt that I didn't really have friends, so true friends. I only had my sister . . . my brother stopped talking to me and it was difficult . . . I would miss him a lot and I would try

to get out of school. When you have a kid, you stop doing things you enjoy doing. I had to stop playing soccer.

Giselle had to stop playing varsity soccer, experienced a loss of friends, and she missed her baby when she had to be in school all day, only weeks after he was born. The shift in priorities resulted in being depressed postpartum and influenced her abilities to focus on her schooling.

Reflecting on her life helped Giselle adapt to her new identity as a student-mother and motivated her to remain committed to her education:

> I have to work hard for him 'cause it's not about me, anymore . . . I said to myself, "I don't want him to have the same lifestyle that I had." . . . I didn't have a father. My father was always in prit-son. I say to myself that my mom was my sister because my mom, she was always working. She would go in at five in the morning, [and not] come out till seven, eight at night, sometimes even later. When I had a question, I would go to my older sister. I said to myself, I don't want that for him.

Because her dad was in prison the majority of her life, Giselle grew up in a single-mother household, and her mom worked over twelve hours each day, six days a week. When she needed guidance, Giselle would resort to her older sister.

Once Giselle had her child, she was able to reflect on her lived experiences and knew that she could secure a career if she earned a college degree. Having a career would benefit her son because she could then be present in his life more. She explained:

> I need to get an education so I can also have time for him. 'Cause if I work in a factory like my mom, I'm not gonna have time for my child and I don't want that. I had bigger goals for myself. I wanted to be a doctor before I got pregnant I know I'm young, I want to grow with my son, together and I wanted to go straight to a university and I had the grades for that. I really did. But when I got pregnant and started missing classes and at first, when it was rocky, I'm like, "Okay, I can't become a doctor anymore 'cause that will take too much of my time, too much school. The work

is gonna be harder." So that's when I said, "Okay, for right now, something small. Think about your child now and get a small little career and go to a community college, if possible." I want to transfer. I still have the big goals, but for right now, I'm settling for something small.

Giselle consistently maintained high educational aspirations, and after having her child, her motivation was even stronger. While she was not considering a medical degree, she was certain that she would transfer to earn her bachelor's degree.

Unfortunately, because she was pregnant, she was not able to access a college preparation course, which aligns with our conceptualization of students being told they do not belong in education. Instead, she was placed in a "pregnancy class," a course designed specifically for pregnant students:

> [My high school] turned into a charter school, so then we started having some classes, CSA. It's a class for them to prepare you to go to college. I didn't have that class because I had a kid and they gave me a pregnancy class so they can show you how to be a parent and all that stuff. But the teacher for that class, she was a big help for financial aid. She basically walked us through the process of applying for financial aid. She was the only one who actually helped me for financial aid.

Giselle was able to apply for financial aid because the teacher guided her through the application process. However, she missed out on the opportunity to focus explicitly on preparing for college.

Giselle's Transition to Community College

When it was time to choose a college, the decision was easy for Giselle. She knew that Pathways College would be a good choice. The college was close to her home and her friend encouraged her to apply: "I actually came to Pathways College because a close friend of mine, she told me about [the] First-Year program. She said, 'They'll help you get your classes, everything.' I'm like, 'Okay, I'll give it a try.'" While in high school, she did not receive guidance from a counselor or instructor beyond applying for financial aid.

Instead, it was her friend who told Giselle to enroll at Pathways College and explained the benefits of being in the First-Year program.

In college, she met only once with the college counselor, who taught her how to search for courses. Upon taking the math assessment, she "scored really low," which reinforced her belief that she was "really bad at math." Although she was in the First-Year program, Giselle was not sure what math courses she would need and explained that she had "a paper that they gave" her, but she was "not really sure which ones" to take. Nevertheless, she benefited from being part of the First-Year program, which helped her "a lot."

In terms of academic expectations, Giselle was comfortable navigating college-level work. She recalled: "It wasn't really much of a challenge because sometimes I felt that the class was easy but my only challenge was my child . . . I didn't want to leave him there and so I was like that." Giselle believed that navigating the courses was doable but she was challenged because she wished she had better care for her son. Being a student-mother from a low-income background meant that she balanced college, work, and parenting responsibilities:

> A typical day was for me to wake up, sneak out of the house so my baby won't see me, and then come to class. Once I would come out of class, go straight home, running home and being with my child. I would sometimes pray for him to be asleep so I could do my homework or have to do cleaning or stuff like that. Then he would be awake. I would play with him for a while. Then I would have to go straight to work . . . Come out of work, pray for my kid to be awake so I can see him before going to sleep and then just go to sleep and wake up again the next morning and do the same thing.

With the constant need to work, parent, and be in class, she would often have to do homework when her child slept or during class.

Continued Sources of Inspiration and Support

When identifying who served as a support system, Giselle did not highlight any institutional resources; instead, she identified various sources of support within her extended family. She recalled:

The people that have helped me a lot have been my sister. She's always been there for me, always. My father-in-law. Even though my mother-in-law is not so great, my father-in-law, he's been a big help. My uncle that unfortunately got locked up not too long ago, he was like a father to me, too. He always been there for me. When he was born, he was there, everything. My mom, 'cause even though she didn't really spend time with us . . . She always tried her best to give us everything that we needed. We struggled a little 'cause we didn't have money but in food-wise, clothing, somewhere to live, we always had that because of her. She plays a big part in my life. I always say she's my hero 'cause she had to deal with three kids all by herself.

Although she was the first in her family to pursue a college degree, Giselle was confident that she had access to a community of support. In her brief summary of individuals who helped her, she noted that her uncle, who had served as a father to her since she was born, was incarcerated. Both her dad and uncle were incarcerated, which highlighted the interconnectedness of the matrix of domination and matrices of power.[28] Nevertheless, she had access to other individuals who provided her with support. Among them was her husband. Giselle reflected: "He's the one that holds me up."

Although her mom continued to work six days a week and she saw her rarely, Giselle explained that her mother's hard work motivated her to continue pursuing her degree:

Not too long ago, I was in the house and she was—she had a big headache, 'cause my mom has always had severe headaches and it's sad to see her like that because all she wants to do is lay down, and that has been happening for five years already. I went to my house and I remember when we were smaller, she would play with us. When she had the time, she would run around with us, every-thing like a mom would do. Seeing her sick, like a week ago, she told me that her legs hurt and I massaged her legs. I wanted to cry because her legs looked like they were tired . . . It hurts to see my mom like that. I don't want him to see me like that. I want him to see me with energy all the time.

Having worked in factory jobs for years, Giselle's mom was often not feeling well but could not stop working. Her mom's suffering fueled Giselle to continue pursuing a college degree because she wanted to make sure that her son would not see her hurting like Giselle saw her mom.

Her son not only motivated Giselle to pursue a college degree but also helped her select a major: "Like I said, I love kids. I believe that if I major in something that has to do with children, I could be closer to my child, so that's basically why I chose child development . . . My biggest goal is to have my career straight, have my job and everything, and be with my son, watching him grow. I know I'm young, I want to grow with my son, together. I want that." She was majoring in child development both because she was interested in working with children and because she would be able to learn more about her son and how to support and interact with him.

Giselle also viewed college as a time for growth:

> [College is] preparing me for who I want to become in life 'cause of your career, your classes you're taking, people you're meeting that are gonna help you towards the things that you want to become. That's what it means to me . . . I just want to get my units that I need to transfer to Long Beach and I want to start to see how my life is gonna turn out. I think in a community college, you find yourself, who you're gonna be, who you are, what you're like. So that's what I want to accomplish here.

Giselle understood that college was an opportunity for her to continue developing on academic, professional, and personal levels, and she looked forward to her college journey.

Encountering Ongoing Obstacles in Community College

However, as a Chicana from a low-income background with a dependent child, Giselle experienced and anticipated various challenges in pursuing her college and career goals, the majority due to financial need. While she received financial aid to pay for her classes and additional expenses, it was not enough to cover all costs and she felt the need to establish a savings account: "They gave me . . . almost $2,000 but it went by quick . . . With the money, I made a savings account 'cause for an emergency or something, and basically, my financial aid money went for that, for a savings account." Her financial aid consisted of $2,000, which was supposed to last her one semester (four months). She shared that if she had sufficient funds, she would purchase a computer: "I do have a computer at home but I don't really like using it 'cause it's inside one of my sisters-in-law's room. That's what I'm working on, trying to get a computer right now." Without a personal computer, Giselle often had to arrive on campus before her classes, in hopes of finishing her work. In addition to having to purchase $200 worth of books, she had to cover other expenses: "I was struggling because my car had just got—it wouldn't run. I had to pay that and then I had to pay bills and it was hard to get that book. Sometimes I feel that money will be an issue." Giselle enacted her facultad to anticipate likely obstacles due to finances.

As such, she began working a second job at McDonald's to ensure that she could afford college:

> I want to try to get into the work here and the childcare program coming up. I just don't know how to get there. I'm trying to leave the job that I have 'cause I work at McDonald's and I want to see if I can get a part-time job here in the childcare so I can also bring him along here in El Camino. But I don't know where to go and get the help from . . . I'm scared that I'll go and they'll tell me, "Oh, you don't have what you need. You don't have the expectations that we need for you to work here."

Giselle knew that she would be better off working on campus at the childcare center because she would gain career experience and she would be able to bring her child to campus. Although she had changed her major to child development, she had yet to take any courses in the major and believed that would prevent the childcare center from considering her application.

Giselle also knew that she could encounter academic obstacles—which she felt more comfortable overcoming, in comparison to financial concerns. In regard to her First-Year program English course, she explained: "If I would need help, I know one of my classmates might know the answer and I could go to them instead of having to go bother the professor."

However, that was not the case in every course: "In my nutrition class, even though I started making friends, you don't feel like that 'cause you don't know everybody . . . Sometimes to get to the professor, you have to make an appointment." Giselle also had friends who could help her in the nutrition course, but it was larger than the English course and the sense of trust and community was not as present. Her nutrition professor was also less available than the English professor, which she felt was not supportive of her academic success.

As a first-generation college student, Giselle anticipated obstacles related to accessing the correct information to support her transfer aspirations. Even though she was in the First-Year program, she was uncertain about receiving the information she needed: "Sometimes the information doesn't get to me . . . I have to go and ask a friend, 'Have you heard anything?' 'Cause lately, we haven't heard nothing about the FY program so we don't know how—we have our classes for the spring. They helped us get them. But I don't know if they're going to come and contact us in our English classes like they did before." She also wondered what would happen her second year in college, when she would not be part of the program: "It is the first year. I don't know if they are gonna be still there with us, pushing us to come to the office and stuff like that . . . I've heard that people who just come in, they have it harder to get in classes." While she may not be able to have priority registration, she felt comfortable knowing that she could still ask for guidance in the future: "I know that even though it's just a year, I can come back and ask them for help to register for other classes that I need or making my papers to transfer out of [this college] going to [a CSU school]. Yeah, I'll be coming back to them asking them for help."

As a student mother, Giselle had to balance college with motherhood—but she did not see that as an obstacle because she enjoyed pursuing her college aspirations:

> I don't have it as hard as other teenage moms do. I have two friends, besides the one that helped me come into [Pathways College], that had children and they stopped going to school so they can be with their kids. I see them now and I feel like they're struggling more than I am because even though I have that in my mind that I have to go to school, I have to take care of my child, and I have to go to work, I feel that I'm not as stressed out as the other teenage moms

that don't go to school and are just there at home. 'Cause they have that frustration that they're at home all day, every day. I can say I'm in school. I'm living my life like I'm supposed to be living.

It was evident that being a mother helped her enact la facultad so that she felt confident in navigating her college plans, as opposed to stopping out of college.

Nepantlera Building Bridges Toward College

Being in college for almost a year had already started to shift Giselle's decisions as a student. She explained that she went from being on campus only for classes to being an involved student: "When you get involved, you start talking to people or you stay after class a little bit to talk to your professors, it helps you be more confident in yourself . . . To me, being a successful student is to come to class every day, being on time, doing your homework, basically what they tell you but also being involved in things in the school and your community." Giselle viewed her involvement in college as beneficial not only to herself but also to her community. Her perspective exemplified the development of her nepantlera abilities, which became evident in her efforts to pursue a degree that would benefit others.

For example, she chose to major in child development with the aim to support children with special needs:

I just changed my major. I was thinking about a minor for [special education]. I want to study them 'cause that idea came to my head 'cause I have a neighbor that's like that . . . He has a teacher that goes to his house and he's afraid of her. He kind of gets scared. I notice when I talk to him and I tell him sweet things, he smiles at me. So, I thought to myself, "Why is he afraid of that person and why isn't he afraid of me if he just met me?"

As a nepantlera, her desire to be a caring educator to children with special needs and her desire to raise her son in a loving home influenced her decision to pursue a degree in child development.

Giselle's nepantlera lens also led her to support her younger brother so that he would understand the importance of pursuing a college degree: "I push him a lot 'cause he's graduating this year . . . He got accepted to Long Beach . . . That's where I want to transfer but he's a really smart young boy. He had a girlfriend that was making him ditch a lot, so I'm like, 'I don't like her for you. Don't do anything that would—not ruin your life but make you stop doing things that you could have done.' I push him a lot so he can have big goals." Although she was not able to attend a CSU campus immediately after high school, her younger brother was admitted, and she wanted to guide him so that he would continue to remain committed to his education.

Just as she motivated her younger brother to pursue college, she also planned to ensure that her husband returned to college:

> He went there for two semesters only and that's when I got pregnant. He was still going but then once the baby was born, he stopped going 'cause he had to get a job . . . He was planning to transfer to Kansas University . . . They really wanted him to over there but he was gonna get transferred over there but he stopped playing . . . Our plan is for me to graduate and get a small career and him—while I'm in school, he's working. And once I finish school and I start working, he goes back to school . . . He's the one that's saying he doesn't want to go back to school, but I'll make him go either way.

Giselle understood that it was important for her household that both she and her husband earned college degrees, which is why she intended to encourage, support, and plan for her husband to complete a college degree. Giselle knew that he was passionate about coaching soccer and she wanted to support his career dreams. She understood that her pursuit of a college degree would have greater implications for those around her and aimed to serve as an example to support others.

Enacting the Chicana/o/x Dream

The two participant narratives shared in this chapter highlight the complex, layered, and intersectional experiences of Chicana/o/x students as they maintain hope, resist marginalization, and succeed academically in the community college sector. We selected to share the lived experiences of Javier and Giselle because they provide insight into the intersection of marginalizing systems. The experiences of Javier and Giselle serve as reminders that the prison industrial complex has concrete influences that can hinder lived experiences, access to schooling, and the economic futures of Chicana/o/x individuals—reinforcing the idea that they are atravesadas/os/xs. Their experiences in higher education were further impacted by being student-parents from a low-income background. As such, they had to navigate their colliding responsibilities as both parents and students.

While previous research argues that "incarceration is an experience that often incites an inner will to change," these narratives highlight that becoming parents motivated the students to enact their facultad to pursue higher education pathways and engage in the process of atravesada/o/x nepantleando.[29] While incarcerated, Javier pursued a high school diploma and then a college degree because of the education programs offered to him as a previously incarcerated individual. However, his daughters fueled his hope for the future. Giselle understood the implications of the severed relationships with her father and uncle due to the prison industrial complex and of never seeing her mother because she had to work. Similar to Javier, Giselle pursued a college degree and hoped to earn a bachelor's degree so that she could be present for her son.

Javier and Giselle moved beyond being atravesadas/os/xs by enacting the forms of facultad accessible to them because of their intersectional identities. Javier's resistance was evident in his persistence in education. Earning a high school diploma while he was incarcerated represented a form of resistance to the marginalization that he was experiencing due to the prison industrial complex and the classism present in the juvenile justice system. Had it not been for the structural opportunity to access schooling while in the juvenile justice system, he would not have been able to resist in that form. As he pursued a college degree, his facultad included knowing that upon earning a college degree he would likely be seen as an atravesado when trying to secure employment. Nevertheless, he planned to apply for employment at NASA because it was his dream and he knew that his welding abilities made him eligible to earn a position there. Along her educational journey, Giselle also resisted her status as an atravesada; pursuing a college degree knowing that she would be the first in her family to attend college represented a form of resistance. Furthermore, earning a high academic GPA while pregnant in high school and applying to college also represented her resistance. While the schooling system framed her as an atravesada for being pregnant and did not offer college guidance, she was able to apply for financial aid with the support of *one* teacher. Once in community college, she had access to the institutional support offered by the First-Year program, which also fostered a community of peers. By pursuing a bachelor's degree and planning to support her husband with his return to higher education, Giselle was an atravesada nepantleando.

Through their experiences, Javier and Giselle exemplify that persistence in schooling and higher education represent a form of resistance to the intersecting contexts that frame Chicana/o/x students as atravesados. In their cases, the marginalization came primarily through the prison industrial complex and capitalistic system of underemployment, but intersected with lack of access to childcare and affordable housing. Both Javier and Giselle enacted their facultad by knowing that they had to persist in the education system because it would, ultimately, provide their children with a better future. Being successful in higher education went beyond academic grades for Javier and Giselle. Academic success as a nepantlero for Javier included supporting his peers, which strengthened his sense of belonging, and ensuring that he could navigate higher education as a father who was present in the same home as his daughters, both while he was in college and in the future. Giselle also tied her nepantlera identity to her academic success because she aimed to be academically successful and earn a bachelor's degree so that she could be a role model to her brother, support her husband with his higher education journey, and pave the way to a better future for her son.

With loved ones fueling their aspirations and having access to institutional resources, Giselle and Javier were guided by their facultad and persisted in higher education with the intent to earn a college degree so as to serve as atravesada/o/xs nepantleando who support future generations. While many would not bother to consider the possibility of success represented in the cases of Chicana/o/x community college students whose lives have been affected by the prison industrial complex and teenage pregnancy, we argue that these students represent a key example of hope, resistance, and success within the structurally intersectional marginalization processes present throughout the United States.[30]

Chapter 4

Community College Students Re-envisioning Success in STEM

The scientific story—which has no way of measuring subjectivity—is losing validity . . . Science has to change its story; it must accept information that goes beyond the five senses. So right away you get into subjectivity, the inner life, thoughts, and feelings. You get into intuition, which is a very maligned sense; in fact, people don't even think of it as a sense . . . Traditional science has such a grip on us, it's become the only way to describe reality . . . If science is going to continue as the reigning paradigm, it will have to change its story, change the way it controls reality, and begin acknowledging the paranormal, intuition, and subjective inner life.[1]

WHILE THE NUMBER of Latina/o/x undergraduate students has more than doubled from 1.4 million to 3.2 million, their representation in STEM degrees remains dismal. In 2010, Latina/o/x students represented 24 percent of awarded certificates, 12 percent of associate degrees, eight percent of bachelor's degrees, four percent of master's degrees, and three percent of doctoral degrees in STEM.[2] With 46 percent of first-time Latina/o/x students enrolling in community colleges and 35 percent of Latina/o/x students who enroll in four-year colleges attending a Hispanic-Serving Institution (HSI), these institutional types are key in shaping pathways toward earning a bachelor's degree.[3] More specifically, 61 percent of Latina/o/x students who earned a bachelor's degree in a STEM field were enrolled in a community college at some point in their trajectory.[4] Despite the majority of Latina/o/x students attending HSIs and community colleges, there is a gap in the literature focusing on retention of STEM students within these contexts.[5] In particular, Crisp and Nora noted a "critical need" for studies that examine how community colleges and HSIs may "serve as institutional pathways for Hispanic students interested in STEM fields."[6]

In this chapter, we share the narratives of Francisco and Yesenia, first-generation students who decided to pursue STEM degrees once in community college. Both Francisco and Yesenia were first-generation students who attended the local community college in a rural, Southern California community. Their experiences speak to navigating high school (and community college) while feeling like atravesados in the education system. Nevertheless, they maintained hope and aspirations to pursue a degree. Their marginalizing experiences fueled their facultad, and they resisted inequities by accessing multiple institutional resources, which helped prepare them to pursue STEM degrees. By being at institutions that allowed them to retain their multiple identities, they were able to develop academic homes as STEM majors in both community college and four-year college. At the same time, their commitment to serve their family and local community fueled their pursuit of being successful in higher education because they aim to serve as nepantleras/os/x with their communities.

Francisco Navigating Autism, STEM, and the Community College as a First-Generation Student

At the time of the interview, Francisco was thirty-five years old. His parents immigrated from Mexico. His dad attended elementary school in Mexico and arrived in the United States at the age of twelve, at which time he began working. When Francisco's older siblings were enrolled in Head Start, his mother began to serve as a volunteer there. She eventually began to pursue a college degree, but stopped out in order to retain her union benefits. Francisco recalled his mother's experiences:

> [She] was a migrant student all the way through high school . . .
> She ended up getting her GED after . . . She didn't go to a four-year
> university, but she did take some classes in trying to her creden-
> tials, back before they required a bachelor's degree . . . Her job was
> so fulfilling, and her job was usually the job that kept food on the
> table for us. So, I saw the stark difference between what it meant
> to have an education versus my dad, who had very little education.

My mom always emphasized that an education should be something you strive for and so did my grandfather.

Early on in his life, Francisco understood the importance of a higher education and the implications it would have in terms of his economic future and career satisfaction.

Francisco attended a high school in rural Southern California; over 90 percent of students at the high school identified as Latina/o/x and over 80 percent received free and reduced lunch. His ninth-grade cohort consisted of about 2,200 students and, Francisco recalled, "just under five hundred of us graduated." High school was a challenging time for Francisco. He "didn't enjoy high school at all" because "it was a very awkward period." He explained:

> I enjoyed the learning; I especially loved my science classes. It was funny taking science classes in high school because I was going to school when STEM wasn't being pushed as heavily. We had very little facilities, no one really cared about science. It was just one of those things you had to take, and I loved it. It made it really challenging because so many of the teachers were just very, "Here is the textbook, read it, don't read it, I don't care. Just don't disrupt the class." I had teachers who were really dedicated and who really wanted us to learn and I had the teachers who, "I'm here to collect the check, don't bother me." I really had an interest in science, but I became painfully aware of the fact that education wasn't for me just because I couldn't do it very well.

Inexplicably Atravesado in preK–12 and Community College

Francisco experienced an education that included inequitable access to science lab facilities, and he encountered indifference from many of his teachers. He acknowledged that his high school did not have the best resources and that some teachers did not care, which is a common experience for Latina/o/x students in the preK–12 education borderlands. The marginalizing practices in the education borderlands influenced Francisco to feel like he did not belong in the education system because he struggled in ways that he could not explain. Although he felt like an atravesado, he understood the importance of earning a college degree, which fueled his choice to enroll in the local community college after graduating from high school.

Once in community college, the lingering effects of the preK–12 education borderlands followed Francisco and hindered his abilities to transition from high school. He recalled: "That was a horrible transition . . . Yeah, in community college it was really overwhelming because I was so used to the structure of preK–12 and, in community college, it was just like, the counselor saying, 'Here, figure out what you want to do.' And, how do you do that? Well everyone else does it. So, what do I do? I just have to take classes toward doing that." Within the preK–12 education borderlands, Francisco was trained to follow the rules and follow specific directions, which aligns with the traditional experiences of Latina/o/x students.[7] However, to navigate community college successfully, Francisco was expected to make decisions independently and choose from various options.

At the same time, he was also struggling socially, which exacerbated his academic challenges. He explained, "I was used to having everyone I had known practically my whole life because I grew up and went to K to 8 at one school and the majority of us went to the same high school. I knew a bunch of the people I was with and college was the first time I walked into class and I didn't know anybody. I didn't realize how much I relied on knowing people in the class to make it feasible. So, my first two semesters were resounding failures, and, so, then I just stopped going." Francisco stopped out from community college for almost ten years.

Stepping into His Facultad

During that time, Francisco was the primary caretaker for his younger brother, who was diagnosed with epilepsy and autism. He explained:

> Well, at that point, my brother's epilepsy, he was starting to have trouble with it at school, because I was struggling myself, I volunteered to stay home. So, the two of us just spent those ten years just hanging out. But in that time, he was growing up, and he was almost nonverbal, and he was very idiosyncratic about the way he wanted to do things, and about the things he would and would not do. But in that time we spent together, I realized how much we

had in common. Because I had always been the one who was better suited to work with him and we didn't understand why. A big part of it was that I did everything the exact same way. We were so focused on making sure that his seizure condition was under control that everything else kind of fell by the wayside. When he got more comfortable, the seizures lessened, so we started seeing a psychiatrist. Well, actually I had started seeing the psychiatrist first and then I turned eighteen and I lost insurance, so I only got to see him for about six months. We were so impressed with the experience I had that we started seeing him for my brother and see if there was anything they could do, in terms of the seizure medication. He did a lot for us and that's when he proposed the idea that both of us were autistic and that was why we stood out from the other members of our family and that's why we were so close. That changed my life a little bit, because then a lot of it made sense. I realized why everyone else seemed to be okay with what was going on, because it wasn't going on for them.

Encountering academic and social obstacles in his transition to community college allowed Francisco to be a primary caretaker for his brother, which is a common experience for others with younger siblings who have autism.[8] Through that experience, Francisco was able to learn that he also had autism, and it served as an *arrebato* (breakthrough moment) because he understood that he saw and experienced the world differently than others.

This breakthrough moment encouraged Francisco to pursue a college degree again. He explained: "I thought, 'I really want to go back to school.' Now that I know the problem, it's easier to mitigate some of the stuff that was going on. It was really hard to do but I eventually got to the point where I was able to go school full-time." Once he learned that he had autism, Francisco was able to understand how to navigate community college differently. Because he enjoyed science, he pursued a STEM degree and began to enjoy the college experience. He noted: "I was like, 'Wow, this is kind of feasible,' and I started to get more involved in the science activities that happened at school and got involved with some of the science programs and learned about [the STEM Scholarship]." While in community college, he transitioned from feeling like an atravesado who did not belong in education to someone who felt that he could navigate a STEM pathway.

Nepantleando in STEM

However, the transition did not happen alone; Francisco had support from various institutional agents, peer communities, and programs. He explained: "They had a summer internship through NSF (National Science Foundation) running out of the community college. I always heard about it, but I thought it was too much for me, I'm not going to live in some strange place for ten weeks. But the more I started thinking about it, I was like, 'I really should find out what this group does.' It was the MESA program that had all the ins and outs about the NSF program. I actually learned a lot and made a lot of friends, which was really cool. But it was a very new experience for me." Through the Mathematics, Engineering, Science, Achievement (MESA) program at the community college, Francisco was able to develop friendships with his peers, learn about scholarships and opportunities, and access faculty mentorship. In MESA, he learned about and applied to a summer research program that required he live on campus at the local four-year college, and he developed friendships with peers who were also pursuing STEM degrees.

Upon participating in the summer research program, he learned about another NSF-funded scholarship program and he applied. Francisco noted:

> Essentially, that's how I found out, because I joined the STEM club at the college. They were like, "These are all the scholarships going on right now," and I applied thinking, "I probably won't get it, but I'll apply, why not." And then I got it and I was really surprised and I thought, "Wow, this is kind of scary because that puts college . . ." because I always go in with the idea that, "I'll go as far as I can get and then I'll be okay with getting as far as I got." So, when they told me I get this dollar amount for this many years, I thought, "Wow, that makes going to a four-year university very feasible." And I was like, "Hey, this is getting real."

Francisco's pursuit of a college degree became a realistic option when he received a scholarship to fund the rest of his undergraduate education in STEM. While he noted earlier that pursuing a college degree was "kind of feasible," receiving the NSF scholarship allowed him to believe that he would be able to earn a bachelor's degree. Although he had already been admitted to the local four-year California State University, it was the scholarship award, not the admission offer, that allowed him to believe he would earn the bachelor's degree and reinforced the notion that he belonged in education.

Francisco's Transition to a Four-Year College

Francisco accepted the scholarship and enrolled at the CSU campus. During the transition in his first year, he experienced various challenges adjusting to the new environment. He explained:

> It's been interesting; it's been good. I have to mitigate a lot of the stress that comes with being in rooms full of different people, because I developed such a community at the school I was at before; I was in classes with many of the same people. So, generally, one of the things I tend to do it, I sit in the back of the classroom because there are times when I do have to periodically have to get up and walk outside for a little bit and I don't want to be disruptive and I also want to make that getaway as quick as possible. But also, because I like to see who's in the classroom. I like to see familiar faces. And the first quarter was tricky because there were no familiar faces. I was like, "Oh, I remember this feeling" and the campus was really big but also really small in that there weren't any real places where you can go and study consistently. Every building you go into and when you want to go, and study is like playing musical chairs because you're always trying to figure out where people are and aren't.

At the community college, Francisco had to navigate a similar transition, but he developed a strong peer community where he could study at specific places, which resulted in academic success. As a student with autism, Francisco had to adjust socially and academically to the new environment at the four-year college. He struggled the first quarter because there was no designated study room for STEM students, and he did not feel comfortable studying in new spaces where new students would likely enter.

The change in environment resulted in having to transition and adjust to a new routine; he had to learn how to navigate a new world. He recalled some of the difficulties he encountered with the transition: "The school I was at before, I knew where I was going to go and here the first quarter, I spent so much time walking around, trying find a good spot . . . I predominantly do a lot of my studying alone . . . I'm seeing a lot of familiar faces and people are really friendly. I wish I could just be that friendly back, it's really hard to so I don't spend a lot of time trying. Usually I just spend my time alone." As someone with autism, Francisco struggled to find a space where he felt like he belonged. Although he encountered friendly peers, he did not feel comfortable with socializing when his intent was to study. This experience interfered with his academics because he wanted to find a space that was quiet, had familiar faces, and where he could sit in the same area. Eventually he did find a space where it was quiet, but he would have benefited from a study area specific to his major.

Family Relationships in Transition

During his first year as a transfer student, Francisco began to understand that his academic success had implications for his family. The transition to a four-year college also meant he was navigating transitions at home. At the time, he went from being the primary caretaker for his younger brother to enrolling at the local community college to commuting to the university multiple days a week. He recalled: "It's been, really something else. Because being here, this is one of the weeks where I've been on campus all five days. I've tried to set up my schedule so I can have at least one or two days to be home, and I'll study but I have the option to study in the same room as my brother. He's interested in the things that I'm doing but mostly he tries to get me to do things he wants to do. So, there's a nice little interplay there." Spending time with his brother continued to be important to Francisco and, for the most part, he managed to balance being a four-year college student with being a sibling. His navigation of multiple worlds continued because he balanced his identity as both a four-year college student and an older brother.

At the same time, learning more about STEM meant that Francisco had to navigate a transition with his older siblings, which was also challenging. He explained:

My relationship with my other siblings is kind of interesting because they now, it's kind of tricky because I know my brother, after high school, he started working and he has a great job and he has a house, just about to get married. But I also see the way our conversation changed about things, because when we were little, we both loved science, we both loved all the things that were going on. But now it's such a very different conversation because there are times when he'll talk to me about stuff and I'll be like, "Oh, well this is how it actually works." It's never an animosity but I don't like sometimes the feeling of being, the feeling I get from him, where he might kind of feel like I'm leaving him behind. And when we were younger, we would always compete about the different ideas we would learn about and we would break out the encyclopedia and we would go look it up. And now, I almost have a degree in this field, so he's kind of just, it's tricky. It's an odd interplay.

Francisco navigated a space of nepantla because he shared the knowledge that he gained in college with his older brother, but this would cause contention. As a nepantlero, Francisco aimed to develop a bridge between his STEM knowledge and his family. However, he was navigating the multiple identities and had to grapple with a change in the relationship.

Regardless of the transitions with his siblings, Francisco continued to receive support from his parents to pursue a bachelor's degree:

My mom is super excited and really nervous just because when I started going back to school, it was one of those things where, she didn't say it, but I would imagine as a parent you really wonder, "How far my child can go and, if he can't go as far as he wants to, is that going to be a problem?" I think she's really excited to see all the things I'm doing. I know when I started to take genetics, she was like, "Wow, that's really something else." And I tell her, "I know, right? Who would have thought?"

The continued support from his parents encouraged and motivated Francisco to pursue a bachelor's degree and beyond. His experiences with engaging in discussions regarding his genetics course challenge the deficit notion of Chicana/o/x families not caring about an education. In taking the time to explain the STEM courses and pathway that he is pursuing to his mother, Francisco merged his colliding worlds together; he became a nepantlero who would bridge STEM higher education with his family. Francisco's ability as a nepantlero to engage in a discussion about his STEM materials with his siblings and mother was rooted in his desire to include his family on his journey and the joy that he experienced in learning. While academically "successful" students are traditionally expected to leave the family behind to pursue higher education, Francisco's decision to include his family on his learning journey represented a form of resistance to the traditional student integration model.[9]

Enacting Facultad to Pursue a PhD

Francisco's sharing his STEM knowledge and his joy of learning represented only part of his resistance. His decision to pursue a master's degree and PhD was another form of resistance. He explained the moment when he began to take STEM courses in community college and realized that he was enjoying learning. He recalled: "It was surreal because, you know, I was just having so much fun just taking the classes. Then there was a point where I realized, 'Oh, hey, if you are really going to go as far as you can, then you're going to have to start setting yourself up to get there.' That was one of the reasons I did [another NSF-funded STEM program] before I came over, because what I really want to do is teach." In his STEM courses, Francisco was able to transition from feeling like an atravesado in the community college to experiencing academic success. He also felt that he could earn a bachelor's and master's degree. Through the MESA program, he was able to learn about an NSF-funded STEM program that provided the opportunity to conduct research over the summer at his local four-year college. He applied to the program with the intent to begin preparing for a teaching career in a community college.

He explained that his reasons for becoming a community college professor were not based in self-interest. Instead, it was his father's trajectory and his rural community that inspired him to pursue the possibility of becoming community college faculty:

I really want to be that springboard. Because every morning my dad, before taking us to school, would stop in the fields; I grew up in the fields. I didn't have to work them like my parents did and I was realizing that that little push that I've had from my parents, from the teachers I've met, those little pushes got me thinking, "Hey, you could do this." I really want to be that kind of push; I want to be able to give that kind of guidance to people. The community college makes a lot of sense and it's such a difficult transition, I've seen so many of us get to the four-year part, being so anxious to get there because they don't like being at the community college, there is this negative stigma about being there and some transfer too early and come back.

Growing up in the agricultural fields influenced Francisco's facultad, and he understood that there was a need to provide guidance to students in his rural community. Francisco was also able to understand that his academic success was attributed to both his parents and to faculty supporting and guiding his educational aspirations.

In particular, community college professors served as institutional resources to help him strengthen his aspirations and navigate the transfer pathway and pursue graduate school. He recalled:

There are so many of the professors that have the goal of getting you there that I was fortunate that I had biology professors, specifically Dr. Simone, who was really like, "Hey if this is something you want to do, let's look at it, let's see how feasible it is." So, we sat in her office and we were going over like, the PhD program at a UC and how to get there and the things you'll need. Just in that one meeting I realized, what I wanted to go to do was get a master's degree and then go to school and teach and that was it—and be happy doing that. But she's just like, "You're so innately good at the things you do that I would be remiss if I didn't tell you to try for a PhD and if it doesn't work out then you can get a master's and go on as you were, but I know you can get a doctorate. And you'll be so much more competitive as a doctor, especially with the emphasis on STEM that continues to grow. You'll have so much more weight, more research experience, and you'll have a better base with which to communicate to get to where you got to."

While his family and passion for STEM helped to establish his aspirations to transfer to a four-year college, Francisco's access to a faculty mentor who provided guidance and concrete information helped to scaffold his preparation to pursue a PhD.

Nevertheless, it was his facultad that fueled Francisco in his persistence and commitment to pursuing a faculty pathway. He appreciated the support that he received from professors, but he was able to see beneath the surface and acknowledge that, although both the community college and the four-year college were Hispanic-Serving Institutions, not one faculty member in either one looked like him or his peers.[10] He recalled:

A lot of my peers look like me, but a lot of the professors don't. I haven't had a single negative experience with a professor. But it's one of those things that I'm constantly aware of, I think I've only had one Professor of Color so far and it was for race and racism . . . I couldn't help but notice that all the STEM professors don't look like me. That was one of the other things that at my school, and all the bio faculty weren't People of Color, although one of them was a woman, and I thought that was amazing. But it's one of those things that—I want to be that person that when they walk into the class, they can be like, "Oh, hey, he looks like me." Especially [at my community college] and its proximity to [other towns], which is mostly agricultural, I want to be able to be like, "I've had the same experiences you've had. I grew up in the fields with my dad and I ended up getting my PhD and coming back." That is one thing I haven't had the opportunity to have somebody to actually connect with, like students yeah, and you find out quickly how many grew up in campesinos or how many people were in migrant programs. But in terms of professors, they have such radically different experiences.

His passion for STEM and access to guidance helped to establish a PhD as a pathway, but it was his facultad that reinforced his interest in becoming a professor at a Hispanic-serving community college. Francisco hoped to be a role model for students who, like him, had experiences growing up in the agricultural fields. Francisco's facultad allowed him to see the need for a faculty member who comes from the agricultural fields because they are able to identify with students from a similar background. His ultimate goal in pursuing the faculty pathway was to be a role model to Chicana/o/x students who grew up in the fields, like himself, and guide them to also pursue a PhD.

Yesenia, Navigating Autoimmune Disease, STEM, and the Community College

Yesenia's parents did not complete high school and immigrated from Mexico to the US. For the majority of Yesenia's life, her mom was a homemaker and her dad worked in construction. Yesenia attended a high school that was only ten miles away from Francisco, but in a different school district. About 50 percent of the school's 2,500 students received free or reduced meals and the school did not qualify to be classified as a Title 1 school. In 2018, about 70 percent of all students identified as Latina/o/x and 20 percent identified as white. Of those graduating in 2018, about 50 percent of Latina/o/x students met the admission requirements for UC/CSU compared with over 70 percent of white students; it seemed that Yesenia attended a school within a school.[11] She began high school by being tracked into college preparation courses, and she joined the Health Academy at her school because she had always "been interested in helping people."

However, she encountered academic obstacles due to her health conditions and her grades began to suffer. She recalled:

> In the beginning of high school, I was kind of a good student but towards the end of high school I wasn't doing so well, to be honest. So, I definitely didn't have mentors or anything like that . . . I don't know. I guess I was tired of being really good. Besides that, I also started to get some health issues. I have hypothyroidism. Yeah, so, when you're not feeling so good it's like you can't really do good . . . I just started to like get some of the symptoms of hypothyroidism . . . I started getting a lot of them, not all of them. I would hear

teachers say that high school is the best time of your life. It's a fun time and stuff like that. I just thought to myself that I didn't feel like that. There's more, like, I could have a better life than this.

Yesenia's hypothyroid condition affected her physically so that she was tired often and she could not navigate schooling with the same enthusiasm that she had when beginning high school. She recalled not having mentors because she did not share her symptoms and diagnosis with institutional agents at her school. Having an experience that was contrary to what teachers would share as the norm added to Yesenia's stress. Therefore, being diagnosed and treated for hypothyroidism brought her relief. She explained: "I think just knowing what's going on, it helps you to be like, 'I'm not crazy,' or something. You learn ways to cope with it and stuff like that." Yesenia not aligning with the traditional high school experience influenced her to believe that she did not belong. However, once she was treated for her health condition, Yesenia was able to enjoy schooling and learning again and (re)commit to her goal of pursuing higher education.

Yesenia credited her parents and her older sister for inspiring her to attend college. She noted: "Well, it was a combination of my sister and my parents. They wanted us to do better than they had." Her parents and sister fostered the aspirational capital to pursue a college degree, and her high school provided institutional resources to support students with the college application process.[12] She recalled: "In high school, they had specific days to help us out with community college. So that also helps you I guess head towards that direction . . . We were all in a lab and we each had our own computer. We were just doing it on our own. If we had questions, we just, um, there was people there. There was help." Although she did not have access to a mentor or a counselor who guided her with the college preparation, application, and transition process, the school ensured that students had access to an institutional agent if they had questions when applying to and enrolling in the local community college.

Maintaining Hope upon Entering the Community College

Yesenia graduated high school in 2012 and began attending the local community college in the fall. At the community college, she chose a major, without any guidance. She explained her thought process behind choosing her major: "I've always liked math and science. I started doing really well in math again and I just got a little bit motivated. At first, I was planning on majoring in math . . . I was interested in math. I didn't have any career goals or a choice in major really. I don't know. I guess it was like that was the next step. Oh, I guess I didn't want to get into any type of job. I wanted to get a good job. I thought I would go to community college and see where it'd go from there."

As Yesenia shared her story, the lack of guidance and mentoring became more apparent. She clarified: "I was undeclared at first. Then I was just continuing with math to see how it works. I guess you could say I was a math major for a while but um then I ended up leaving . . . Um, I just felt like. I don't know. I just felt like it was getting too complicated. It wasn't fun anymore. Also, there were many questions and I would go to tutoring. They would mess up a lot." When math classes became too challenging, Yesenia would reach out for help at the tutoring center, which is what is expected of students. However, the tutoring center was not helpful because she was taking an advanced math course. When she began to struggle academically, she did not stop out; instead, she changed her major. She recalled: "Well at community college there's a lot of boring classes but last semester, I just took one class that I actually needed to and the rest of them were just kind of like fun. I just wanted to see other things. I didn't want to have to quit college yet. I still wanted to take classes but I wanted to have some time to think and I ended up becoming a music major actually . . . I played the classical guitar." Her commitment to pursuing a college degree did not allow her to stop out when courses were too challenging and uninteresting.

In her efforts to earn a degree, she changed her major from math to music but realized that was a mistake. She recalled:

> After that one semester of taking required classes, then I went straight into taking music classes. When I took it for, I don't remember too much but it was a while, maybe two years. I was almost going to graduate as a music major . . . It was so fun but I just felt like playing the guitar was more of a hobby for me. I don't know. I just feel like if you're going to be in a career like music or something in art, you have to love it. It's the only thing they could

ever do. There's not that many jobs anyways and you want passionate people to be in those fields. I did enjoy it, but I thought of
it as more of a hobby.

Again, a lack of mentorship influenced Yesenia to spend two years pursuing a music major, but she did not complete the degree because she did
not believe that a degree in music would facilitate her goal of securing a
career. Instead, she saw music as a hobby that she enjoyed but that would
not allow her to earn a livable wage.

Self-Reflection as Resistance in Choosing Biology

An arrebato occurred for Yesenia when she had to register for college and
her mom was not present. She explained:

> I was just thinking one day and actually I was pretty busy dur-
> ing that time because my mom had gone to Mexico. I had to like
> register towards college. Then I started realizing that this wasn't
> the right direction for me. I guess, I kind of remember like what
> I actually liked from school which was math and science. I've
> always liked it, enjoyed it. But then I just started thinking like,
> "Well, I don't want to do math because no." Then I just thought
> about science and umm, I just remember that I took a biology class
> in college and I really liked it. That's how I got like, "You know
> what, this is what I want to do."

For years, Yesenia searched for the "right direction" in selecting a major,
and she switched from math to music to biology. Throughout this time,
her parents were supportive with the transitions and she was able to reflect
on her interest and passions. Given the pressure to complete a degree as
quickly as possible, part of Yesenia's resistance included taking the time to
find a major that she enjoyed.

Once she decided that biology would be her major, she was prepared
to commit to the degree. She explained: "I loved it. It was so fun. I loved
it because it was challenging but in a different way. I just kind of realized
that this was right." While math was also difficult, Yesenia noted that

biology was challenging in a way that she could enjoy and felt that she belonged. She also explained, "The only challenge was eventually to start going higher in science. The classes are hard. Yeah, so, they started to get really hard and a lot of homework. That's not completely fun all the time but I tried to find, I guess, good in it like fun in it." She worked hard to maintain her academic grades and refused to change her major when the materials became difficult. Yesenia had to take additional coursework and reflect on her time at the community college to realize that biology would be a major she enjoyed. However, she was grateful that she was able to choose biology. She shared: "I feel like I'm in the right major. I feel complete, I guess you could say. Yeah, because when I was a music major there was something; I didn't feel right I guess." Yesenia understood that math and music did not align well with her goal, but while majoring in biology, she felt "complete."

However, unlike when math was challenging and she did not receive adequate support at the tutoring center, Yesenia had various sources of institutional support once she was majoring in biology. She explained: "I just had a lot of support at this time. I was like a good student. I would actually go to office hours and get a lot of help from teachers. I would also get help from classmates like doing homework together. Sometimes I did struggle with the second semester of calculus. It was years ago. It was pretty challenging but that final support really helps . . . I just feel like, if you do it on your own, you'll take so long. When you have help, they're guiding you. I don't know. I just started making connections with teachers and classmates." As a biology student, she had access to a community of support with her instructors and peers. Thus, when she encountered academic obstacles in her courses, she was able to ask for help and receive guidance from multiple reliable sources.

At the same time, she became involved in extracurricular activities. Yesenia stated, "I didn't work at community college, but I was part of some clubs. I was part of ballet folklórico. Also, I was part of the biology club and STEM club." Yesenia's decision to engage in ballet folklórico and STEM-focused extracurricular activities speaks to her being in nepantla, in between different and possibly conflicting spaces that maintain contradicting values. Like Francisco, Yesenia joined MESA at the community college, which influenced her pathway in STEM. She explained, "[Through] the MESA program in the college, I learned about the scholarship that NSF offers, the STEM scholarship. I always like going to the meetings because I always learn about new opportunities." She understood that the MESA meetings were beneficial to her future, and that is where she learned about the opportunity to apply for the STEM scholarship. When she applied, she was "pretty confident" that she would receive the award. Her reasoning was clear: "I knew I was doing good in school. I was working hard and I had like mentors, you could say, connections with teachers. When I asked them for a letter of recommendation, I kind of felt like they would put good effort to recommend me." When she received the scholarship, it reaffirmed Yesenia's decision to pursue biology and she "felt really happy" because "it was the biggest scholarship that [she] ever received." Receiving the scholarship reinforced her pursuit of a bachelor's degree and her sense of belonging in biology.

When it came time to select a four-year college to transfer, Yesenia knew she would not go far. She explained:

> Well for me, I just wanted something close by to be honest. I'm a family person so I didn't want to go too far away. For me, my options were definitely [the local CSU and UC]. They were like my top two considerations. Well, I also applied to other ones just in case. I guess what made me choose UC was mostly because I did want to go into research and stuff. I felt like I might get more opportunities at UC in undergraduate research and stuff like that. Also, the CSU didn't have the major that I actually wanted, which was microbiology. That was another big [reason], yeah.

For Yesenia, choosing a four-year college was a simpler process than choosing a major. Although she applied to multiple colleges, distance from home delimited the colleges that she would consider attending, and ultimately her choice of major influenced where she would enroll. She also understood that the UC option would likely have research opportunities that she may not readily access at the CSU option, which aligned well with her interest in research.

Although choosing a four-year college was an easier process than choosing a major, Yesenia still encountered difficulties, but she had a support system throughout. She explained:

It was a difficult decision because my sister went to a Cal State. I didn't know how UCs, like how much more expensive they would be. I did receive help from going to MESA. They really helped you and wanted us to transfer. They did tell us about how UCs have the blue and gold opportunities which pays for like your tuition. I thought that would be a great move. Also, one of my teachers, one of my math teachers was also helpful. He went to UC and he highly recommended it. Then I knew that I had to go right here.

As noted earlier, Yesenia had the support of her MESA community and community college faculty. She had access to role models and individuals who she could turn to when she was having any fears or doubts, which led to choosing the UC campus.

Despite feeling confident with her decision to major in microbiology, Yesenia shared that she had to overcome instances when she doubted whether she belonged. She credited her Chicana identity as a motivating factor: "I don't know. I guess just being a minority gives you more umm, how do I say it. I want to say it in Spanish. It gives you more *ganas*, like 'Keep going and to do better.' I guess, just showing people that we could do it too . . . I guess sometimes like STEM is more male dominated. But I guess biology isn't. Biology is mostly women, the majority. I don't know, sometimes I just feel like people think that if you're Mexican you could not be as smart or something." As a Chicana in a male-dominated field of science, she felt she had to prove herself. She understood that biology was not as male dominant, but she still had to grapple with her identity as a Chicana. In searching for how to describe the feeling she had as a Chicana pursuing a STEM degree, the only word she could use to describe the motivation she felt to continue was *ganas*, which is similar to what other Chicana/o/x and Latina/o/x students have described.[13] Engaging with *ganas* exemplifies her resistance when navigating her pathway a Chicana in STEM.

Yesenia shared that she encountered microaggressions from peers when in high school. She attributed this to a combination of her ethnic identity and her ability to speak English: "It might not be because I'm Mexican or something. It might be because of the way I speak. I guess one of my academic weaknesses is English. I just don't, I speak very. I don't know how to explain it. I don't know if it had anything to do because I'm

Mexican or they thought I was dumb or something. It might just be the way I speak. I'm not sure." Her identities as a Chicana whose first language was not English influenced her self-perceptions of her academic abilities: "Sometimes, when I'm in a group people don't think I'm that smart or something. It might be just me thinking that or it might be what it is. I don't know . . . I guess classmates but also ugh, I've been training at the research program in the research lab. Well, the graduate student, the one that's teaching me. She's, well I don't know. She has her own thing. She's kind of like impatient. Sometimes I feel like she thinks I'm dumb. I don't know if it's my own insecurity or if it is." In other words, Yesenia understood that others view Chicanas as intellectually inferior and she had to navigate such perceptions from others. These experiences positioned her as an outsider, an atravesada within STEM, and sent the messages that she does not belong in her field of study.

Despite having to overcome what she felt were insecurities because of her identity as a Chicana during her first year at the UC campus, Yesenia had access to various resources to support her transition. In particular, she had access to a peer mentor: "I have received some help right here in UC. I'm in this transfer program. It's called STEM Connect. Part of the program is to have a peer mentor. That would be someone who is a transfer student and has like a year of experience or more than you. Well, she's been helping me a lot, I guess guiding me a little bit and giving me those connections." By being paired with a peer mentor who was also a transfer student and who Yesenia could identify with, she was able to develop new relationships and connections at the UC campus.

In addition, she did have the opportunity to pursue her interest and refine her research skills. She explained: "I'm actually taking two units for undergraduate research and so I do actually have to present. It's only for the people in our lab. We have to present in front of them by the end of the quarter and explain what we've been doing so far. It won't be a project. It's just all the training and what I've learned. I haven't done it yet, but I will do it in the future." As she shared earlier, Yesenia had various experiences with microaggressions, which sometimes made her question her abilities to be in STEM. With access to a course in which she honed her skills as a researcher, she was able to continue developing her confidence so that in the future she could continue with her journey. Having access to various institutional resources influenced Yesenia's self-confidence. She stated: "I guess they feel confident about what I'm doing now. I feel like I'm more stable when it comes to school, my major, and everything like that, including career goals." As a nepantlera, Yesenia navigates multiple worlds that often collide and may not always be welcoming, sometimes leading her to be an atravesada. However, due to being able to access institutional resources, she was able to regain her confidence in pursuing her academic and career goals.

In doing so, her family continued to support her academic journey but could not understand why she had to work so much. Yesenia recalled: "They're supportive, but I guess my mom doesn't like how it's too much homework and stuff . . . She doesn't like it because sometimes, well, when I was living over there, she would be like ugh, I don't know, we would want to go out or something and it's not that I didn't want to but I didn't have time. I would be studying for a test and sometimes she didn't understand that. She just didn't like that, that umm, you have to make some sacrifices." Yesenia had to explain to her mother why she had to miss family events. The family unit is a priority in the Chicana/o/x culture, but higher education and STEM courses did not honor time for family; this was a challenge that she navigated.[14] As a nepantlera, she had to navigate conflicting worlds: one that prioritizes family and one that prioritizes individual sacrifices and gains.

After getting married and leaving home, Yesenia did not experience as much difficulty when having to balance family with college expectations. Her husband was a student majoring in computer science at the same UC campus, and she explained: "We understand each other and how hard it can be." Therefore, she did not have to explain why she had to spend hours studying or sacrificing her social and family time to complete academic assignments. However, she did have to focus on how to spend her limited time to meet all of her commitments. She reflected: "I think my only struggle now a days is just having to do so many things. I have to work, then I have to go to school, and it's quicker. Also, there's more responsibilities now that you're not living with your parents like you have to do grocery shopping for food and all these things. It could be a lot . . . So, I think the only thing I've been struggling with and I've been working on is organization. You know, finding times for responsibilities but you have to have time for fun. You can't be miserable." As an independent and married student, Yesenia had to transition to adulthood and ensure that her time would also include basic tasks, such as grocery shopping. She also had to find a way to balance her academic work with her job. At the same time, she understood that she had to find a way to maintain a balance between work and having fun. Being able to understand the need to maintain a healthy balance speaks to her facultad and her being a nepantlera; for her, success did not only entail earning a specific GPA in her courses. Instead, her success included being able to maintain a balanced life in which she could maintain a marriage, pursue a research career in STEM, and find time to enjoy life with her family.

After earning a bachelor's degree, Yesenia aimed to pursue graduate school: "I'm thinking about going to graduate school, to get a PhD [in] microbiology." Her desire to earn a PhD was rooted in her identity and her desire to help others. She explained:

> Well, I guess I was kind of thinking about all of my interests like priorities and things in life. Well, for me, I just know that I love math and science. I just love that you could find new things. That's what I really like about it. I guess something that is giving more of a direction is that I'm also in Student Help and I know how to help people. That's why I was interested in microbiology specifically. Well, since I have an autoimmune disorder or disease, I just wanted to find ugh, I guess that's what I wanted to research. I wanted to find the correlation between micro- and autoimmune diseases or something similar to that.

Similar to when she chose a major, Yesenia engaged in self-reflection when it came to thinking about her STEM career goals. As someone with an autoimmune disease, she wanted her research to contribute finding a cure for such diseases—not so that she could get fame or credit, but because she was interested in helping others with similar conditions. As a nepantlera in STEM, the bridges she aimed to build were founded on doing research that would benefit a wider community of individuals.

Enacting the Chicana/o/x Dream

STEM is rooted in a work culture that is white, masculine, male-dominated, and culturally incongruent for Students of Color, including

Chicana/o/x students.[15] Such a "historically exclusionary" system can contribute to framing Chicana/o/x students as atravesadas/os/xs[16] who do not belong in STEM fields. Given the hostile environment in STEM, receiving support from peers, mentors, and faculty is critical to succeed in STEM education.[17] Both Francisco and Yesenia exemplify the success that can result from accessing interconnecting and complementary institutional resources. Because they were at Hispanic-Serving Institutions, they were not subjected to a hostile-campus racial climate; such a climate decreases a sense of belonging for Latina/o/x students, particularly in STEM.[18]

Francisco and Yesenia exemplify that their commitment to support future generations is interconnected with both their goal to be professors who reflect the same background as students and to make a difference through their research. This highlights the need for faculty to help students understand the connections between pursuing graduate school and supporting Chicana/o/x communities.[19] This is key, given that student identities, including their religion and culture, can be used to validate STEM identities.[20] For Francisco and Yesenia, developing a sense of belonging in STEM happened because they were able to embrace their invisible disabilities, and they could navigate their pursuit of higher education while maintaining and balancing their multiple identities, pushing back on the notion of being an atravesada/o/x. As such, they hope to serve as atravesadas/os/xs nepantleandos when they become faculty and guide the next generation of Chicana/o/x students in STEM.

The Chicana/o/x student's dream is representative of the process that the participants underwent. Each transitioned from an atravesada/o/x in higher education to an atravesada/o/x nepantleando in a STEM field. In order for this to occur, they had to tap into their facultad and multiple identities as they accessed institutional resources and developed a sense of belonging in both STEM and higher education. When they encountered obstacles, which made them feel like an atravesada/o/x, their ability to maintain the hope that they would be able to pursue higher education represented a form of resistance. Upon learning that they each had a disability, they gained new insight to navigate higher education; in other words, their facultad was strengthened. Through la facultad, they navigate multiple worlds as a nepantlera/o/x by ensuring that their families continued to be part of their education process.

The process is representative of the dream that Chicana/o/x parents have for their children: to maintain hope despite having to resist marginalizing experiences and to understand that success is encompassed by more than individual gains. Instead, with the support of institutional resources, such as caring faculty and peer mentors, Francisco and Yesenia were able to pursue their bachelor's degrees and prepare for graduate school, with the goal of helping others in the future. With access to support and guidance from institutional agents and programs, their aspirations will become a reality so that they can create bridges for future generations of Chicana/o/x scholars.

The Chicana/o/x Dream in the Four-Year University Borderlands

Chapter 5

Empowerment and Success Among Four-Year University Chicano Male Students

The truth is that I am an American citizen born in the soil that once belonged to my indigenous ancestors who were here way before they themselves were colonized. I am the product of hard-working immigrants and I am proud of what they stand for: hope, determination, and dedication. Aside from being of brown skin, I am honored to say I am a first-generation Latino high school graduate who is the first in his entire family's bloodline to attend college. One might see me at the University of California campus and think, "Oh, he was a lucky one whom had mentors and economic support," but they are wrong. If only those who doubted me took a moment to hear me out and learn about the struggles and accomplishments in my path to becoming a student at the University of California, then maybe, just maybe they too could have a change in opinion and accept that fact that descendants from Mexican immigrant parents simply want what is the best—an education.

—Miguel, first-generation Chicano college student

THE CONTEMPORARY AMERICAN EDUCATIONAL SYSTEM employs seemingly discrimination-free approaches in educating youths of diverse backgrounds—especially the compulsory primary and secondary educational enrollments, which supposedly offer opportunities for upward social mobility to socioeconomically disadvantaged minoritized students. However, education has never been separated from the larger societal inequalities in the United States: from boarding schools for Native American children to racially segregated schools, the American educational system has served minoritized students unequally when compared to their white counterparts.[1] Such unequal and dehumanizing treatment of students of minoritized status is just one of many pieces of evidence showing that the contemporary American educational system is built upon coloniality and continues to marginalize, misrepresent, and erase histories and lived experiences of Students of Color.[2]

In this chapter, we focus on the *testimonios* of three Chicano students' experiences of marginalization in their educational pursuits and the resources they used to overcome adversities and achieve academic success. Coloniality in the US public educational system not only oppresses and erases Chicana/o/x students' histories, cultures, and language from its curricula, but also affects each Chicana/o/x student differently along various axes of the social worlds in which they are situated.[3] For example, even though the three Chicanos in this chapter share certain characteristics, such as being members of minoritized ethnoracial groups and children of immigrants, their experiences of marginalization differ by level of socioeconomic precariousness, exposure to violence, disability, and sexuality. As intersectionality scholars have argued previously, multiple forms of inequality and subjugation affect individuals' experiences and perceptions of the worlds around them differently according to the varying degrees of penalties and privileges they accrue in their everyday lives.[4]

Thus, we employ intersectional approaches to shed light on the multiplicative nature of social marginalization that Chicano students have experienced in their educational pursuits through the testimonios of three Chicano first-generation college students.[5] Testimonios are first-person narratives of the experiences of sociopolitical inequality, oppression, and trauma.[6] By placing these testimonios at the center of our analyses, we aim to reveal the social processes and mechanisms through which Chicano students reject coloniality and enact la facultad—that is, their ability to see beneath the surface of inequities. Subverting the systems of coloniality via la facultad leads Chicanos to become nepantleros.[7] As nepantleros, they are able not only to perceive multiple, overlapping, and conflicting social worlds in which they live, but also become agents of larger social change by bridging these social worlds.[8] This ability to see beyond surface realities, to turn adversities into resources and opportunities, and to further create and merge social worlds that reflect multiplicative realities allow Chicano students to empower not only themselves, but also others who share similar experiences of oppression.

In this chapter, we highlight the ways in which three Chicano students enact la facultad to reject the colonial atravesado designation and become nepantleros who not only propel their own success, but also become leaders who represent and instill the Chicana/o/x dream of hope, resistance, and success in others. In so doing, we focus on three systems of oppression that students have to navigate—ableism, racist nativism, and heteronormativity—and how Chicanos turn them into sources of self- and community empowerment by enacting la facultad.

Testimonios of Chicano *Atravesados Nepantleando*
Esteban's Story: Lessons Learned from Ableism

Esteban is a first-generation college student and fourth-generation US-born Chicano, whose great grandparents immigrated from Mexico to California over a hundred years ago. Even though such latter-generational status makes him an American indubitably and Esteban does not really see his Mexican heritage as a source of marginalization, his journey to higher education still largely mirrors that of other poor, first- and second-generation Chicanos, who have to persist against all odds. More specifically, despite his latter-generation status, Esteban experienced extreme hardships and uncertainty due to poverty. Growing up with a single mother who could barely afford to provide for her three children, Esteban learned what it was like to live in poverty and be treated as if he did not belong in the community and the larger society:

> There was no "home" that was permanent; we were always having to move. Section 8 only allows you to live in an apartment that costs no more than x amount to rent. If the rent were to be raised even one dollar over the set amount, we were forced to move out and find another place to live that met Section 8's guidelines. Since Section 8 only pays for a fixed, often low amount of rent, these locations were never in a good neighborhood. Though we did our best to move in the safe neighborhood free from drugs and gangs, many times [we] would be unsuccessful as the cost of these good neighborhoods were too much, as per the guidelines.

His account shows how poverty and socioeconomic marginalization, much like ethnoracial inequalities, labels certain individuals as the transgressors of the society, atravesados, who do not belong in or deserve to belong in "good" neighborhoods. To make matters worse, Esteban was diagnosed with Lyme disease shortly after his birth, a rare neurological disease that attacks his nervous system. With Lyme disease came involuntary jerking of muscles, pain, learning disabilities, and other complications. His medical condition required continuous monitoring and caused multiple debilitating symptoms.

Yet this disability status came with an additional Supplemental Security Income/Disability (SSI) support from the government, which provided his family with limited relief from potential immediate financial crises. Helpful and understanding doctors and nurses also provided all the medical services, care, and attention that Esteban needed during his childhood and adolescence. Moreover, Esteban was able to access any and all institutional resources available at his elementary, middle, and high schools to pursue education undeterred by his medical conditions.

Esteban was an exceptionally gifted student, testing at twelfth-grade level when he was only in sixth grade, and was able to take advantage of programs like the Individuals with Disabilities Education Act (IDEA) and Individualized Education Program (IEP): "IEP was the holy grail to my academic career as I was able to receive all the help I personally need in order to be a successful student. With my IEP active, the [middle] school was able to work with me and allowed me to complete the schoolwork at home. With the IDEA and IEP, all the staff and teachers were able to work with me." Because his medical condition required many sudden surgical operations, Esteban had to miss school a lot more than other kids. Somewhere along the way, he also began developing noticeable memory problems and eventually was diagnosed with a learning disability, too—a part of his health complications. Thankfully, the IDEA and IEP participation prevented him from falling behind. Other than not being able to participate in physical education classes and extracurricular sports or having limited social interactions with his peers due to his disability, Esteban's educational experiences seemed to have prepared him to be successful in college.

Upon graduating from high school, Esteban enrolled in a local community college with hopes of transferring out to a four-year institution upon finishing the transfer requirements. However, Esteban's transition into adulthood was marked by various atravesado experiences. He faced further adversity when he turned eighteen years old and his SSI checks stopped suddenly because of the bureaucratic loophole that assumes that children's disabilities "disappear" upon entering adulthood:

> When I turned 18, my income was taken away without warning. Upon further investigation, [I learned that] my income was taken away because they believe my disability "disappeared" upon turning 18 . . . they were in the wrong as I am clearly a candidate. We had to fight my case, which took a long time as they wanted doctors' notes, visit reports, scans, images, and much more from the time I "became disabled," which was right after birth. I was required to fax every single page to multiple different departments. I was expected to pay for every paper faxed while I had no source of income, even though it was over ten thousand pages. It took a total of two years to reach the final decision.

With his additional income unavailable, Esteban worked part-time as a sales associate at Walmart. However, his medical conditions started worsening due to the physically demanding nature of the work. Between his job and additional visits to the doctor's office, Esteban's academic performance at the community college suffered. To make matters worse, his worsening health put him in critical care at one point, prolonging his hospitalization more than expected. As a result, Esteban missed a lot of classes, which became an issue for many of his professors:

> Although some professors worked with me, there were two that did not. They were very by the book and told me via email that if I was not in class, then I will be dropped and failed. I was told to submit the assignments in person and not online. Reading those messages while hospitalized was devastating. It confused me as to how they expected me to attend. I could not understand how a professor would not be able to see my perspective and my inability to attend class despite my mom sending all my paperwork and doctor notes from the hospital.

As these accounts show, Esteban was labeled a transgressor, an atravesado, due to his disability status in multiple societal domains. Institutional supports, such as SSI paychecks and laws regarding disability accommodation in higher education settings are intended to help individuals like Esteban but do not work well. Instead of assisting Esteban and ensuring that he be able to live his life to the fullest, the larger system forced Esteban to prove that he deserved these supports; once again, he had to assert his belongingness and deservingness in the larger society as a disabled person. Fortunately for Esteban, he had a network of social support and capital available through his mother and a few understanding and helpful institutional gatekeepers, such as doctors, nurses, teachers, and community college deans. As a result, Esteban was able to continue his academic career undeterred by a series of setbacks. Central to his determination was his mother's unwavering faith both in his potential as a student and in education as a way of achieving upward mobility. Despite the myriad obstacles single mothers face, starting from when her children were very young, Esteban's mother was engaged in and supportive of their educational development and pursuits:

> She ensured we were on track for a good academic career. My mother is an amazing person for successfully raising five children while being a low-income, uneducated, divorced parent who did not want us to struggle like she did. In order to keep us from hanging out with the wrong crowd, she was fully engaged in our education and made sure we did not get into any trouble. My mother wanted us to get out of the low-SES apartments and live in our own home without being bound by strict rules or having to watch our backs 24-7 due to the bad neighborhood.

The personal and institutional support Esteban was able to access through his mother, his participation in IDEA and IEP, and various medical and educational agents he encountered throughout his life eventually led to his enactment of la facultad. Despite continuously worsening health conditions, Esteban decided to focus on his academic career. When he doubted himself, he quickly turned to look for a role model in his social network, always learning from those around him who exhibited exceptional work ethics, preparation and determination for a better future, and welcoming personalities.

In addition to the social support and capital he was able to access, Esteban learned to cope with the physical limitations his disability poses in healthy, productive ways:

> Good mental health is important when dealing with a serious medical condition, so I got into drawing, video games, and fishing. Although these hobbies were influenced by my environment, I maintained these throughout my entire life due to their compatibility with me . . . These three hobbies have been my personal tool to get through the day; however, I have had external help with the support from family and friends. Lyme has been a personal struggle and has been something I have to deal with on my own due to how much it has shaped my life.

Esteban's pursuit of hobbies was more than just a distraction: it was his way of enacting la facultad to see beyond the physical limitations posed by his disability and ensure his academic success by proactively taking care of his mental health. In so doing, he developed the mental and emotional resilience to persist not only when faced with health complications and consequent challenges but also when faced with atravesado moments in his social, political, and educational experiences as a disabled Chicano.

Esteban's health conditions have gotten worse; he now has several inoperable tumors in his brain, spine, and ribs, in addition to other health complications he is and has been experiencing. However, he does not see his disability as limiting. If anything, as Esteban asserts, his disability is his identity—one that is not necessarily restricting and oppressed, but characterized by resilience, resistance, and persistence:

> Lyme has become the main part of my identity. I have met so many wonderful people growing up at my hospital or the many charity events I attended. This upbringing has taught me to be nonjudgmental. I have been told many times, "You do not look disabled," or "You look normal." I find that is the case with most people. You do not know what others are going through, which is why I do not jump to conclusion with people and their actions. This upbringing

has allowed me to understand the perspectives of others and treat everyone equally.

As Esteban explains, he understands what it is like to be treated differently and constantly judged, doubted by others—informed by his own experiences of achieving academic success despite being marginalized as a student from a financially poor background with a disability. However, these experiences only fuel his aspiration to become an educator who can support and guide the next generation of marginalized youths.

His personal experiences of becoming invisible in the system, experiencing physical and social challenges in asserting his presence in the mainstream educational realm and the larger society, allowed for his enactment of la facultad, developing the ability to see limited but available opportunities to which disadvantaged students seldom have access. He noted:

> I aspire to be the social worker that makes a significant impact in a child's life. I want to be a youth social worker who positively influences children who are placed at risk. I know what opportunity looks like and I want to make sure every child can see it too. I want to show the next generation there is a chance to grow no matter where you come from. The opportunity to grow from a low-class environment is always there; students just need the scaffold along the way. This is necessary since children cannot think this abstract on their own. Especially when they do not have the proper guidance or support at home. Anything is possible with all the resources out there. I want to make sure everyone has access to them since they are not easily handed out. I aspire to be there for every child to be sure that no one is left behind and motivate every child to learn. I want to be there for students who are suffering from an identity crisis. It does not matter what upbringing, race, citizenship status, SES, or gender you have. All that matters is that you are persistent and you get back up when you are kicked to the curb. No matter how many times you fall—and you will, everyone does—you must get back up and follow your dream.

His ability to see the overlapping but unequal worlds of the larger society and marginalized communities shows Esteban's projected transformation into a nepantlero. Esteban understands from first-hand experiences dealing with bureaucratic procedures and gatekeepers that even the resources that marginalized people are supposedly entitled to do not necessarily become easily available. As an educator, he wants to be the one who connects disadvantaged students to these resources and opportunities to ensure that no deterrence or failure discourages a student. In this sense, Esteban is already able to see the different worlds one may belong to as a result of not only societal marginalization, but also personal identity crises and failures. As a nepantlero, he would be the bridge these disadvantaged students need to see beyond these limitations and enact their own la facultad to resist societal pressures and oppression and, eventually, achieve positive educational experiences and outcomes, which in turn will allow these marginalized students to further succeed in the larger society.

Miguel's Story: An Anchor Baby Not Defined by Mistakes of the Past

Miguel is a first-generation college student at a University of California (UC) school, majoring in history and sociology. As he explained, he dresses well, has good posture, and a strong vocabulary because that is expected of a successful college student traditionally. However, Miguel's journey to academic success was marked by uncertainties, criminality, and scarcities, as he was born to poor, undocumented immigrant parents from Mexico, who were left with no other option than to raise Miguel and his sister in disadvantaged neighborhoods characterized by poverty, gang activity, and a lack of institutional opportunities, expectations, and resources for their youths.

As a result, Miguel's educational journey has been marked by his status as an atravesado, due to institutional agents, such as teachers, expressing disinterest, low expectations, and assuming that students are deviant:

> I vaguely remember my time at Ford Elementary, yet I do recognize the aspects that developed my thoughts growing up. Early on I noticed that educators did in fact want to teach students on how to behave and the basics on education such as the alphabet and numbers. Despite this, those same educators were unable to teach and control every student, and often those students who

caused trouble influenced the instructors' behavior over the other students. Most times teachers where angry at everyone and strict to the point where we could not raise our hand if we had a question. It was a simple dead silent classroom environment. Although there where instructors (in middle school) that were helpful and had high hopes for students, the majority did not see to go beyond their comfort zones to inspire and express that one can be more than they are told. They would simply teach class, tell students that they needed to ask one another if they were confused, which no one ever did, and left campus as soon as the end of the day bell rung.

Despite this school environment, characterized by uninspiring school curricula and disengaged teachers, Miguel found a few teachers who cared for his academic success and volunteered to tutor him before and after school. Moreover, Miguel's parents, not having had educational opportunities themselves but fully understanding the bleak future the lack of education leads to, instilled the values of hard work and education in him and his sister from a very young age.

Being in a disadvantaged neighborhood, Miguel was exposed to a world of violence in middle school, where boys pressured one another to join a gang or a clique with bullying. After numerous incidents of getting bullied and beat up, Miguel decided to defend himself. However, his self-defense propelled him to become a name of sorts on his school campus, leading him to be involved in the same social clique and its delinquent and deviant behaviors that he tried his best to avoid. Ironically, he became an atravesado as a result of his resistance. Miguel recalls: "The self-defense aspect was that which helped me make a name for myself during my first years at LB [Long Beach]. The quiet kid who was picked on was fed up of mistreatment and simply defended himself to the point where the perpetrator was left with a broken nose, bruised ribs, and humiliated in front of his clique. It was then when I was invited to form part of a clique and, thus, led to my hardships in which my grades fail, I lost respect for education." Fortunately for him, the adult figures around Miguel had not given up their hopes for him, despite his delinquent teenage behaviors. One of the teachers from Miguel's elementary school who had cared for him and motivated him to respect and focus on education transferred to his high school as a math teacher. This teacher, instead of simply being disappointed in his transgression, sat Miguel down and checked in on his academic progress, social surroundings, and behaviors, which eventually reignited Miguel's passion for education.

Moreover, Miguel's parents provided immense emotional and psychological support despite not being able to help his academic growth directly. In addition to his parents' continuous sacrifices and support, Miguel also benefited from a local gang leader's protection. Seeing Miguel's academic potential early on, this gang leader, whom Miguel refers to as his second father, barred his gang from initiating him and repeatedly told Miguel that he had a bright future ahead:

> If it was not for my mother, I can honestly say that I would not be in the spot that I am today. She is the one who inspired me to obtain more than the basic high school diploma, the one who always tried to help me with any school assignment even if she had no background knowledge of the topic, and the one who consistently reminded me that my education was going to be the only way out of the low socioeconomic status that we had to consistently face. I was raised by [a local gang leader] since my parents were always at work and my grandmother had to take care of my grandfather, and I would always be outside and hanging out with his kid and himself. Despite obtaining a first-hand look at how he managed the gang, he told me that I had a bright future ahead of me and forbid that I be initiated . . . Despite going down the wrong path early on, it was my instructors' motivation to keep pushing and their willingness to listen to my struggles, my parents' constant work ethic, and my second father's value toward me that made me come back with a better view towards education. I needed to be heard in order for educators and my parents to know the best way for me to succeed, to be involved, and most importantly stay motivated; without a voice, I would not be able to get where I am due to the lack of help.

As Miguel's account shows, the social and emotional capital he accessed via his teacher, parents, and his "second father" allowed him to enact la facultad and pursue academic success.

Whenever he encountered institutional gatekeepers who doubted his potential and treated him as an atravesado who was on his way to either prison or death, Miguel was able to see beyond this surface reality and keep his faith in his chances at success strong. Moreover, having experienced the violence and lack of expectations that other Chicana/o/x atravesados are also subjected to, Miguel is now able to understand that his parents are also victims of cultural and structural forces that oppress and limit minoritized individuals' pursuit of opportunities. Miguel learned that asking for help was not a sign of weakness, but something that could assist and propel his achievement.

This realization was especially profound for Miguel, who has always struggled with the Mexican cultural notion and norms of machismo, coupled with the Western hegemonic notions of patriarchy and masculinity, which influenced his father and grandfather to become absent, hard-to-approach breadwinners of the family:

> Understanding my grandfather's way of being with his children allows me to ease my views as to why my father decided to plant a seed within my head that constantly put the notion that working and earning money was more important than obtaining education, the thought that men do not need to cry or seek help when facing issues on a daily basis, and the notion that we are no better than what others say we are. I can understand that being undocumented brings challenges when trying to obtain a good job, puts you under the law enforcement's radar, or that you are in a country that is new to you and are still maneuvering around this new world, but I will not accept the fact that my father is the way he is with my family and I for the simple reason that his father was like that with him.

This is another example of Miguel's enactment of la facultad: he was able to see beyond the stoic, emotionless, day-to-day expressions of his father and grandfather and understand that capitalism, patriarchy, coloniality, and a lack of economic opportunities had shaped their world views and the ways in which they interact with others. With his understanding of the struggles of his poor, undocumented parents contextualized by his own experiences and la facultad, Miguel joined his UC campus's chapter of Moviminiento Estudiantil Chicana/o/x de Aztlan (MEChA), a historic organization created around the civil rights movement to raise awareness of social and political issues that the Chicana/o/x community face in this society.

His participation in MEChA, coupled with his previous experiences, his parental sacrifices, and the social, cultural resources that he obtained through college curricula, drove Miguel's aspirations to help the next generation of Chicana/o/x/Latina/o/x youths as a nepantlero:

> Understanding the struggles and witnessing firsthand the hardships that can present themselves at any time I have made it my goal to give back to the younger generations with MEChA . . . For this reason, I have made it my mission to reach out to the younger Latina/o/x generations with the goal of exposing them to the vast opportunities that are out there willing to be discovered by them. They only know so much yet have the interest to learn from those who have been there and who have succeeded in overcoming obstacles. Like my parents, who are undocumented, are a success and overcame many obstacles. Being undocumented is a status placed on humans, not a cultural marker; it's socially imposed and not born with. I am a reflection of their success and I will pass along my knowledge to others that follow.

Miguel's dedication to the next generation of disadvantaged Latina/o/x youth is exemplary of the role nepantleras/os/xs play in marginalized communities. As a Chicano who has struggled with the gender socialization norms of machismo and patriarchy—which led him to question his father's and grandfather's relationships with the family and nearly become another troubled Boy of Color with delinquency problems—Miguel was able to make sense of the overlapping worlds of Mexican culture and American institutions and understand that Chicana/o/x youths could be caught between these two worlds, doubting their own abilities.

Moreover, seeing that undocumented status could impede not only immigrants' but also their children's economic chances, Miguel is now determined to pass along the knowledge he has obtained through his enactment of la facultad to the next generation of youths who may be facing difficulties and problems similar to those he experienced. In this sense, he is truly becoming the bridge that connects the positive aspects of overlapping social worlds of disadvantaged immigrants and unwelcoming institutions and the larger society that labels minoritized populations as atravesados, showing that it is possible to resist oppressive social and cultural forces and actualize one's potential with one's own academic success and future aspirations.

Carlos's Story: Finding Pride as a Gay Chicano from the Barrio

Like many other children of poor Mexican immigrants, Carlos's journey to academic success cannot be fully explained without mentioning his parents' hardships and dedication. However, Carlos's story is also a bit different in that his father's authoritative parenting style that intimidated his siblings actually provided a strong foundation for Carlos's future academic probing and problem solving. As Carlos explains, his father's upbringing as a poor, uneducated Mexican child who had to become a "man" at a young age in the absence of his father or a father figure greatly impacted Carlos's aspiration today. Carlos's grandfather left the *rancho* in Mexico to pursue economic opportunities in the United States under the Bracero program and left his young family behind—including Carlos's father.

Growing up, Carlos tried to understand his often violent and aggressive father, but it was not easy:

> Not having the guidance of his own father, he consequently never learned how to raise kids as a dad. Instead, as he was always out working and only saw my grandmother's caretaking skills after work. My dad's teaching style is mostly a result of observations and experiences he has learned vicariously through his parents or scripture. Avoiding my dad after he came home from work was like dodging a heavy rain of thought bullets or attempting to avoid an agitated wasp inside a phone booth. His logic would consume your reality, and you would have to wait until he was satisfied that we learned our lesson. If we resisted, he would interrogate us. If we confessed to doing "wrong," the punishment could end painfully quick or indefinitely dreading.

The absence of Carlos's father's father speaks to the root of familial trauma that is informed by the capitalism and coloniality between the United States and Mexico. Nonetheless, this parenting style of Carlos's father caused his siblings to challenge everything he did and believed in. They condemned and resisted against his use of violence and his religious beliefs, and his father responded with more aggression and violence; as Carlos explains, his father interpreted such challenges from his children as a threat to his position as a father and the leader of the household. Carlos further interpreted his father's actions based upon his father's positionality in the US structure, whereby he had little power outside the home: if his children challenged him, he would also have little power at home.

The relationship between Carlos's father and his siblings became so strained that his dad isolated himself from the rest of the family. However, upon his brother Ricardo's arrest, the family dynamics changed. They began communicating and motivating one another to work hard, help each other, and carry on as a family unit. Ricardo's arrest had a further impact on Carlos as they shared a sexual identity as gay Chicanos. Seeing that a lack of safe space led Ricardo to make a series of poor choices that eventually led to his incarceration, Carlos came to understand the different kind of atravesado experience the gay identity brings into the lives of marginalized Chicanos. Determined to not repeat his brother's mistakes, Carlos enacted la facultad to challenge the surface reality buttressed by religious doctrine:

> To my dad, *la verdad* is a universal wisdom dispensed only to those who completely surrender to the will of God. This truth can only be understood through the will of God . . . Part of the lesson behind *la verdad* is the idea that being true with oneself is being in good standing with God and his will. My dad believed that if one is honest and good, God will guide their choices because he is honest and good. I liked the logic behind it, I just had a problem with religion as an oppressive institution. It was during high school, when I was attending an evening indoctrination class once a week. Four hours of indoctrination instructors partaking in deficit thinking by assuming children in the ghetto need God, not recreational opportunities. Four hours of indoctrination

instructors preaching about moral integrity, while they subscribe the oppressive stereotypes fixing gender roles . . . Instead of rebelling at home, I figured I would use the interrogation methods I learned from my dad, after ages of lectures, to challenge and question the validity of my Catholic indoctrination instructors. Lectures upon lectures on universal truths and moral relativity later, I was anything less than a saint in class.

Instead of passively accepting religious doctrines as the absolute truth, Carlos challenged them with logic and rigor. Surprisingly, his aggressive—yet eloquent and logical—expression of resistance to oppression resulted from dealing with his father's persistent questioning of his children's wrongdoings, which accompanied his authoritative and violent parenting style. To avoid what Carlos calls *existential homilies*, he was challenged to think critically, beyond his own moral failings and their consequences, to consider the larger society and other individuals' interests and/or needs. As a result, even after relentlessly challenging his indoctrination instructors, Carlos was praised for his eloquence and told that he challenged adults to grow stronger in their faith while correcting their own biases and mistakes.

Carlos's ability to think beyond the immediate situation—his *facultad*—led him to understand that his father's use of aggression and violence were motivated by good intentions for his children. Even though his father was unable to show any affection to his children because of his own upbringing and the intersecting forces of machismo, global patriarchy, and coloniality, Carlos understood that his father cared deeply about and for his children. His use of violence was the only way he knew how to express this:

> His use of violence was a due to panic, for he understood the opportunities his lack of education was costing him. Opportunities he believed could have led us away from the struggles of poverty . . . I know my dad feels guilty for using force, but in reality, his pedagogical approach through the 1990s was effective. None of us joined a gang, but the suffering he created is far from over. Retrospectively, I remember seeing the level of violence escalate from fist brawls to gunshots, so my dad's behaviors could

also be a fearful reaction to the violent environments around us. He thought that any disrespect of authority will result in gang participation, and he thought a strict rule of law could preserve this respect.

In addition to protecting Carlos and his siblings from the street gang violence that was prevalent in their community, Carlos's father's parenting style also assisted Carlos with his success in school, both indirectly and directly. To avoid his father's aggression and the strained family relationship at home, Carlos turned to school and everything the school space had to offer. He went to school early and stayed there until 7:00 p.m. almost daily; he was focused on his academics during the day and occupied himself during his free time in the band room after classes, teaching himself how to play instruments. Staying at school inadvertently led Carlos to stay away from the same environment that led his brother Ricardo to make a series of poor choices.

Carlos's father's probing and lecturing equipped him with the critical thinking abilities that led a couple teachers to see the potential in him, despite his circumstances, which could have easily marked him as another potential troublemaker atravesado student in the classroom:

> Ms. Williams and Ms. Rodriguez worked hard to get me to challenge myself to my fullest potential, and they did their best to hold me up to high standards. Sometimes higher than those expected of my peers. At times it felt unfair how hard my teachers criticized my work, but my social capital was more than substantial. All of my teachers were women, and even though they did work to help us fight the logic of oppression, my friend Brandon and I always received the most attention. His whiteness and my competitiveness monopolized much of the attention left for others.

Even as he was benefitting from his teachers' attention and high expectations of him, Carlos knew that his nonwhite racial status distinguished him from his peer, Brandon. Such perception is also informed by his first-hand experiences with violence and poverty that labeled many Chicanos, including his brother Ricardo, as atravesados and marked them with criminality.

As shown in these accounts, Carlos learned to enact his facultad in both positive and negative circumstances, which led him to interpret the social worlds around him from multiple perspectives beyond his own. For instance, even though Carlos thinks he personally benefited from the machismo culture in a way, he does not discount its negative effects on gender inequality within Latina/o/x communities: "I want to work towards a place where little Latina/o/x girls can have the same dreams as boys. I, however, cannot act like the effects of machismo have been entirely negative on my life. I would dare say that my father's ideals have given me thick skin and the ability to be unaffected by the unfortunate events in my life." With such critical and expansive understandings of the larger society and how the educational system itself, in addition to other structural and cultural factors, perpetuates existing disadvantages of many poor Chicana/o/x and Latina/o/x children of immigrants, Carlos aspires to be a teacher. Apparent in his aspiration is the role that he seeks to take on as a nepantlero for disadvantaged youths. He understands that "good" school environments are not easily accessible for Students of Color. Instead, he wants to bring the "good" school experiences as an attentive and engaging educator to minoritized students. Further, he hopes to set an example for his students and to highlight that he, too, has experienced such hardships and persisted.

In this sense, he aims to bridge overlapping worlds of good and bad schools, of Chicana/o/x and Latina/o/x culture and the mainstream one, and the invisible, yet ever-present oppressive social structure and individual lived experiences—and this aspiration is the main characteristic of nepantleros who further contribute to the larger social change by taking necessary small steps:

> I want to be a teacher. I don't want to take the easy route that I have seen many others take. They get their credentials, and start teaching at "good" schools, where the pay is better and is convenient to them. That is not what I want to do. I want to go back to my community and educate students like me. I want students to feel proud of who they are and accept themselves—yes, even their sexual identity. I want to be able to teach students and give them a sense of comfort I sometimes did not have as a gay Chicano from

the *barrio*. I want my students to be able to ask questions and trust me as an educator without having to force that trust upon them. I want them to be able to talk to me because I look like them and I know their struggles. I want to teach students that know I can understand them. I want them to know that I have walked in their shoes.

Enacting the Chicana/o/x Dream

As shown in the testimonios in this chapter, lived experiences of coloniality, oppression, and overcoming adversity greatly influence the ways in which Chicano first-generation college students navigate through educational institutional settings and the larger society. In their pursuits of academic achievement and success, the three Chicanos introduced herein found ways to make sense of the structures that restrict their marginalized positions in US society. The processes through which they subvert adversarial and colonial discourses into opportunities and successes reveal that those labeled as deviant and transgressive—as atravesados— need to access resources and opportunities for themselves, beyond the immediate circumstances that present obstacles in their pursuits of success, by enacting la facultad. The enactment of la facultad allows for these individuals to become nepantleros not only for themselves, but also for others, and ultimately to create a strong community to resist systems of oppression together.

Even though Esteban, Miguel, and Carlos share similar experiences of social inequality, as they all grew up as marginalized Mexican Americans in disadvantaged neighborhoods, their testimonios reveal that there are multiple ways of being labeled atravesados and overcoming adversity with various supports in place. Yet as unique and distinctive each of the three Chicanos' lived experiences are, they share certain commonalities in the ways in which they enact la facultad. For instance, the uniquely Chicano cultural gender socialization through machismo led Miguel and Carlos to understand the colonial worlds around them (and those of their fathers and grandfathers, by extension), while simultaneously enabling them to reject machismo, coloniality, capitalism, and patriarchy as transgressive sociocultural discourses. This realization has been especially important

for Miguel and Carlos as they were able to see beyond the restrictive definitions of masculinity and the realities to which machismo often exposes
Chicano boys (such as violence, social isolation, etc.), leading them to
seek out necessary help and resources in their families, communities,
and beyond. Such enactment of la facultad grounded in critical understandings of machismo, coloniality, capitalism, and patriarchy shows
that ethnic culture—both its negative and positive aspects—provides
unique tools to minoritized groups to interpret the social worlds around
them and modify existing ethnic cultural discourses to further empower
themselves.

The ways in which they find guidance in their parents' experiences
of marginalization and perseverance further allow them to see the positive dimensions of their own experiences, such as the fact that they are
benefitting from compulsory primary and secondary education and have
opportunities their parents could only dream of but never access, which is
a central characteristic of la facultad. They further supplement their facultad with available resources and assistance in their communities, often via
a few helpful adult figures and institutional actors. For instance, all three
Chicano reported at least one helpful and engaged teacher inspiring them;
in Miguel's case, the protection and guidance of a local gang leader further
prevented him from continuing his delinquent behaviors, which he notes
could have led him to prison or caused his death.

The structural and cultural processes through which Esteban, Miguel,
and Carlos similarly enacted la facultad also led them to share a common
nepantlero aspiration to create a safe community for the next generation of
Chicana/o/x and Latina/o/x youths. More specifically, all three Chicanos
aspire to be educators and leaders who can provide access to institutional
resources and develop critical consciousness for all youths. Thus, the enactment of la facultad, partnered with institutional resources, allows them to
become agents of change and resistance who could bridge the mainstream
and marginal social realms to inspire others and help provide the social
and cultural capital one may need in one's own pursuit of success. As
Carlos puts it, they have "walked in [the future generation of Chicana/o/x
and Latina/o/x students'] shoes" and they can understand their needs and
struggles. The transformation from atravesados to nepantleros shown in
the three testimonios represents the Chicana/o/x dream—persisting in the

American educational landscapes that is characterized by its coloniality and achieving hope, resistance, and school success.

Esteban's, Miguel's, and Carlos's testimonios reveal the processes through which atravesados who are subjected to multiplicative forms of social marginalization, which additionally vary by one's location in the larger social structure, enact la facultad to resist coloniality and become nepantleros. By employing testimonios as a theoretical and empirical tool, we have shown not only that coloniality perpetuates systems of oppression and inequality in almost every social, political, and cultural domain and adversely impacts minorities disproportionately, but also that individuals make informed decisions and use resistance tactics based on their own and their families' lived experiences. The testimonios allow us to situate marginalized individuals' own accounts at the center of our analyses, rather than approaching them while centering our analyses on the concept of marginality. As a result, we were able to ensure that each individual experience was representative of one's intersectional experiences of coloniality and oppression, apart from the larger structures of coloniality that establish and reinforce academic and social hegemony, which renders marginalized individuals' experiences invisible in mainstream discourses.

We have shown that the systems of coloniality not only are present in the mainstream American educational institutions of today's society, but also actively influence minoritized students' educational experiences and outcomes by reinforcing existing inequalities. However, minoritized individuals do not passively succumb to the pressures and systems of coloniality and oppression, as shown in the lived experiences of Esteban, Miguel, and Carlos. Instead, they actively and assertively challenge and resist coloniality (enactment of la facultad) to become agents of change (nepantleros). These individual transformations from atravesados to nepantleros represent the Chicana/o/x dream, characterized by hope, resistance, and school success; becoming nepantleros via la facultad not only empowers on to turn adversities into opportunities, but also allows individuals to further instill a common sense of hope and agency in their home communities, as well as in other marginalized communities, by setting positive examples. In this sense, the personal is and always has been political: the seemingly personal experiences of being atravesados, enacting la facultad to resist coloniality, becoming nepantleros, and achieving the Chicana/o/x dream result from colonial social processes, and yet they simultaneously establish alternative, inclusive sociopolitical processes and discourses at various levels of society to resist and challenge the system of coloniality and oppression in the mainstream educational system, as well as in the larger American society.

Chapter 6

Intersectional Journeys of Four-Year University Chicana Female Students

Every time we go out, it is a risk we take, but as I gain knowledge of how society works against some, I realize that I must not be afraid, and while I have some sort of temporary legal status, I must fight and protect my parents and any other person who has even less of a voice than I do. Life has taught me that good things come to those who sacrifice themselves for others, just as my parents did for me, and that is why I proudly and openly say that I'm an immigrant, undocumented, and unafraid.

—Rosa, first-generation college student

EDUCATIONAL INSTITUTIONS are presumed to employ seemingly race-, sex-, and class-neutral sociopolitical discourses in their curricula while cultivating knowledge in today's youths. However, numerous studies have shown that the contemporary American educational system is built upon coloniality and does not adequately capture or even accommodate histories and lived experiences of marginalized groups.[1] Ethnoracial minoritized groups are perhaps the most directly affected by this unequal, colonial, and discriminatory educational system. In particular, Chicana/o/x students' histories, cultures, and language have been oppressed and erased from the US public educational system since the late eighteenth century.[2]

Yet coloniality and marginality do not affect all members of the Chicana/o/x community in the same manner. Intersectional scholars have previously argued for the multiplicative nature of social marginalization.[3] More specifically, multiple forms of inequality, along various axes of the social world, affect individuals' experiences and perceptions of the world around them.[4] As for Chicana/o/x students, their marginality is rooted in their structural positionality as ethnoracial minorities and immigrants/children of immigrants in the Eurocentric American society. Additional subjugation as women, sexual minorities, undocumented immigrants or children of undocumented immigrants, and people with disabilities further burdens many members of the Chicana/o/x community. The ways in which these different forms of subjugation affect individuals vary by different penalties and privileges they acquire and experience in their everyday lives in multilayered systems of oppression.[5]

Although Chicana students face many socioeconomic, political, and even discursive obstacles in their educational experiences, many of them still successfully obtain bachelor's degrees and eventually achieve upward social mobility.[6] Scholars have identified immigrant optimism and gendered educational experiences and outlooks as the driving factors behind Chicanas' eventual success.[7] Nonetheless, there exists little information regarding how Chicanas themselves make sense of their experiences, and in this chapter we aim to fill this gap in literature. More specifically, we are interested in how Chicana first-generation college students subvert existing coloniality and/or disadvantages to propel their academic success. By taking an intersectional approach, we put their experiences at the center of our analysis.

This chapter presents the educational experiences of Chicana first-generation college students and how their experiences vary due to distinct forms of marginality. Utilizing testimonios, we center the voices of three Chicanas whose experiences are often erased in mainstream sociopolitical discourses.[8] The aim is to reveal the ways in which these women enact la facultad to both proactively and assertively claim their belongingness in the educational system despite their marginalized positions as colonial subjects and persist when faced with adversity. We identify different ways in which three nepantleras made sense of the marginalities they experience as atravesadas and how they enacted la facultad to persist and succeed in their educational pursuits. In so doing, we explore three identities pertaining to their marginalization—one's own undocumented status (and DACA status), disability, and sexuality—and how these Chicanas turn them into sources of self- and community empowerment to promote hope, resistance, and success.

Testimonios of Chicana *Atravesadas Nepantleando*

Rosa's DACA Experiences: Proudly Immigrant, Undocumented, and Unafraid

Rosa is a twenty-year-old first-generation college student who migrated from Mexico with her family at a young age. Rosa's parents were born in and met each other in Mexico. Prior to their move to the United States, Rosa's family lived a relatively comfortable life: both of her parents had steady jobs, they owned the home the family lived in, and her grandparents lived across the street from them, offering much-needed childcare support. Yet upon hearing about better opportunities available in the United States, Rosa's father decided to cross the border without proper legal paperwork in 1997, when Rosa was only a few months old. Her father's pursuit of the American dream changed everything for Rosa's family. Even though Rosa's father entered the United States illegally, he found work soon and was able to obtain a worker's visa. However, the family's separation became a big concern, which propelled Rosa's mother to move to the United States with Rosa and her older sister. Rosa and her family's first experiences as atravesadas began as they attempted to obtain a tourist visa:

> We went to our appointment to request a tourist visa, but it was denied due to the laws, which were becoming more and more strict over the years when immigration began to become a "problem" to some people in the US. After that day we went home disappointed, and a few days later we went back, but this time asking for a worker's visa, for which my sister and I were listed as my mom's companions. Once we obtained our visas, we bought our plane tickets, and that was the first and last airplane that I have ever been on in my life. *This shows that all of my family entered the US legally with the exception of my dad's first time, but either way we are still viewed as illegals.* (emphasis added)

As Rosa points out, the racist and xenophobic popular discourses against Mexican immigrants immediately labeled potential immigrants as "illegal," and such discourse affected Rosa's family's pursuit of a better life in the United States even before their arrival.

After this initial experience, the fear of getting their visa renewal applications denied led Rosa's family to overstay their visa and remain in the United States as undocumented immigrants. Even Rosa's father, who had been going back to Mexico every year to renew his worker's visa, stopped doing so. As undocumented immigrants, Rosa's family lived in fear and encountered many institutional barriers to accessing resources, information, services, and opportunities. For example, Rosa remembers the fear she encountered with her father and sister almost daily on their way to school while growing up: "Living in the US without documentation for most of my education was also a hardship, because there was a time when my dad was driving my sister and me to our school and it turned into a time of great fear when a border patrol vehicle began to follow us around. My dad was trying to stay calm, but at the same time he was frantically trying to drive into areas where he knew that he could lose them." Despite such experiences, however, Rosa and her family persisted. Most importantly, Rosa's parents put tremendous emphasis on the value of education, and Rosa herself also was well aware of the opportunities she could obtain through education. She also benefited from having encouraging and supportive teachers who "made learning fun and entertaining," especially during her early educational experiences. Upon obtaining entrance into the Deferred Action for Childhood Arrivals (DACA) program—which offers temporary relief from deportation to undocumented immigrant youths—Rosa was able to pursue higher education without worrying about deportation or paying out-of-state tuition.

However, the additional bureaucratic steps required for DACA students like Rosa once again made her feel as if the higher education system was not designed for immigrants like herself—that atravesadas like Rosa are not welcome:

When I was filling out my college applications, I was also shocked because I would have to pay a much higher tuition compared to an American citizen. I would almost have to pay double if it weren't for an extra form called AB-540 that I had to fill out, which would grant me California in-state tuition. I feel like I had more struggles and a longer application process to obtain higher education than the average student. This was difficult because at the time the topic about legal status was a sensitive issue to talk about, so I did not know anyone else who was in my situation and had to figure out where to apply and how to fill out my financial aid, which was different to everyone else's. Sometimes I see those who are American citizens or who are at least documented not appreciate the education and privileges that they have, while I know that I would be very lucky if I had citizenship in order for me to gain more opportunities.

Rosa did not have access to the social capital required to navigate the complicated college application processes as a DACA and AB-540 student. Even after successfully enrolling in a prestigious public four-year university, Rosa faced many anti-immigrant adversities in various aspects of her college life. When Trump was elected president, it was Rosa's first encounter with a large group of racist and xenophobic white people; this experience led her to think of her home community as a safe Latino "bubble" and exposed her to the harsher reality of the larger society. Moreover, President Trump's new immigration policies and punitive treatment of immigrants discouraged Rosa from pursuing a study-abroad opportunity, which her sister had done without much fear during the Obama administration.

Despite such constant reminders of her undocumented, unwelcomed atravesada status, Rosa persisted in college, driven by her parents' love, support, and sacrifices:

I live a very comfortable life with just the minimum necessities and nothing more. First of all, I appreciate my lifestyle because my parents make sure to give me all of the necessary things in order for me to be well equipped and motivated to continue my education. Something that my dad says to me every chance he gets is to work hard so I don't end up like them working in the blazing 120 degree heat in the desert sun doing something that I am not passionate about . . . In a way, I value education much more because since my parents help me, I feel like it's not just a step in my life that I need to put all of my efforts into. My education is something that I need to complete because I feel like it's a sacrifice that I need to make in order to give back to my parents,

even though all the help they have given me was done with no
intention of getting anything in return. I feel like they deserve it
because of all the sacrifices they made for my sister and me, basically living a life without their parents and siblings being around
for most of their lives.

It is this parental sacrifice, support, and love that led to Rosa's enactment
of la facultad. Her experiences of illegality led Rosa to see that US systems of coloniality across various institutional domains—from immigration policies to educational opportunity structures—make Mexican
immigrants, like herself, feel like criminals who do not belong and do
not deserve access to resources and opportunities. Yet her experiences of
marginality also allow her to see clearly that, despite everything, she has
more privileges than others. This realization further drives Rosa to succeed in the United States, against all odds, to benefit not only her parents,
but others, too.

In fact, as Rosa puts it, she sees it as her responsibility to help her parents and other undocumented immigrants who are going through similar
experiences as her family's:

I have had first-hand experience of life with lack of resources and
I want to give hope to those who are not given a fighting chance
or do not have the opportunities needed to succeed. Since I experienced a lot of hardships when applying to scholarships with
DACA, I want to help those who are covered by it by funding a
scholarship which would help them pay for school, books, food,
and a place to live because it is hard to obtain the money to cover
all of these costs. This has always been one of my major goals
because since I did not get any help or scholarships, I know how
discouraging it can be to see those who didn't take advantage of
their education receive financial aid and those who do left to fend
for themselves. I would also want to help anyone with DACA or
illegal status obtain opportunities in research by funding them in
any way that I can. These are the most important goals that I have
because I want to give back to my community and help my own
people reach new heights because I know that its not something

that's expected of us but that we can accomplish with a little help from others.

In this sense, the enactment of la facultad not only allowed Rosa to achieve academic success that would further assist her and her family's upward social mobility, but also led Rosa to become a nepantlera, who navigates the educational system and fosters bridges for others to follow.

More specifically, Rosa's atravesada experiences not only propel her own enactment of la facultad, but also allow her to see beyond each individual fragmented reality of marginalities and coloniality. She now realizes that economic precariousness, immigrant documentation status, and the unequal opportunity structure all go hand in hand with limiting minoritized individuals' chances at success. Consequently, she is inspired to help others see these intersecting worlds and experiences and become a bridge that connects other undocumented and marginalized individuals to resources and opportunities in the larger society as a nepantlera.

Araceli's Story: Accessing the Inaccessible Despite Facing Ableism

Araceli is a senior at the University of California, majoring in sociology and ethnic studies. Araceli's life experiences are unique due to her disability status: she was diagnosed with neuromuscular scoliosis at the age of three, which influenced the ways in which she and her family navigated through her educational pursuits. Other than her disability status, Araceli's childhood and adolescence mirror those of many other children of poor, undocumented Mexican immigrants. Araceli's father never received formal schooling in Mexico and immigrated to the United States when he was seventeen years old, looking for better economic opportunities. Similarly, Araceli's mother only received basic elementary education in Mexico and left her hometown to pursue economic opportunities first in Mexico City and then in San Diego. Both of Araceli's parents arrived in the United States illegally, but her father was able to obtain residency through the Immigration Reform and Control Act of 1986. Araceli's mother, on the other hand, migrated to the United States after the 1986 reform and therefore remained undocumented until 2001, almost a decade after she married Araceli's father. Being poor, uneducated, and undocumented, Araceli's parents had difficulties securing stable jobs and navigating through the American society in general:

> Not knowing the English language has made it difficult for my parents to obtain job opportunities that they would otherwise obtain with their residency status. My mom has been a victim of discrimination because she does not know the language. We were always pushed to assimilate into this culture and American lifestyle however, my parents were very traditional and firm to the values they had growing up. . . . Despite everything, a general value they both inseminated in me, was the value of perseverance. Even if they were miserable and struggling, they taught us to withstand the pain and simply get through situation as best as we can. In a country that made them feel foreign, while having children native to that country, they feared us losing our values and our roots, which is why they have always been resistant to assimilation.

The pressure to assimilate stems from the racist, xenophobic popular discourse that labeled Araceli's parents, as well as other similarly situated poor immigrants and native Spanish speakers, as atravesados. Or perhaps, because they understood their atravesado status, Araceli's parents were able to resist such pressure and successfully instill ethnic authenticity and values in their children. Such perseverance further assisted Araceli in her educational experiences, where the curricula and environments are not designed to welcome or accommodate many minoritized students—especially with disabilities like Araceli:

> I was four years old and was getting ready to start the new school year. My mom attempted to enroll me in the local elementary school; however, they would not take me because they were unsure of my status as someone with a disability. They were unsure of whether I had a learning disability and thought other schools would be better equipped to provide me with the resources I needed. I was sent to school farther away from home, but I still qualified for free transportation. I spent my kindergarten and

first-grade years in a special education program where I was eval-
uated to see whether I had the ability of performing well in the
classroom. There was a wide array of children with disabilities
in the classroom. We were all taught the same curriculum but in
different ways. There was a special ed gated bungalow located in
the back of the school, and we were not allowed to leave the area.
We did not get to go play in the yard with everyone else or even
have lunch with them. We were a bit secluded. Unlike the rest of
the school, we had a playground and actual toys and tricycles we
were allowed to use.

As Araceli recalled, finding a school that could provide special education and accommodate students with disabilities was a struggle. However,
Araceli was able to pursue mainstream school curricula once she entered
second grade and thrived. She even participated in afterschool hip-hop
and ballet classes. Even though her experiences in these classes made her
become aware of the extent of her physical limitations as a disabled person, Araceli remembers these days fondly. Behind such fond memories are
Araceli's parents' continuous efforts and perseverance to provide the best
care and education for Araceli. However, her disability posed more than
just a physical limitation once she entered middle school:

Physically, elementary and middle school were not challenging
for me; however, my self-esteem detrimentally took a toll in middle school when I began to get bullied. As a middle schooler who
still did not understand disabled identity, who felt self-conscious
about my appearance and was constantly attacked in the beginning stages of social media and rapid advancement of technology,
I hated myself. Every day consisted of sneaking my way through
the front gate of the school despite being very visible because of
my crutches, or I'd begin to get humiliated in front of the whole
school. I did not raise my hands or participate in class and I did
not try too hard for fear of being called a smartass or a teacher's
pet. People wrote about me in the restroom walls for all to see. I
was bullied at school and at home with kids from the block. I had
no escape. I questioned why I was disabled and why people bullied
me. I was not good at school, and I had a troublesome time finding

something to like about myself. I was struck with depression in a household that did not believe in mental health. I did not communicate any of this with my family since we never talked about our feelings or checked in with each other. I did not feel supported anywhere and had suicidal tendencies. Eventually, my bullies grew tired of attacking me and I was simply glad the attacks were over, although I still had to see them every day.

Even though Araceli was a good, promising student, her peers did not see her as a social equal. In this sense, Araceli's atravesada experiences were rooted in her disability status: in mainstream society dominated by able-bodied individuals, she was an outcast who did not belong or deserve equal opportunities. Despite the spirit of perseverance Araceli's parents instilled in her, she fell into depression and started doubting herself, both socially and academically. Even though it is hard to tell if Araceli really was "not a good student" as she claims in her interview, the experiences of bullying and self-questioning seem to have functioned as a form of self-fulfilling prophecy and negatively affected her high school achievements.

Araceli admits that she "did not work [her] way up to college" and that she "barely felt [she] belonged and that teachers were courteous with [her] grades." With not many academic achievements or aspirations, Araceli initially was not interested in pursuing a college degree. Moreover, she lacked social and cultural capital to navigate through the complicated college application and admissions processes, which is a common experience among many poor children of immigrants and first-generation students. However, all of this changed when Araceli serendipitously stumbled upon an internship position that provided her with much-needed social and cultural capital, as well as the strong drive to succeed:

While working on a school project, we needed a space to work and discuss. The library did not let us speak; therefore, my friends introduced me to a program they attended in order to use their space to work. The center was small in people since it was barely starting up. I met the director, and she conveniently said that they released applications for interns that day. The internship was paid, and we would work in programming activities for younger kids in the summer. I was hired and interned there the summer after my junior year. The director and the staff decided to work with us high school students as well and began asking what our plans for college were. She and the staff realized we were all first-generation students who did not have any knowledge of college. The rest of the summer they spent planning college trips for us and preparing to advise us on the college application process. By September, which was the beginning of my senior year, we had already begun to draft our personal statements. With the help of fee waivers, I ended up applying to four Cal State Universities, three UCs, and four private schools.

Araceli was eventually admitted to a University of California school, but feared that the institution and overall postsecondary educational system were not designed to accommodate someone like her—a poor child of immigrants who is a first-generation student with a disability. One of her high school teachers explained that the systems of inequality work to disadvantage students like Araceli and her classmates. The teacher explained that Araceli's experiences as an atravesada were not a result of her personal failure but of the way the larger educational system works to marginalize and ostracize students from ethnoracial, socioeconomic, and other minoritized backgrounds. Nevertheless, Araceli continued to suffer from imposter syndrome, believing that she did not deserve to be admitted to a prestigious UC school. However, the program director at her high school internship helped Araceli remember the values of perseverance that her parents had instilled in her; her parents also believed in Araceli. In this sense, if the social and cultural capital she accrued from participating in her internship program allowed her to be admitted to a prestigious university, then the emotional support and aspirational capital her parents and the program director offered further helped her overcome her fears and anxiety and find the determination and drive to be successful in college.

Once Araceli started her college career, a different obstacle hindered her academic success: accessibility. Even though she was academically performing well, the inaccessibility of her college campus left her physically exhausted at the end of every day. Neither the on-campus Disability Services Center nor her academic advisor could find a way to provide Araceli with mobility support, such as a power scooter or other transportation services. However, upon hearing about her struggles, the director of her internship program contacted individuals near campus, using their already established institutional network, to secure a power scooter donation from a local couple. Again, Araceli's social capital available through her old internship position supplemented what her family and school could not provide her to ensure her academic success. Once the issue of mobility was resolved, Araceli quickly adapted to the new college environment and found a welcoming community in her campus's chapter of Moviminiento Estudiantil Chicana/o/x de Aztlan (MEChA), a historic organization created around the civil rights movement to raise awareness of social and political issues that the Chicana/o/x and Latina/o/x community face in this society. Her involvement in MEChA was crucial in her enactment of la facultad:

> My mentor from MEChA at the time served as the executive secretary of student government. She introduced me to the realm of activism, where I quickly found my voice within the disability justice movements. All my struggles in relation to my identity were all making sense to me now. I was fired up and wanted to make change. I participated in a few protests to fight against tuition increases and against the school-to-prison pipeline. The biggest campaign I participated in was the protests in solidarity with the campus service workers who were getting pay cuts and being laid off. In every and all the spaces I interact with on campus, I educate on disability and bring consciousness to accessibility and accommodations. There is a lot more awareness of disability from what I have seen since my first year, but there is still a lot of work to do. Politics and social justice issues have been engrained in my college experience, and I became very intentional with the spaces I chose to be involved with.

As Araceli recalls, her extracurricular involvement in MEChA allowed her to tap into a whole new set of important resources and social and cultural capital. This experience not only allowed her to become involved in the disability justice movement, but also opened her eyes to the intersecting struggles and marginalities individuals experience as ethnoracial minoritized people, workers, and other marginalized persons. Thus, Araceli's involvement in MEChA led to her enactment of la facultad, seeing beyond the surface of the oppression she lived with as a child with disability whose mother was once undocumented. Enacting la facultad led her to reject the ways in which the larger society labels her an atravesada. In so doing, Araceli was able to turn all adversities she's faced into lived knowledge and positive reinforcement of her aspirations.

Today, Araceli not only continues to enact her facultad, but also aspires to become an important asset to marginalized communities as a nepantlera. Her experiences and involvement in various grassroots social movements via MEChA allows her to see the complicated, intersecting social realities that marginalize and oppress individuals along different axes of power and domination; she sees all these struggles as connected and wants to be a bridge that connects these social worlds, empowering other disabled individuals and people who experience different forms of social marginalities and inequalities. She concludes her life history with big dreams of becoming the person who could connect underprivileged individuals to necessary social capital, much like the program director at her old internship and her parents had done for her:

> Now that I am graduating, I want to take a break from academia ... My identity as a disabled Chicana who is first generation has motivated me to find better ways to support marginalized communities. In today's political climate, it is easy to get disheartened by seeing the fear in my community's eyes upon deportations. It is hard when I go back home and help my nine-year-old neighbor with her homework and notice how she struggles to read, while nine-year-olds in San Diego are writing poems and reading *Harry Potter*. Along with socioeconomic challenges, there are educational disparities that affect students and their learning. I want to return to my community and help provide accessible resources that will help educate the community, that will tackle issues of gang violence and crimes. I especially want to support the disabled community that is prevented from obtaining an education solely because of structural barriers rather than their ability and willingness to learn. I have been challenged in every way possible and I need a break. I want to work and help support my family while

gaining experience that will help me apply to graduate school for disability studies or multicultural education in the future.

Christina's Story: Community as a Form of Queer Resistance

Christina is a first-generation college student and a third-generation US-born Chicana, whose parents are of Mexican heritage but born in the United States. She self-identifies as a "beautiful, smart, sexy, voluptuous, queer Chicana." Her parents were children of Mexican immigrants who settled relatively successfully in the United States and owned properties, enjoyed childhood and adolescence experiences typical of middle-class families. However, Christina grew up in much more deprived circumstances. As Christina explains, her parents were barely "adults" when she was born: her father was a high school graduate and her mother a high school dropout, and neither of them had transferable skills to secure salaried jobs to support a growing young family. Christina's family enjoyed a comfortable life for a while, thanks to her paternal grandparents' financial assistance, but this all changed when the recession began and Christina's dad lost his job. To make matters worse, Christina's mother's health quickly deteriorated. Christina recalled this time of her life:

> When my dad lost his job, my entire family lost our health insurance. Luckily, there were government programs in place to make sure that my brother and I could get insurance, but my parents didn't qualify for any more help. My dad was alright—he hated the doctor anyway—but for my mom, it almost resulted in her death . . . Eventually, she was diagnosed with lupus, an inflammatory disease that makes your own body attack itself . . . Without insurance, the medicine was extremely expensive, but we needed it to keep my mom functioning. Her immune system, however, could not keep up, especially with all the added stress. She got pneumonia, and with no health insurance, we had nowhere to go. My own doctor agreed to see my mom because he understood our situation. He prescribed her the medicine she needed and gave her advice to manage it. I was only seven, but suddenly I was responsible for even more. I had to make sure I got myself and my brother

to school on time. I had to make him feel better about what was going on. I had to be an adult. When you have a sick mom, you're usually prepared for these types of things. You tell your teachers in advance, you make sure you'll be able to get extra time for the homework, but with everything going on at once, it all felt impossible.

Thus, despite their native-born status, Christina's family was effectively ostracized from any institutional support for her family members' health and well-being due to their low socioeconomic status, which was worsened by the economic recession. In such an environment, school was an outlet, a solace of sorts for Christina that allowed her to ignore and forget about her unstable home life. However, concerns about her family's financial stability and economic livelihood kept worrying young Christina, even though she was passionate about learning. When she needed to buy school supplies, such as printer paper or volleyball shoes, Christina felt especially guilty for needing them. To make matters worse, Christina's only outlet, school, became a place of suffering instead of an escape:

I realized that attending school itself was so much work. Just existing at school required a form of work that didn't even account for the assignments given to me by my teachers. School can be very stressful outside of the academic part of it because teenagers are learning how to interact with each in very often brutal forms of socialization. As a fat, queer Chicana, I was subjected to a lot of bullying as a kid, but going to high school made it worse. Even the thought of walking to school made me anxious. Every night before I went to bed, I made a very specific plan about my route to school. I took the longer path, trying to avoid intersections so that I was visible to less people. The thought of going to school exacerbated my anxiety and gave me panic attacks. This wasn't even about the demand I faced for work; this was solely based on the action of going to school. Once I started taking more demanding and difficult classes, I was affected in different ways. If I didn't understand something the teacher had tried to explain to me, I was out of luck. There was nowhere else for me to go. My parents couldn't afford tutoring, and they couldn't help me either.

Despite feeling out of place for being different, and despite not having the immediate familial resources to support her increasingly demanding high school coursework, Christina was able to persist with the help of her parents and other adult figures. In particular, Christina's mother was determined to push her daughter's educational pursuit further, hoping that Christina would not repeat her own decisions of dropping out of high school and becoming a parent at a young age. Moreover, caring teachers not only made sure Christina did well in school, but also provided her with food and emotional support as needed. With support and encouragement from her parents and teachers, Christina was able to access valuable social and cultural capital that was not immediately available in her disadvantaged neighborhood. One of the most crucial moments of accruing such capital to assist her academic success came just in time, right before she began applying for colleges:

Even though I was clearly on the path to attending college, none of the counselors reached out to explain what I should be doing, and this was mirrored in the experiences of my fellow classmates as well. Despite this inadequacy, I was one of the lucky ones. Because I knew it was important to be involved, I had access to a lot of things other students didn't. I had good relationships with my teachers, and I could depend on them to help me with things from personal statements to school stuff. They couldn't all get that personal help with college applications. My parents didn't complain when I'd be at school until 10:00 p.m. I was also given the opportunity to participate in UC's Early Academic Outreach Program. This program was designed for first-generation, low-income students who wanted to go to college. When they contacted me and told me to apply, I was so excited. I came home from school and immediately told my mom. They took us to visit colleges, let us stay on UC's campus, gave us advice, and helped us with our applications. I was able to meet UC's admissions officers to go over my personal statements and get feedback. This was so valuable to me, and their willingness to help made me feel like college was actually attainable.

These experiences not only propelled Christina's academic success, but also allowed her to understand her marginality differently. Even in college, despite continuing financial struggles and feeling isolated, Christina was able to persist and be successful due to the support she had from her parents and the communities in which she grew up.

These experiences led to her enactment of la facultad. Rather than passively accepting her fate as a minoritized student with limited resources, Christina actively sought out role models from media and in her social networks. She explains that her parents' sacrifices, the social and cultural capital she accessed with the help of her teachers, and other similarly disadvantaged individuals' experiences of navigating through adversities gives her not only hope, but also the drive to build a better future for herself and for others. Various role models assisted with Christina's aspiration: Hillary Clinton, President Obama, and even coparticipants in UC's Early Academic Outreach Program. Christina was able to fight her fear of and anxiety in embarking on a path that no one else in her family has been on—that is, succeeding in higher education and becoming an educator herself—because, from these role models and from her own experiences, she was able to see the importance of supportive communities for marginalized individuals:

I saw how deeply a lack of education affected people's discernment of information. I saw just how critical it is for educators and the community to take civic engagement and education seriously. There are so many different ways to approach this; I am thinking that my path might lead me to becoming an educator . . . I know that there are very real barriers in place to prevent the students in my community from making these changes, but I want to help bring an understanding so they can fight too. I am constantly in limbo between these choices. They're all interconnected, but they all are very different paths. While I know that hope alone will not fix anything, it is something that is driving me work to make things better. I believe that eventually I can do for someone what so many of my teachers did for me. . . .

Despite poverty, I came from a strong community. *The emergence of the community as a form of resistance* reminded me of my community's work to ensure that despite my high school's lack of funding, we still had opportunities. Parents and teachers came together to make sure that students had food before AP [Advanced Placement] testing, that they didn't need to buy calculators, and that students weren't taken out of class for insignificant interruptions. . . . importance of the community in making sure a school district was responsible for implementing a model of restorative justice in schools. I constantly challenge myself as an economically disadvantaged queer Chicana. My life showed me that there was more to my educational journey than I ever thought, and it even gave me a voice in college to back it up. In college, I gained a better understanding of how my life affected my education, and it showed me what I can do to counteract these things in the future. I can now approach my education fully understanding what it means for me to be here.

As Christina accurately and succinctly puts it, existence is a form of resistance for atravesadas like her. Social and cultural capital and resources she was able to obtain with the help of her parents and teachers led her to this conclusion and further drives her enactment of la facultad to subvert her marginality to empower not only herself, but also other similarly marginalized people.

In this sense, Christina's "pay-it-forward" mentality, via which she is prepared and willing to extend the help and support she has benefited from to other members of her community, represents her personal growth as a nepantlera, ultimately contributing to the emergence of the community as a form of resistance, as she puts it. As an educator, she will able to guide others to also enact la facultad and see beyond the immediate adversities they are facing and contribute to emerging communities to resist coloniality together.

Enacting the Chicana/o/x Dream

What do we make of the testimonios of Rosa, Araceli, and Christina? Even though society does not value them as trained social scientists or policy makers (yet), their lived experiences provide valuable insights into how coloniality shapes marginalized persons' experiences in the mainstream educational realm and beyond. In this way, these young women empowered themselves by turning adversities into opportunities with the support of institutional programs and supportive adults. These accounts provide powerful vernacular examples of individuals who have been subjected to coloniality, and were therefore labeled as atravesadas, can move beyond the realities surrounding them to perceive positivity, potential, and success in their present and future selves by enacting la facultad and ultimately becoming nepantleras despite institutional and cultural barriers and precariousness.

Clearly presented in the three testimonios in this chapter are the multifaceted experiences of being labeled transgressors, atravesadas, who are deemed undeserving of and unbelonging in the mainstream educational, cultural, and popular domains in the contemporary American society. Rosa's, Araceli's, and Christina's narratives show that in addition to their ethnoracial minoritized status, their sex, the immigrant documentation status of themselves and their family members, their sexuality, and their disability statuses further complicated the ways in which they encountered, navigated through, and overcame adversities. Yet as unique as their experiences are, these Chicanas similarly benefitted from accessing and accumulating emotional, aspirational, social, and cultural capitals that were available through families and communities in their pursuit of success in education and beyond.

For instance, all three Chicanas benefited greatly from familial resources: their parents not only sought out appropriate help and resources in the community, but also provided emotional and aspirational capital whenever their daughters doubted themselves or faced a roadblock. In their secondary and postsecondary educational experiences, they benefited from having access to extracurricular involvements, whether in the form of a student organization or external internship program. These opportunities widened their social networks and helped them access social and cultural capital—such as work and networking opportunities, direct involvement in social movements, and more—that they could not have accessed otherwise. We argue that these instances of accruing capital through familial and community-based networks led to the enactment of la facultad, by which these three young women were able to develop a sixth sense of awareness to see beyond the surface reality of coloniality and inequality.[9] Such deepened awareness and conocimiento allowed Rosa, Araceli, and Christina not only to anticipate difficulties in their postsecondary educational pursuits, but also proactively respond to and resist such difficulties in empowering ways.

What is apparent in these three Chicanas' life histories of overcoming adversities is that their enactment of la facultad leads them to become agents of change for others. All subjects in this study exhibit a pay-it-forward mentality characterized by their eagerness to reciprocate whatever assistance and advantages from which they have benefited back into their communities of origin as educators and scholars. In so doing, they are contributing to the emergence of communities as a form of resistance, as Christina argues. Such a phenomenon represents more than these three individuals' personal growth; it captures how the enactment of la facultad leads individuals to become nepantleras. As nepantleras, Rosa, Araceli, and Christina are developing understandings of their own lived experiences, as well as how all forms of inequalities and marginalization are interconnected as they support the system of coloniality by alienating individuals who are deemed deviant and as having transgressed from society. Based on such awareness that goes beyond the surface realities, they are able to persist in their own pursuits of success and provide others with the necessary social and cultural capital to resist coloniality. Thus, the enactment of la facultad among atravesadas like Rosa, Araceli, and Christina that leads individuals to become nepantleras, shown in the testimonios, hints at what we dub the Chicana/o/x dream, characterized by hope, resistance, and school success in marginalizing educational landscapes.

Chapter 7

Conclusion

Developing *Nepantlera/o/x* Critical Consciousness Among Educators to Foster the Chicana/o/x Dream

> The nepantla mindset eliminates polarity thinking where there's no in between, only "either/or"; it reinstates "and." Because our perceptions and thinking contain subtle and hidden biases, we need a nepantla brain to prompt the questioning of our usual assumptions and beliefs. Such a brain would facilitate our ability to look at the world with new eyes. Navigating the cracks is the process of reconstructing life anew, of fashioning new identities.[1]

THROUGH *The Chicana/o/x Dream*, we shared the narratives of students as they navigate from feeling like an *atravesada/o/x* in the education system to accessing institutional resources, enacting their *facultad*, and being a *nepantlera/o/x*. In doing so, what becomes apparent is that students challenge meritocracy because they do not undertake their journeys alone. They do not achieve academic success because they pull themselves up from their bootstraps or because they resort to grit: instead, the Chicana/o/x students in these studies maintain hope and create bridges because their family members, caring educators, and friends provide encouragement, information, and support. Combined with institutional support and guided by la facultad, Chicana/o/x students engage in their critical consciousness to challenge traditional notions of success.

We began this book with a brief overview of the history and theory connecting coloniality with the contemporary experiences of Chicana/o/x students in the education system. We contextualize our analysis and empirical results within a higher education system that fails to account for intersectionality; in so doing, we centralize the experiences of students as they maintain hope, enact resistance, and re-envision educational success. As such, we recommend specific practices, pedagogical approaches, and policies that address the experiences relevant to the intersectional identities of students and that support the development of the *Framework of Atravesados Nepantleando* that Chicana/o/x students exemplified throughout the book. We now challenge educators to do the same.

In the next sections, we encourage educators and administrators to develop student-centered schools and colleges by fostering opportunities to develop critical consciousness and support Chicana/o/x students as they enact their facultad and nepantleando abilities. In particular, we reflect on these questions: What skills do educators and leaders need to foster a Chicana/o/x-student-centered college? What elements would a Chicana/o/x-student-centered college entail? As we begin to consider the answers to these questions, we reflect on the argument established in chapter 1: the US education system is founded on coloniality and deservingness. If our aim is to challenge the heteropatriracial roots of higher education, the issue of coloniality and decoloniality must be addressed.[2] Although decolonization has been a contested word because of its increased use in recent years, we discuss decolonization as defined by Joel Modiri, who argues that decolonization "entails nothing less than an endless fracturing of the world colonialism created."[3] Maldonado-Torres acknowledges the contention between the term decolonize (to give back land) and decolonial by defining decoloniality as "a direct challenge to the temporal, spatial, and subjective axis of the modern/colonial world and its institutions, including the university and the state."[4]

With that in mind, we focus on developing a pragmatic framework of nepantlera/o/x consciousness based on a two-pronged approach focused on educators, educational leaders, and students. The two-pronged approach requires a *nepantlera/o/x praxis* for educators and educational leaders and a sense of belonging for Chicana/o/x students; together, the two-pronged approach decenters the heteronormative white standards and institutional racism present throughout higher education institutions in the US.[5]

Nepantlera/o/x Praxis

The aim of a nepantlera/o/x praxis is to interrupt and fracture colonial structures. A nepantlera/o/x praxis bridges theory with action for educators (e.g., counseling staff and teachers/faculty) and educational leaders through a cycle of being open to learning, self-reflexivity, and outward action. Nepantlera/o/x praxis entails the process that an individual engages in to develop a nepantlera/o/x brain and foster an environment where other individuals can navigate the colliding worlds present in nepantla. We argue that a nepantla praxis can also serve to explain both the intersectional institutional contexts that Chicana/o/x students navigate, in addition to the education borderlands, and the skills that would benefit students. What follows is an explanation of how a nepantlera/o/x praxis can assist educators in developing a nepantla mindset.

In alignment with Anzaldúa's call for individuals to rethink ourselves "in more global-spiritual terms," we propose a nepantlera/o/x praxis as a framework to encourage all educators and educational leaders to "step into consciousness."[6] Educators and administrators in under-resourced prepreK–12 schools and colleges—which enroll a majority of Chicana/o/x students and underrepresented Students of Color—enter the education borderlands and have the opportunity to engage in nepantla. In other words, even if educational leaders and educators come from privileged backgrounds, they are able to learn both through the second-hand experiences of Chicana/o/x students and through their first-hand experiences as educators in a prepreK–12 school or college that is limited in its amount of institutional resources. However, without stepping into consciousness, educators will only reproduce deficit educational environments for Chicana/o/x students. Doing so could often entail a shift in perspective and epistemology. As Anzaldúa explained, "Nepantleras use competing systems of knowledge and rewrite their identities."[7]

Guided by Anzaldúa's work, we propose four overlapping and interconnected spaces to engage in such a fundamental shift: (1) dismantling stereotypes, (2) reflexive engagement in creative acts, (3) avoiding replicating marginalizing structures, and (4) (re-)envisioning a socially just reality.

(1) Dismantling stereotypes. The first space is guided by the notion that "dismantling identities entails unlearning stereotypical labels and questioning consensual reality."[8] We apply this by asserting that in order to unlearn deficit thinking, individuals need to be open to (un)learning—that is, unlearning stereotypes and learning about intersectional systems of oppression. This process was revealed in every chapter by the Chicana/o/x students who unlearned various stereotypes through their personal experiences and by learning from the experiences of their family members. In this space, individuals must dive inward to reflect on their experiences with systems of oppression and consider how they have served both to reproduce and to challenge marginalization based on racism, sexism, racist nativism, and other isms. This step requires being open to engage in learning from individuals who share their histories and experiences with marginalization and from reading literature that documents the lived experiences of underrepresented People of Color. This process cannot happen in a short period of time but is instead a continuous long-term experience.

(2) **Reflexive engagement in creative acts.** Along with the (un)learning process, nepantleras/os/xs must engage in a reflective process as the second space. Anzaldúa explained, "As intermediaries between various *mundos* [worlds], *las nepantleras* 'speak in tongues'—grasp the thoughts, emotions, languages, and perspectives associated with varying individual and cultural positions."[9] Within a nepantlera/o/x praxis perspective, after individuals step into consciousness, the process then entails an asset-based and culturally responsive understanding of Chicana/o/x students.[10] From such a perspective, a nepantlera/o/x praxis calls for educators to self-reflect on what they know about the local communities and students they are supposed to serve. The educator must be able to understand both the deficit rhetoric to understand stereotypes and the intersectional systems of marginalization in which stereotypes are rooted. Finally, they must consider the various ways in which they have benefited from not aligning with stereotypes. The educator must shift her perspective to be centered on acknowledging the assets and various forms of community cultural wealth that are present in the Chicana/o/x communities.

Anzaldúa argues that the reflection required on the path toward consciousness (*conocimiento*) can be led by engaging in creative acts. She explained: "Conocimiento is reached via creative acts-writing, art-making, dancing, healing, teaching, meditation, and spiritual activism-both mental and somatic (the body, too, is a form as well as site of creativity). Through creative engagements, you embed your experiences in a larger frame of reference, connecting your personal struggles with those of other beings on the planet, with the struggles of the Earth itself."[11] By engaging in creative acts, individuals deepen their understanding of their own experiences with marginalizing structures and reinforce their appreciation of interconnecting injustices. However, this cannot happen if the educator has not engaged in the first stage of (un)learning stereotypes. Through this process, individuals have the opportunity to engage in a reflexive process in which they continue to bridge theory with lived experiences so as to continue strengthening their critical consciousness.

Praxis can engage in a cyclical nature when individuals bring others into the nepantla praxis process. For example, when those interacting with students directly, such as teachers and faculty, incorporate such creative acts within their coursework, they begin connecting "personal struggles" with "other beings." This in turn supports the students engaging in such acts on their journey toward consciousness. Engaging in reflexive creative acts becomes a reciprocal process in which educators continue to grow and strengthen their understanding of intersectionality and dismantling stereotypes. With this in mind, the following reflexive questions can assist with the process toward nepantlera/o/x praxis:

1. *Making the common and everyday seem strange and problematic.* When did you learn what to expect when you interact with someone based on their race, gender, sex, class, immigration status, age, ability, and/or other identities? What stereotypes and misunderstandings do you have related to race, gender, sex, class, immigration status, age, ability, and/or other identities? How will you engage in searching for accurate information to challenge stereotypes and misunderstandings?

2. *Critically examining the culture, organization, and structures of privilege.* What structures does your school or college have in place to reach out to Chicana/o/x students and develop a critical consciousness? How can you understand and support the intersectional demands of students, given that their lived experiences are erased within both prepreK–12 and higher education contexts? How does

your school/college ensure that students have access to the institutional resources that these students need, given intersectional contexts?

3. *Challenging marginalizing and nondominant structures.* How do *you* ensure that Chicana/o/x students have access to financial, academic, and socioemotional institutional resources? How do policies and practices that you propose and implement reinforce intersectional marginalization of Chicana/o/x students?

4. *(Re-)envisioning a socially just reality.* What institutional supports can be developed that account for intersectionality? What are the local organizations that you can collaborate with and invite into your school/college so that students have access to a wider social network and resources?

(3) **Avoid replicating marginalizing structures.** Anzaldúa also reminds us that nepantleras/os/x must prevent reinforcing or replicating marginalizing structures. She states: "Las nepantleras recognize that we're all complicit in the existing power structures, that we must deal with conflictive as well as connectionist relations within and among various groups. Ensuring that our acts not mirror or replicate the oppression and dominant power structures we seek to dismantle, las nepantleras upset our cultures' foundations and disturb the concepts structuring their realities."[12] For educators and educational leaders, this point is particularly important when considering the practices and policies they develop that will affect Chicana/o/x students (and other underrepresented Students of Color). Thus, the aim should be to "disturb" the marginalizing structures present in higher education. As faculty, staff, and administrators, there are plenty of opportunities to disturb these structures, such as speaking up in service committees, restructuring coursework expectations, allocating funds to hire tenure-track faculty at a fair salary, leading faculty cluster hires that focus on social justice perspectives, and challenging deficit-based approaches.

(4) **(Re-)envisioning a socially just reality.** Finally, in considering the steps needed to create a *nepantlera/o/x* praxis, the need to re-envision a new reality is required. Anzaldúa theorized that as agents of awakening (conocimiento), nepantleras/o/x must resist marginalization, envision solutions, and create a socially just reality. Thus, a nepantlera/o/x praxis

entails individuals envisioning a new and just reality. As such, they propose policies, programs, and practices that dismantle traditionally marginalizing spaces so as to transform them into consciousness-building, asset-based environments for Chicana/o/x students.

For example, measures of success must be reframed. Previous scholars call for the field of higher education to reframe measures of success that go beyond graduation and time-to-degree rates.[13] In addition to students earning a college degree in a timely manner, institutional success should be measured by the percentage of Chicana/o/x students (and other underrepresented Students of Color) who have access to and engage in the various opportunities mentioned earlier. Institutional success should be measured by reporting: the percentage of students who participated in paid research and/or internship/externship opportunities, the percentage of students who had access to faculty mentors, the percentage of students who have a sense of belonging in both the institution and major, the percentage of students who feel prepared to contribute to their communities, and the percentage of students who have strengthened their critical consciousness. The field of higher education is well beyond serving the "traditional" (wealthy white male) student; colleges must be held accountable for new measures of success that will benefit the increasing Chicana/o/x first-generation student population.

In addition, instead of perpetuating the notion that Chicana/o/x students are not adequately prepared for college-level math or writing, college leaders and faculty can re-envision the traditionally deficit area of developmental education. Various models exist for college to engage in learning communities, cocurricular support, accelerated programs, and curricular reforms, and California leaders have started to re-envision developmental education with Assembly Bill 705.[14] The California Community Colleges system has moved away from the traditional model of developmental education, but individual campuses still continue to enroll students in math and English courses that are below college level. Moreover, although the developmental education system may be redesigned, the college-level math and English courses may still entail classroom environments full of microaggressions and interactions with faculty who are deficit-minded; just like Chicana/o/x students experience in developmental education courses.[15] Thus, re-envisioning such marginalizing spaces could entail engaging all administrators and faculty in a nepantlera/o/x praxis during departmental meetings and new faculty orientations. If college leaders and faculty are expected to develop their critical consciousness, the reflection and discussion begins with the aspirations, assets, and strengths that students bring to college. While various professional development workshops and lectures are tailored to faculty, few require faculty to engage, reflect, discuss, and, ultimately, challenge their deficit perspectives.

Of course, not all faculty and administrators will be able to engage on a pathway toward a nepantlera/o/x praxis, but such practices would be part of the process so that they may also re-envision the classroom context: something as simple as preparing faculty to integrate writing or math assignments that consider intersectionality. For instance, guided by research-based practices, writing assignments can engage students in writing about their fears of navigating college, academic fears and beyond. Previous research establishes that engaging in self-reflection and a discussion of issues related to being low income can benefit the academic outcomes of low-income college students. Therefore, by centralizing the social identities of students—including race, gender, class, sexuality, and immigration status—within an intersectionality framework, students can become inspired to pursue a college degree with social justice as a primary motive. In other words, faculty and students will acknowledge marginalization experiences due to social identity but reflect on and perceive earning a college degree as a form of resistance. Similarly, such work can be done in some mathematics courses, particularly as it relates to college costs, financial aid, and anticipated financial returns upon earning a college degree. In alignment with Anzaldúan theories, we argue that this re-envisioning requires collaboration with others who are also on the journey toward consciousness.

That journey toward critical consciousness includes connecting contemporary education institutions to their historical roots of coloniality: it requires that educators and educational leaders go beyond simply developing asset-based epistemologies. They must aim to stand on the shoulders of previous scholars, activists, and students who challenge inequitable and marginalizing structures that continue to represent obstacles for Chicana/o/x students. We challenge educators and educational leaders to avoid "benevolent neglect" by simply sending such recommendations to ad hoc committees or task teams, resulting in meaningless recommendations that are not enforced.[16] Instead, we call for educators and educational leaders to take action after engaging in the ongoing inner work required for them to develop an asset-based critical consciousness based on a nepantlera/o/x praxis. We argue that such action entails taking steps to develop a school and college environment that fosters a sense of belonging for Chicana/o/x students so that they persist in college.

Nepantla as a Sense of Belonging for Chicana/o/x Students

Throughout this book, we shared various examples of students feeling like atravesados who do not belong within higher education, as well as moments that help them feel like they do belong. With the Framework of Atravesadas/os/xs Nepantleando, we identified that Chicana/o/x students maintain hope, resist subjugation, and reframe success. As such, we propose that educators and educational leaders are responsible for fostering environments that contribute to Chicana/o/x students developing their abilities to become nepantleras/os/xs. To disrupt unwelcoming campus climates, prepreK–12 and college administrators must contribute to a sense of belonging for Chicana/o/x students by developing a sense of membership in school/college.[17] A *sense of belonging* has been defined as a "psychological or normative sense of academic and social integration in their transition to college."[18] In other words, a sense of belonging means students feeling like part of a particular community as they are, not by fitting into a specific mold. However, if Chicana/o/x students experience exclusion, it likely hinders their development of a sense of belonging.[19]

While research traditionally separates preK–12 and higher education contexts, we choose to merge recommendations for the two in efforts to create a much-needed bridge between the systems. Providing completely separate recommendations would be repetitive and continue to divide the preK–12 and higher education systems. As such, we provide seven interconnected elements that are essential to fostering a sense of belonging for Chicana/o/x students, which can support the FAN process. These seven elements are centered on cocurricular experiences, curricular experiences, and out-of-school/-college time.

1. Guidance counselors/advisors. The first element in contributing to a sense of belonging for Chicana/o/x students centers on ensuring that students have access to guidance counselors and advisors who prepare them to choose college, transition to college, prepare for transfer to a four-year college, and pursue graduate school pathways. At the high school level, this aligns with the notion of a college culture, which emerged in the late 1990s and early 2000s, particularly in under-resourced urban high schools. A college culture was adapted from majority white wealthy schools and aims to prepare all students to make informed postsecondary decisions.[20] But it does not account for intersectionality (nor education borderland contexts) and it has been found that inequitable schooling continues to reproduce opportunities based on socioeconomic status.[21] In other words, while a college culture may support Chicana/o/x students on their quest to be admitted to college, it does not prepare them to navigate inequitable opportunity structures. In addition, the college choice process must be supported by guidance staff to account for the multiple postsecondary options; students must receive information from a critical perspective to understand the short-term and long-term implications of choosing among a for-profit college, two-year college, four-year college, vocational program, work, and the military. For example, while a Chicana may have been advised to apply for financial aid, she will probably be unprepared to navigate likely financial hardships. The student narratives presented in this book reaffirm the importance of accounting for intersectional identities, engaging in students' critical consciousness, and preparing students to seek out resources.

Similarly, at the college level, counselors and advisors must provide information and guidance in ways that prepare students to transfer from community colleges to four-year colleges. In a time when neoliberal policies have produced pressure for higher education institutions to reduce the time to degree and increase the number of students completing in a timely manner under financial divestment, we urge educational leaders to consider what it means for students to be the first in their family to pursue a college degree and the level of guidance that would support their degree completion. For example, if it were not for the determination to seek out a major that aligned with their interests, some of the first-generation college students discussed in this book would not have been able to major in STEM. Within this neoliberal context, guidance counselors/advisors easily can be expected to conform to advising processes that aim to rush the completion process and, ultimately, hinder the college-going pathways of Chicana/o/x students. Instead, a decolonial approach would engage in intersectionality and prepare students to make an informed decision by considering the relevant institutional contexts that students have to navigate.

Guidance at the college level includes not only logistical information about what courses to take, but also the knowledge to navigate two-year and four-year college contexts that continue to be higher education borderlands. As such, counselors and advisors should contribute to Chicana/o/x students being prepared not just to critique institutional marginalizing policies and practices but also to seek out appropriate resources to navigate inequitable college pathways. Supporting students to pursue and navigate transfer and graduate school pathways entails much more than dispensing information. As shared by students, interactions with faculty during advising sessions allowed them to envision and plan for graduate school as a realistic pathway. Such experiences spoke both to the students' academic abilities and their intersectional identities. Thus, the notion of validation is also essential during counseling and advising sessions, which leads to the second element.

2. Teachers/faculty and staff. The second element includes validation from faculty and staff, which supports Chicana/o/x students in developing a sense of belonging. Student narratives highlighted the importance of teachers, faculty, and staff validating their social and academic skills. "Validation is an enabling, confirming and supportive process initiated by in- and out-of-class agents that fosters academic and interpersonal development."[22] Given the various examples of Chicana/o/x students made to feel like they do not belong in education, it should come as no surprise that they benefit from validating experiences, particularly from teachers/faculty. However, it is also no surprise that not all teachers/faculty are prepared to foster moments of validation for Chicana/o/x students.[23] Therefore, educational leaders, including college presidents, college deans, department chairs, district superintendents, and school principals, must be prepared to challenge the traditional standards of a what constitutes a "high-quality" teacher/faculty member.

Educational leaders must be prepared to establish validation as part of their mission statements and strategic plans, integrate validation into teacher/faculty orientations, and provide professional development opportunities to engage in workshops. With the increasing focus on graduation rates and the pressure to increase completion rates, educational leaders must be willing to shift institutional expectations and scaffold opportunities for teachers/faculty to provide academic validation for Chicana/o/x students.

3. Academic experiences. The third element consists of ensuring that academic experiences prepare students for a nepantlera/o/x praxis to be enacted outside of the education system. In other words, preK–12 standards and colleges need to align with student learning objectives that prepare students to dismantle lingering colonial contexts. To do so, we recommend a focus on strengthening students' critical consciousness. Critical consciousness has been defined as "increasing one's consciousness of the systemic, institutionalized inequities operating in society, and subsequently gaining the motivation and skills to confront those structures." Ethnic studies courses are essential in providing students with opportunities to strengthen their critical consciousness. These courses prioritize the development of a critical consciousness to understand and navigate institutional inequities and can represent a key starting point for preparing students to navigate higher education borderlands and beyond.[24] It is important to highlight that requiring students to take ethnic studies courses also entails ensuring that ethnic studies departments are funded properly and an urgent need to increase the number of tenure-track faculty.

Guided by critical theory, ethnic studies in preK–12 aims to develop, examine, critique, and challenge structures of oppression.[25] Ethnic studies courses both explicitly center intersectional identities and aim to develop a critical consciousness to understand institutional inequities.[26] Unlike the majority of courses, ethnic studies courses "are centered on the knowledge and perspectives of an ethnic or racial group, reflecting narratives and points of view rooted in that group's lived experiences and intellectual scholarship."[27] Ethnic studies courses are designed with the aim to develop academic and civic engagement.[28] Civic engagement, in particular, aligns with our findings of Chicana/o/x students maintaining hope and engaging in resistance because they are motivated to contribute to their communities, families, and society writ large.

A preK–12 and college context that aims to foster a sense of belonging for Chicana/o/x students would entail requiring *all* students to take ethnic studies courses. A number of qualitative and descriptive studies have found that such courses result in numerous academic benefits, both in high school and in college.[29] While ethnic studies courses develop the critical consciousness of students, at the college level these courses also support students while they focus on developing their *conocimiento*, which "allows individuals to venture into a journey of coming to new ways of thinking that requires self-reflection and attention to sociohistorical and political realities."[30] In addition, ethnic studies courses increase graduation rates, and "ethnic studies faculty members spend more time on advising and supplemental education."[31] As such, the courses would foster a Chicana student to strengthen her facultad, to pursue her nepantlera pathway and engage in critical consciousness. If a student has a critical understanding of her positionality within intersectional systems of oppression and can resort to her facultad to resist by advocating for adequate resources, she will be better positioned to navigate higher education.

We acknowledge the need to foster the critical understanding of inequality in students, which is why we recommend the implementation of an ethnic studies requirement in preK–12 and in higher education.[32] Unfortunately, over the last decade, ethnic studies courses have been at the center of national controversy in the United States, and in 2010, the Arizona legislature passed House Bill 2281, which eliminated the Mexican American Studies program. Similarly, although various stakeholders in California have led local and statewide efforts to implement ethnic studies as a graduation requirement and allow school districts to access funding from the State Department of Education to develop ethnic studies programs, Governor Brown vetoed Assembly Bill 2772 in 2018 after it was amended and approved by the state senate. Nevertheless, twelve school districts in California offer ethnic studies either as an elective or as a requirement for high school graduation. Finally, as the largest school district in Texas, 62 percent of students in Houston Independent School District identify as Latina/o/x, and in 2015 the district was approved to offer a Mexican American studies course. With a continued commitment and leadership from various activists and stakeholders, access to ethnic studies in preK–12 is slowly expanding, and the State Board of Education in Texas approved creating curriculum standards for an ethnic studies course. Similarly, in 2019, the California State University system—the largest public university system in the nation—is currently debating Assembly Bill 1460, which would require students to complete one ethnic studies course to graduate.

   4. Equitable distribution of institutional resources. The fourth element we propose includes ensuring that legislators, educational leaders, and administrators ensure the equitable distribution of institutional resources so as to facilitate access to faculty mentors and next-step peer mentors.[33] This would entail restructuring the funding away from high-level administrators and toward tenured and tenure-track counselors and faculty. However, it is vital to ensure that students have access to faculty mentors and next-step peer mentors who can identify with students. Legislators, educational leaders, and administrators must allocate funds to ensure both that faculty are compensated adequately and that students can engage in extracurricular programming that is rooted in intersectionality.[34]

With governmental and private funding, leaders must be able to envision and fund mentoring efforts that account for intersectionality. First, such a vision includes Chicana/o/x students having access to next-step mentors who have graduated from the institution, come from a similar background, and can provide guidance based on their experiences. Within the preK–12 sector, school districts can hire alumni to return to schools as mentors and student assistants for teaching and counseling staff. Doing so would benefit both the preK–12 students and the alumni.[35] Second, a faculty mentor can serve as another individual who provides validation and guidance through research opportunities. This allows for Chicana/o/x students to learn more about pursuing research and scholarly pathways in preparation for graduate school. In partnership with graduate studies and the career center, the institution should require workshops for students participating in research opportunities so that they can apply for graduate school.

5. Restructure hiring practices. We assert that the fifth element of fostering a sense of belonging for Chicana/o/x students entails institutions hiring faculty, administrators, and staff who enact decisions from a critical consciousness standpoint. We agree that it is important to hire faculty who align with student backgrounds,[36] but it is also essential to ensure that faculty reflect an asset-based perspective and critical consciousness so they can support the development and retention of Chicana/o/x students. This highlights the importance of college leaders, particularly at Hispanic-Serving Institutions, to ensure that incoming students have access to Chicana/o/x faculty who are critically conscious. In other words, if colleges are to facilitate providing access to faculty mentors, as noted earlier, there is a need to ensure that the faculty will foster a sense of belonging rooted in socially just actions.

Such expectation would require not just sharing a similar background but also maintaining a critical consciousness. As Maldonado-Torres argued:

> At times, it is faculty members hired to support the new spaces and projects that turn against them, which should not be surprising given that they were trained in the university and that they work for the university. Indeed, initiatives for diversifying the faculty sometimes turn into surreptitious efforts to find these kind of scholars, who will then "normalize" the new spaces by aligning them with the traditional standards, and who will also play a major role, from the inside, in keeping them as subordinates to other areas or in gradually making them disappear.[37]

Taking into consideration the reality that faculty can subvert institutional processes, it is important to ensure that the hiring processes connect back with a nepantlera/o/x praxis. In other words, when hiring new educators who represent and relate with the Chicana/o/x student population, the institution should have structures in place so that all new hires engage in the nepantlera/o/x praxis process because they then can be better prepared to contribute to a sense of belonging for Chicana/o/x students.

6. Fostering familial peer relationships. Guided by the importance of social validation and familial relationships in Chicana/o/x communities, faculty and staff should be trained and required to foster supportive peer relationships within and outside of classroom environments. As indicated in chapters 3 to 6, students benefited from developing relationships with peers because they gained academic and social validation. As such, faculty can develop a sense of belonging for Chicana/o/x students by fostering an environment where students collaborate with and support one another. At the same time, student narratives provide an important reminder about developing inclusive collaborative environments that account for different abilities.

Student experiences provide insight into how faculty developed inclusive and collaborative classrooms. Possible approaches include allowing for students to learn from one another in small groups. As indicated in chapter four, students can benefit from both academic validation and developing supportive peer relationships by working in small groups in

classroom activities; this can happen easily in both preK–12 and postsecondary contexts, whether through online or face-to-face instruction. As
indicated in chapter three, collaborative study areas around campus can
be helpful for students once they become comfortable with the learning
environment. Collaborative areas can include ensuring that "white boards
outside of classrooms" are available to students so they can work on math
problems or draft essay ideas.[38] Collaborative areas can also include a
designated classroom for the Math, Engineering, Science, Achievement
program or a space designated by other colleges on campus, such as social
sciences, liberal arts, and humanities.

In addition, while organizing potlucks can encourage a sense of
familial peer bonding, it can marginalize low-income and impoverished
students and families. Instead, the school and college leaders should collaborate with local restaurants and grocery stores to sponsor potlucks for
courses throughout the term. This would help destigmatize students who
cannot afford to contribute to a potluck and students who may be experiencing a food shortage. Moreover, student participants also emphasized
the importance of extracurricular groups such as MESA and MEChA.
Therefore, it is equally important to provide adequate support for such
groups to thrive.

**7. Community engagement through paid career/research intern-
ships.** High school and college leaders must provide access to career and
research internships that pay a wage in line with the local standards of
living. As indicated by research participants, the opportunity to engage
in research opportunities made it possible for them to believe that they
could pursue college. While various school districts throughout California
provide paid summer internships, the focus is traditionally on vocational
career opportunities. Career and technical education pathways can be
one postsecondary opportunity, but equitable educational opportunities
would entail providing students with the mentoring and guidance necessary to pursue a bachelor's degree. In addition, these opportunities are
often competitive and require an in-depth application process, meaning school district leaders must ensure that students receive the guidance
needed to access opportunities or must open them up to all students.

Colleges who serve first-generation (Chicana/o/x) students should
receive funding from state and federal levels to establish more than the traditional career center. At the college level, paid research internships allow
for students to engage with faculty, which increases the opportunities to be

mentored and to build their social network.[39] Similarly, career internships provide students with skills to increase their abilities to compete in the job market upon graduation. It is important to ensure that students participate in paid apprentice and career internships in which they increase their skills to enter a career in their field. This initiative would require college administrators to set aside adequate funding to ensure that students have access, and increasing federal work-study opportunities would be one option to reduce costs.

Considering that Chicana/o/x students maintain a commitment to their communities, which informs their abilities to maintain hope and resist marginalization, institutional agents must ensure that the research opportunities are relevant to that commitment. In other words, if an institution begins an undergraduate research program and students do not seem interested in participating, faculty need to work on "translating" what it means to conduct research and the potential to engage in research to make a difference in various communities. This can be as simple as providing a concrete example of research making a difference. For instance, Francisco (chapter 4) aimed to pursue a STEM degree because he wanted to serve as an example to students from migrant rural communities. Similarly, Yesenia (chapter 4) wanted to pursue a PhD because she wanted to develop research findings that helped to address autoimmune diseases. They exemplify the Chicana/o/x dream through their drive to pursue undergraduate and graduate degrees so as to engage in research that aims to support their local communities. However, without support from faculty, counselors, and NSF-funded summer research opportunities, they would not have experienced research nor embraced their abilities to lead research studies in the future.

For first-generation college students, research is often an abstract concept that is challenging to fully understand, but as evidenced by the shared lived experiences of Chicana/o/x students engaging in and understanding research, they were able to use research as an additional source of motivation to fuel their aspirations and resistance.[40] However, it is also essential that students experience a validating context when partnering with faculty and staff supervisors.

The student narratives highlight that intersectionality matters; for example, in order for Chicana/o/x student-parents to participate in such opportunities, they must have access to affordable childcare facilities. While many colleges have excellent early education childcare centers, the lack of access and affordability creates another obstacle that students must overcome, and it inhibits their sense of belonging. Thus, institutional leaders must ensure that they do not essentialize identities and instead understand the various student populations.

Disrupting the Colonial Space in Education

Our recommendations challenge the recent trend in higher education to focus on student success initiatives and student success services by instead emphasizing the role of faculty in this process.[41] In doing so, we question the patchwork benefits of the student success approaches[42] and cocurricular or supplemental support systems if they do not address toxic and invalidating classroom environments.[43] As Maldonado-Torres explained in describing coloniality with higher education:

> It should not be strange, then, that educators do not even realize the extent to which their students may find themselves breathless as they sit in their classes and listen to their lectures and the comments of their peers, as they go to libraries and find symbols that over-glorify certain bodies and societies and dehumanize others, and as they walk through campus to constantly be reminded of their place by the symbols of white power and control, now presented in liberal forms as representatives of pure excellence.[44]

By focusing on educators and educational leaders, we aim to disrupt the colonial space that is often forgotten when institutional leaders develop and implement policies targeting student success. Instead, we acknowledge the richness and importance of engaging in a nepantlera/o/x praxis to develop a sense of belonging for Chicana/o/x students—and the narratives shared in this book highlight the imperative of institutional resources to do so.

We are not the first to make such recommendations, and we build on the findings of previous studies that advocate for similar institutional resources. These recommendations are key as we potentially enter times of financial hardships due to natural disasters, like the COVID-19 pandemic. It becomes ever more important that educational leaders, faculty, and staff understand the implications of intersectionality as Chicana/o/x students engage in online learning. Ultimately, if the aim is to foster the sense of belonging and academic success of Chicana/o/x students, then institutional leaders must ensure that quality, equitable, and relevant resources are available at the school and college level. It is time for institutional leaders to lead institutions and foster an environment that is rooted in nepantlera/o/x critical consciousness to ultimately enrich the Chicana/o/x dream.

Conclusion

As we conclude this book, it is important to consider the economic implications of COVID-19 and what it will mean for the funding available to preK–12 and higher-education sectors. COVID-19 is one of numerous excuses to decrease and cut education funding: previously, it was the deindustrialization era in the 1970s and 1980s, the downturn in the stock market during the early 2000s, and the economic recession in the late 2000s, among others. However, it is in the face of economic hardship, pandemics, and natural disasters that educational leaders, faculty, and staff need to work even harder to ensure that technological needs, additional financial aid, and access to support staff are distributed equitably, in a manner that prioritizes the students with the greatest need.

Education borderlands are the nexus of deficit and marginalizing practices, policies, and ideologies present in the education system that Chicana/o/x student confront. Within such a reality in the US, Chicana/o/x students likely represent atravesadas/os/x (transgressors) who navigate colonial schooling structures, which were not established for their success. And though the education borderlands prepare students to view the world from a deficit Eurocentric perspective, their experiences with marginalization allows them to enact la facultad to see the underlying US structures of inequality. Chicana/o/x students are in spaces where they are othered and under pressure, but they are able to enact la facultad as an ability to survive within these hostile environments. We call for educators and educational leaders to consider that through the Framework of Atravesados Nepantleando (FAN), intersecting identities allow Chicana/o/x students to see various structural inequities and critique institutional processes that reproduce marginalization. Guided by a nepantlera/o/x critical consciousness and praxis, educators can foster an environment where Chicana/o/x students engage in the FAN and have a strong sense of belonging.

Early on in her career, Gloria Anzaldúa explained: "I change myself, I change the world . . . Awareness of our situation must come before inner changes, which in turn come before changes in society. Nothing happens in the 'real' world unless it first happens in the images in our heads."[45] In proposing the various concepts, frameworks, and approaches detailed in this book, our hope is that we help inform both inner changes and changes in the real world. Engaging in such changes builds on a history of resistance, so as to envision possibilities of success for students in US education systems and ultimately realize the Chicana/o/x dream.

Appendix

Methodological Reflections

THE BOOK is based on three unique research projects with low-income, first-generation Chicana/o/x students, in five community colleges and one four-year university classified as Hispanic-Serving Institutions (HSIs) in the United States. Pseudonyms are used to protect participant confidentiality, and institutional review board approval was received at our respective home institutions. We describe briefly each study ahead and offer our thoughts about the utility of each approach and our own roles as Chicana/o/x researchers.

Project 1: The First-Generation College Student Inequality and Opportunity Project

The First-Generation College Student Inequality and Opportunity Project was an exploratory and comparative case study of first-generation students at a large four-year university in the United States. Case study design methodology was employed because it allows the researcher to focus on phenomenon within its real-world context.[1] This project ascertained the factors that five racial and ethnic college students identify as contributing to inequality and opportunity in the United States. This two-phase comparative case study was conducted with assistance from a grant from the *University of California Center for New Racial Studies* at the University of California, Santa Barbara and a University of California Irvine Faculty Research Award.

First phase: interviews for chapter 2. To explore differences in perspectives, the research team interviewed 226 students, from 2014 to 2016, at a selective research-intensive public university classified as an HSI on the West Coast. Twenty-four percent of the sample identified as Chicana/o/x,

21 percent Vietnamese American, 19 percent white, 18 percent Korean American, and 17.6 percent Chinese American. These groups were selected because they were the largest ethnoracial groups of the university. Of the 226 students, the majority were between eighteen and twenty-six years of age. In terms of gender, 50.5 percent identified as female and 49.5 percent as male.

Chapter 2 specifically draws on data from the fifty-four Chicana/o/x college students, 52 percent identified as female and 48 percent as male, of this first phase of the study. All of the Chicana/o/x students identified as first-generation college students in the United States, but not necessarily first-generation born. The majority, 85 percent, of the Chicana/ox/ students were born in the United States of Mexican immigrant parents, several students identified as third-plus-generation US-born, and relatively few students arrived to the United States at an early age as undocumented. A substantial number of Chicana/o/x students were raised in low-income households, based on 94 percent who identified that they received free or reduced-cost lunch during their preK–12 education and based on their parental education and occupation.

Participants were recruited through associations with multicultural education courses, ethnic studies courses, social sciences course, STEM majors, campus organizations, and involvement with community organizations. Snowball sampling, use of social networks, and direct approach in public situations was used. This sampling technique was employed to attain a reflective portrait of the larger population of first-generation college students on the university campus that were also from one of the five ethnic groups under study. The final group of student participants represented a wide range of majors on campus, and the racial breakdown reflected the larger demographic profile of the student body. Of importance to note is that all of these students entered college with similarly strong academic profiles despite mixed preK–12 public schooling experiences, as we will highlight in phase two of the study. The sample reflected primarily upper-class juniors and seniors.

Open-ended interviews were conducted that consisted of three main foci of interest: (1) How students explain inequality and opportunity in America; (2) what ethnic group they believe does best in society and why; and (3) what students believe are the consequences of inequality. Interviews lasted an average of forty-five to sixty minutes, and all interviews were transcribed verbatim. The interviews were conducted at the college, a library, or another quiet location in the community, such as a community-based organization or coffee shop. During each interview, the college students were asked about demographic characteristics, ethnic and cultural identity, perceptions of school success and failure, school academic and behavioral climate, past involvement in high school, and perceptions of social inequality and opportunity in the United States.

The interview data was coded into three different waves. First, open coding was conducted to capture the major themes, recurring words, and phrases that were related to the informants' perception of inequality. Then, the long list of open codes was recoded and collapsed into three significant groups: (1) same opportunity, (2) sources of inequality, and (3) consequences of inequality. Lastly, these three significant groups were further taken apart and coded into thematic responses. We then captured these themes as the percentage of respondents who stated each as a reason.

Second phase: *testimonios* for chapters 5 and 6. To augment the aforementioned interview data, the research team contacted a subsample of the 226 students to conduct more in-depth life *testimonios* to uncover the hows and whys of their perceptions and experiences. The *testimonio* interview process was exploratory and asked broad enough questions to allow students the freedom to offer their unique perspectives of growing up and how their experiences in and out of school relate to their sense of social mobility. The findings therefore emerged organically between the participants and the researchers, and, most importantly, the participants helped construct the final narratives of their lives to ensure credibility, reliability, and validity. This was especially crucial to capture for many research reasons, but most importantly because the first set of interviews ascertained student perspectives (and not necessarily experiences), and the interviews were conducted before the election of Donald J. Trump.

In total, seventy-one students agreed to participate, and a total of sixty-eight *testimonios* were completed among the five original groups under study from 2016 to 2018. Eighteen *testimonios* were specifically conducted with Chicana/o/x college students, eight Chicanos and ten Chicanas. For the purposes of this book, the voices of six Chicana/o/x first-generation college students are presented in chapter 5 on three Chicano male students and chapter 6 on three Chicana female students. Despite using an intersectional lens, we acknowledge that a shortcoming of the book is that it does not engage in all dimensions of the Chicana/o/x experience, particularly as it relates to skin color and those that identify as Afro-Chicana/o/x; this speaks to the need for more research in this area. We nonetheless focus on four main sources of oppression identified in the six *testimonios*—class (capitalism), familial immigrant documentation status (racist nativism), disability (ableism), and sexuality (heteronormativity)—and how Chicana/o/x students turn these into sources of self- and community empowerment to promote hope, resistance, and success.

Project 2: UC/ACCORD Pathways to
Postsecondary Success Project

Chapter 3 draws on qualitative data from the Pathways to Postsecondary Success research project, a five-year, mixed-method study.[2] Specifically, the authors home in on the Los Angeles case study component, which addressed three distinct academic pathways at three community college campuses: developmental education/basic skills, career and technical education (CTE), and transfer pathways to four-year universities. Between December 2010 and September 2012, the Pathways team conducted three waves of semistructured interviews with 110 low-income students at three different community colleges. All interviews took place on each respective college campus, in a reserved private conference room or an empty classroom.

Of the 110 students, 87 percent were between eighteen and twenty-four years of age. The majority of students were raised in low-income households: 87 percent identified that they received free or reduced-cost lunch during their preK–12 education. In addition, of the 110 students, 56 percent identified as female and 44 percent as male. Sixty-six percent of the sample identified as Latina/o/x, 10 percent Asian American, 9 percent African American, 4 percent white, 3 percent Pacific Islander/Native Hawaiian, and 8 percent as "other." Sixty percent of the participants had parents who immigrated to the United States. Approximately 90 percent of students indicated they attended school full-time during the first wave of interviews, which fluctuated throughout the three-interview process. Qualitative data for chapter 3 was derived from interviews conducted during the first wave of data collection with Chicana/o/x students.

After being transcribed, the qualitative data was analyzed through an iterative process that included coding inductively and deductively. Deductive codes included a range of elements, including choosing college, basic skills, and community cultural wealth, among others. After a round of initial coding, we focused on parents as students to examine the experiences of participants with parenting. We found an overlap between student parents and the prison industrial complex (particularly for Chicano men). We then used process coding. These process codes were then grouped into categories through selective coding to answer the research questions.[3]

Project 3: Promoting Pre- and Post-transfer Success in STEM at Hispanic-Serving Institutions

As part of the 2010 America COMPETES Act, the National Science Foundation (NSF) began to fund grants for HSIs as an attempt to increase the number of students of color earning STEM degrees.[4] Chapter 4 draws from a larger dataset from a research study funded by NSF through an S-STEM grant led by Dr. Kimberley Cousins (award no. 1644261) to focus on the experiences of Chicana/o/x students pursuing a STEM degree at two HSI community colleges in Southern California. At Soleado College, 68 percent of students identify as Latina/o/x, and the median household income is $50,000 per year. At El Valle College, 62 percent of students identify as Latina/o/x, and the median household income in the local area ranges between $35,000 and $55,000. Both colleges serve a large percentage of low-income students. Semistructured interviews were conducted during the 2018 to 2019 academic year as participants were preparing to transfer or had just transferred to a four-year college. On average, the interviews lasted about fifty minutes and were conducted over the phone or in a college conference room. Data for chapter 4 was derived from interviews with ten Chicanos and nine Chicanas who were either enrolled at the community college or transferred to a four-year college from the community college.

After transcribing each interview, we wrote analytic memos to reflect on the data. We used initial coding followed by values coding.[5] The values coding was particularly helpful to understand the connection between the intersecting identities of participants and their experiences in STEM. We used selective coding to group the process codes into summative categories, which we developed into themes.[6] Throughout the data-analysis process, we developed a comprehensive codebook.[7]

Multiple steps were taken to ensure trustworthiness. Credibility was addressed through member checking: after transcribing and coding interviews, we shared the transcripts and preliminary findings with the participants and considered their feedback.[8] Transferability was addressed by providing a description of the contextual factors and institutional resources available in the community colleges through the findings.[9] Finally, we considered feedback from colleagues in STEM by sharing preliminary findings.

A Note About the Power and Significance of *Testimonios*

Testimonios have accumulated attention in education research, as they can be a powerful tool to reveal how oppression operates in the lives of Chicana/o/x and Latina/o/x students.[10] The Latina Feminist Group conceptualizes *testimonios* as ways that knowledge and theory emerge through the theorizing of personal experiences as women of color.[11] Testimonios not only make space for nondominant communities to validate their lived experiences, but also become counterstories that resist and challenge sites of oppression, with the ultimate goal of social justice.[12] Unlike traditional research seeking alleged unbiased knowledge, *testimonios* challenge objectivity by linking subjects with experiences marked by resistance, oppression, and marginalization.[13] Thus, a *testimonio* defies dominant notions of what counts as knowledge production and privileges a "voice and perspective [that] has been suppressed, devalued, and abnormalize[d]."[14] This research methodology has engendered new conceptualizations of how communities come together to plan and enact acts of resistance against forces that perpetuate inequality.

Testimonios align with our Chicana feminist framework that foregrounds the reflection, resistance, and silence-breaking from the brown body as a response to social inequality and a stride toward change.[15] Ultimately, Chicana feminism is rooted within the material realities and experiences of those subjected because their experiences give us a more accurate conceptualization of how social forces are manifested in everyday life. Thus, Chicana feminist theory has developed its analysis to include *testimonios* in order to preserve the experiential knowledge of Chicanas/ Latinas, who have often been rendered invisible by colonialism and various political forces.[16]

We utilize *testimonios* as a methodological approach to unravel how the unique identities of these young scholars shape their lived experiences as first-generation college students navigating higher education. As such, we are able to recognize how Chicana/o/x students respond to, heal from, and draw upon their experiences to mobilize academic and personal achievement. In alignment with a feminist methodology agenda, the young Chicanx/a/o scholars are the key sources of knowledge guiding this book. Their *testimonios* rebuke deficit narratives of Chicana/o/x/ students as *atravesados* in the face of myriad obstacles, all the while becoming *nepantleros* that assert their belongingness in the unequal and colonial educational realm. Moreover, many cite the vast wealth from their communities as a tool that has mobilized their navigation through higher education. Ultimately, these scholars openly share their *sueños* (dreams) of utilizing their experiential knowledge to give back to the next generations of young scholars of color.

A Note on Researcher Positionality and Reflexivity

An important component of the role of the researcher in critical research is reflection on the position of the researcher within society and within research. Key understandings of Chicana/o/x education experiences have come from the explicit questioning of whose perspectives are valued and legitimized through the research process. Hence, insights from Chicana/ o/x scholars and Latina/o/x communities have been an important source of expertise into Chicana/o/x education.

Reflexivity among Chicana/o/x scholars has offered insight into important questions and research dynamics tied to Chicana/o/x education. One example of this type of research is Villenas and Foley's review of critical ethnography, where they argued that in order to "reveal oppressive relations of power," researchers must consider collaborating with research gatekeepers while simultaneously moving away from scientific notions of detached objectivity in research.[17]

Echoing Anzaldúa's call for a mestiza consciousness that skillfully negotiates multiple borders, Villenas and Foley described a critical ethnographer's journey as one that straddles academic and working-class Chicana/o/x identities.[18] This often means addressing the limitations of being both the colonized and the colonizer.[19] In fact, bringing forth these tensions underscores the role of reflexivity through the research process. Through such research, perspectives of Chicana/o/x researchers have added to important methodological insights. This is in part due to scholars' own exploration of their insider knowledge, subjectivities, and standpoints to formulate new research queries, provide new frameworks for examining the educational experiences of Chicana/o/x students, and reexamine previous assumptions dominant in education research methodologies.

We do not presume that insider status based on ethnic membership alone provides clearance to make unchecked assumptions about research subjects. Zavella cautioned against assuming that insider status does not diminish class, education, or identity differences that exist and that may permeate the researchers' interactions with the subjects.[20] Peshkin offered that it is not sufficient to simply acknowledge researcher subjectivity; it is also important to "systematically identify" subjectivities so that researchers can critically and methodically "attend to it" throughout the research process.[21] Rather, we acknowledge important insights Chicana/o/x scholars can have through the research process. This falls in line with Maxwell's and Hammersley and Atkinson's arguments that researchers' backgrounds and cultural identities offer an acceptable source of theoretical insights into and valid interpretations of findings. Indeed, scholars' personal experiences provide a valuable source of methodological developments.[22]

Furthermore, Chicana/o/x scholars are in unique positions to understand the lived experiences of Chicana/o/x students because their own lived experiences have involved negotiating different voices, strategies, and identities for survival in educational institutions.[23] Delgado Bernal argued that Chicanas have "unique viewpoints that can provide 'cultural intuition.'"[24] This cultural intuition derives from personal and professional experiences, existing literature, and the analytical process. For Delgado Bernal, cultural intuition allows Chicanas to draw on their own experiences and form the basis of an epistemology that allows Chicana/o/x scholars to reclaim their own knowledge.[25]

As Chicana/o/x researchers, we strongly believe that educational institutions should be places of fairness and equal participation. Our critical stance, we hope, has allowed us to illuminate institutional agents and structures seeking to improve the quality of schooling for all Youth of Color throughout the educational borderlands.

Notes

Introduction

1. *Time* Staff, "Here's Donald Trump's Presidential Announcement Speech," *Time*, June 16, 2015, https://time.com/3923128/donald-trump-announcement-speech/.
2. Lindsay Perez Huber, Corina Benavides Lopez, Maria C. Malagon, Veronica Velez, and Daniel G. Solorzano, "Getting Beyond the 'Symptom,' Acknowledging the 'Disease': Theorizing Racist Nativism," *Contemporary Justice Review* 11, no. 1 (2008): 39–51.
3. We use *Chicana/o/x* throughout the article as a gender-neutral term that resists the gender binary and to highlight that the data derives from students who maintain a Mexican ethnic background.
4. Tanya J. Serrano Gaxiola, Mónica González Ybarra, and Dolores Delgado Bernal, "'Defend Yourself with Words, with the Knowledge That You've Gained': An Exploration of Conocimiento Among Latina Undergraduates in Ethnic Studies," *Journal of Latinos and Education* 18, no. 3 (2019): 243–257.
5. Nancy Acevedo-Gil, "Latina Undocumented Students: A Critical Race Counterstory of Atravesadas Navigating the Education Borderlands," *Border-Lines: Journal of the Latino Research Center*, vol. 11 (2019): 86–109; Aurora Chang, "Identity Production in Figured Worlds: How Some Multiracial Students Become Racial Atravesados/as," *Urban Review* 46, no. 1 (2014): 25–46; Nancy Acevedo-Gil, "College-conocimiento: Toward an Interdisciplinary College Choice Framework for Latinx Students," *Race Ethnicity and Education* 20, no. 6 (2017): 829–850; Susana M. Muñoz, "Unpacking Legality Through La Facultad and Cultural Citizenship: Critical and Legal Consciousness Formation for Politicized Latinx Undocumented Youth Activists," *Equity & Excellence in Education* 51, no. 1 (2018): 78–91; Nancy Acevedo-Gil, "College-Going Facultad: Latinx Students Anticipating Postsecondary Institutional Obstacles," *Journal of Latinos and Education* 18, no. 2 (2019): 107–125.
6. Gloria Anzaldúa, *Borderlands: La Frontera*, vol. 3, (San Francisco: Aunt Lute, 1987), 39.
7. Derrick Bell, "Racial Realism," *Connecticut Law Review* 24 (1991): 363.
8. William Edward Burghardt Du Bois, *The Souls of Black Folk* (New York: Bantam, 1989), 2.

9. Gloria Anzaldúa, *Borderlands: La Frontera*, vol. 3, (San Francisco: Aunt Lute, 1987), 20.

10. Gloria Anzaldúa, "Now Let us Shift . . . The Path of Conocimiento . . . Inner Work, Public Acts," In *This Bridge We Call Home: Radical Visions for Transformation*, ed. Gloria Anzaldúa and AnaLouise Keating (New York: Routledge, 2002), 576.

Chapter 1

1. Gloria Anzaldúa, *Making Faces, Making Soul = Haciendo Caras: Creative and Critical Perspectives of Feminists of Color* (San Francisco: Aunte Lute Foundation, 1990), xxv.

2. Sylvia Hurtado and Deborah Faye Carter, "Effects of College Transition and Perceptions of the Campus Racial Climate on Latino College Students' Sense of Belonging," *Sociology of Education* 70, no. 4 (1997): 324–345; Anne-Marie Nuñez, "Latino Students' Transitions to College: A Social and Intercultural Capital Perspective," *Harvard Educational Review* 79, no. 1 (2009): 22–48; Anne-Marie Núñez, "Employing Multilevel Intersectionality in Educational Research: Latino Identities, Contexts, and College Access," *Educational Researcher* 43, no. 2 (2014): 85–92; Cecilia Rios-Aguilar and Judy Marquez Kiyama, "Funds of Knowledge: An Approach to Studying Latina (o) Students' Transition to College," *Journal of Latinos and Education* 11, no. 1 (2012): 2–16.

3. Walter Mignolo, "Geopolitics of Sensing and Knowing: On (de) Coloniality, Border Thinking, and Epistemic Disobedience," *Confero: Essays on Education, Philosophy and Politics* 1, no. 1 (2013): 129–150; Clelia O. Rodriguez, *Decolonizing Academia: Poverty, Oppression and Pain* (Winnipeg: Fernwood Books, 2018); Riyad A. Shahjahan and Clara Morgan, "Global Competition, Coloniality, and the Geopolitics of Knowledge in Higher Education," *British Journal of Sociology of Education* 37, no. 1 (2016): 92–109.

4. Nancy Acevedo-Gil, "Latina Undocumented Students: A Critical Race Counterstory of Atravesadas Navigating the Education Borderlands," *Border-Lines: Journal of the Latino Research Center* 11 (2019): 86–109; Gina Ann Garcia, *Becoming Hispanic-Serving Institutions: Opportunities for Colleges and Universities* (Baltimore: Johns Hopkins University Press, 2019); Leigh Patel, "Deservingness: Challenging Coloniality in Education and Migration Scholarship," *Association of Mexican American Educators Journal* 9, no. 3 (2016): 11–21.

5. Enrique Alemán and Rudy Luna, *Stolen Education*, directed by Rudy Luna (2013); Gilbert González, "Segregation and the Education of Mexican Children, 1900–1940," in *The Elusive Quest for Equality: 150 years of Chicano/Chicana Education*, ed. José F. Moreno (Cambridge, MA: Harvard Education Press, 1999), 53–76.

6. Kimberle Crenshaw, "Mapping the Margins: Intersectionality, Identity Politics, and Violence Against Women of Color," *Stanford Law Review* 43 (1990): 1241–1299; Leslie McCall, "The Complexity of Intersectionality," *Signs: Journal of Women in Culture and Society* 30, no. 3 (2005): 1771–1800.

7. Crenshaw, "Mapping the Margins," 1241–1299.

8. Arely M. Zimmerman, "A Dream Detained: Undocumented Latino Youth and the DREAM Movement," *NACLA Report on the Americas* 44, no. 6 (2011): 14–17.

9. Gloria Anzaldúa, *Borderlands: La Frontera*, vol. 3 (San Francisco: Aunt Lute, 1987).

10. Jens Manuel Krogstad et al., "Millennials Make Up Almost Half of Latino Eligible Voters in 2016," Pew Research Center, January 19, 2016.

11. Jens Manuel Krogstad, "5 Facts About Latinos and Education, Pew Research Center, July 28, 2016, https://www.pewresearch.org/fact-tank/2016/07/28/5-facts-about-latinos-and-education/.

12. Grace Kao and Jennifer S. Thompson, "Racial and Ethnic Stratification in Educational Achievement and Attainment," *Annual Review of Sociology* 29, no. 1 (2003): 417–442; Gilberto Q. Conchas, *The Color of Success: Race and High Achieving Urban Youth* (New York: Teachers College Press, 2006); Daniel G. Sólorzano, Octavio Villalpando, and Leticia Oseguera, "Educational Inequities and Latina/o Undergraduate Students in the United States: A Critical Race Analysis of Their Educational Progress," *Journal of Hispanic Higher Education* 4, no. 3 (2005): 272–294.

13. Dolores Delgado Bernal, "Critical Race Theory, Latino Critical Theory, and Critical Raced-Gendered Epistemologies: Recognizing Students of Color as Holders and Creators of Knowledge," *Qualitative Inquiry* 8, no. 1 (2002): 105–126; Dolores Delgado Bernal, "Mujeres in College: Negotiating Identities and Challenging Educational Norms," in *Chicana/Latina Education in Everyday Life: Feminista Perspectives on Pedagogy and Epistemology*, ed. Dolores Delgado Bernal et al. (New York: State University of New York Press, 2006), 77–79.

14. Delgado Bernal, "Critical Raced-Gendered Epistemologies."

15. Dolores Delgado Bernal et al., eds., *Chicana/Latina Education in Everyday Life: Feminista Perspectives on Pedagogy and Epistemology* (New York: State University of New York Press, 2006).

16. Glenda M. Flores and Pierrette Hondagneu-Sotelo, "The Social Dynamics Channeling Latina College Graduates into the Teaching Profession," *Gender, Work & Organization* 21, no. 6 (2014): 491–515.

17. Delgado Bernal, "Critical Raced-Gendered Epistemologies."

18. Gilberto Q. Conchas, Leticia Oseguera, and James Diego Vigil, "Acculturation and School Success: Understanding the Variability of Mexican American Youth Adaptation Across Urban and Suburban Contexts," *Urban Review* 44, no. 4 (2012): 401–422.

19. Susan Roberta Katz, "Presumed Guilty: How Schools Criminalize Latino Youth," *Social Justice* 24, no. 4 (1997): 77–95.

20. Victor M. Rios, *Punished: Policing the Lives of Black and Latino Boys* (New York: NYU Press, 2011).

21. Maxine Baca Zinn, "Gender and Ethnic Identity Among Chicanos," *Frontiers: A Journal of Women Studies* 5, no. 2 (1980): 18–24.

22. Aída Hurtado and Mrinal Sinha, *Beyond Machismo: Intersectional Latino Masculinities* (Austin: University of Texas Press, 2016).

23. Leo R. Chavez, *Anchor Babies and the Challenge of Birthright Citizenship* (Palo Alto, CA: Stanford University Press, 2017).

24. Chavez, *Anchor Babies.*

25. Chavez, *Anchor Babies*; Ariana Mangual Figueroa, "'I Have Papers So I Can Go Anywhere!': Everyday Talk About Citizenship in a Mixed-Status Mexican Family," *Journal of Language, Identity & Education* 11, no. 5 (2012): 291–311.

26. Leisy Janet Abrego, "'I Can't go to College Because I Don't Have Papers': Incorporation Patterns of Latino Undocumented Youth," *Latino Studies* 4, no. 3 (2006): 212–231; Roberto G. Gonzales, "Learning to Be Illegal: Undocumented Youth and

Shifting Legal Contexts in the Transition to Adulthood," *American Sociological Review* 76, no. 4 (2011): 602–619.

27. Abrego, "'I Can't go to College'"; Gonzales, "Learning to Be Illegal."

28. Mollie V. Blackburn, "Gender Rules and Regulations as Experienced and Negotiated by Queer Youth," *Journal of Gay and Lesbian Issues in Education* 4, no. 2 (2007): 33–54; Cheri J. Pascoe, *Dude, You're a Fag: Masculinity and Sexuality in High School* (Berkeley: University of California Press, 2011); Didi Khayatt, "Compulsory Heterosexuality: Schools and Lesbian Students," in *Knowledge, Experience and Ruling Relations: Studies in the Social Organization of Knowledge,* ed. Marie Campbell and Ann Manicom (Toronto: University of Toronto Press, 1995), 149–163.

29. Katie L. Acosta, "Lesbianas in the Borderlands: Shifting Identities and Imagined Communities," *Gender & Society* 22, no. 5 (2008): 639–659; Antonio Jay Pastrana, "Being Out to Others: The Relative Importance of Family Support, Identity and Religion for LGBT Latina/os," *Latino Studies* 13, no. 1 (2015): 88–112.

30. Anita Tijerina Revilla, "Raza Womyn—Making It Safe To Be Queer: Student Organizations as Retention Tools in Higher Education," *Black Women, Gender & Families* 4, no. 1 (2010): 37–61; Summer Melody Pennell, "Queer Cultural Capital: Implications for Education," *Race Ethnicity and Education* 19, no. 2 (2016): 324–338.

31. Jane R. Mercer, *Labeling the Mentally Retarded: Clinical and Social System Perspectives on Mental Retardation* (Berkeley: University of California Press, 1973); David P. Prasse and Daniel J. Reschly, "Larry P.: A Case of Segregation, Testing, or Program Efficacy?," *Exceptional Children* 52, no. 4 (1986): 333–346.

32. Brianne Dávila, "Critical Race Theory, Disability Microaggressions and Latina/o Student Experiences in Special Education," *Race Ethnicity and Education* 18, no. 4 (2015): 443–468.

33. Gilberto Q. Conchas, "Structuring Failure and Success: Understanding the Variability in Latino School Engagement," *Harvard Educational Review* 71, no. 3 (2001): 475–505; Kao and Thompson, "Racial and Ethnic Stratification."

34. Nancy Acevedo-Gil, "College-Conocimiento: Toward an Interdisciplinary College Choice Framework for Latinx Students," *Race Ethnicity and Education* 20, no. 6 (2017): 829–850; Aurora Chang, "Identity Production in Figured Worlds: How Some Multiracial Students Become Racial Atravesados/as," *Urban Review* 46, no. 1 (2014): 25–46; Susana M. Muñoz, "Unpacking Legality Through La Facultad and Cultural Citizenship: Critical and Legal Consciousness Formation for Politicized Latinx Undocumented Youth Activists," *Equity & Excellence in Education* 51, no. 1 (2018): 78–91.

35. Lisa Patel, "Countering Coloniality in Educational Research: From Ownership to Answerability," *Educational Studies* 50, no. 4 (2014): 357–377. See also Patel, "Deservingness"; Anzaldúa, *Borderlands.*

36. Maldonado-Torres defines *coloniality* as the "long-standing patterns of power that emerged as a result of colonialism, but that define culture, labor, intersubjective relations, and knowledge production well beyond the strict limits of colonial administrations." See Nelson Maldonado-Torres, "On the Coloniality of Being: Contributions to the Development of a Concept," *Cultural Studies* 21, no. 2–3 (2007): 240–270. As cited in Patel, "Deservingness."

37. Nancy Acevedo-Gil, "College-Conocimiento"; Dolores Calderón et al., "A Chicana Feminist Epistemology Revisited: Cultivating Ideas a Generation Later," *Harvard*

Educational Review 82, no. 4 (December 2012): 513–539; Elsa Ruiz and Norma Cantú, "R(ace), A(gency), I(dentity), S(ocial Justice), E(ducation): Bridging Borders in English and Mathematics Education," *Journal of Latino/Latin American Studies* 5, no. 3 (2013): 156–166; Muñoz, "Unpacking Legality"; Daniel G. Solórzano and Tarra J. Yosso, "Critical Race Methodology: Counter-Storytelling as an Analytical Framework for Education Research," *Qualitative Inquiry* 8, no. 1 (2002): 23–44.

38. Critical race theory (CRT) in education guides the development of the proposed framework by providing us with "a greater ontological and epistemological understanding of how race and racism affect the education and lives of the racially disenfranchised." See Laurence Parker and Marvin Lynn, "What's Race Got to Do with It? Critical Race Theory's Conflicts with and Connections to Qualitative Research Methodology and Epistemology," *Qualitative Inquiry* 8, no. 1 (2002): 7. CRT in education serves as an analytical framework to "challenge the dominant discourse on race and racism as they relate to education by examining how educational theory, policy, and practice are used to subordinate certain racial and ethnic groups." See Daniel G. Solorzano, "Critical Race Theory, Race and Gender Microaggressions, and the experience of Chicana and Chicano Scholars," *International Journal of Qualitative Studies in Education* 11, no. 1 (1998): 121–136. Critical race theory in education is guided by five tenets informed by Solórzano: (1) centrality and intersectionality of race and racism, (2) challenging the dominant perspective, (3) commitment to social justice, (4) valuing experiential knowledge, and (5) maintaining an interdisciplinary perspective. See Solórzano, "Critical Race Theory." See also Dolores Calderon, "Anticolonial Methodologies in Education: Embodying Land and Indigeneity in Chicana Feminisms," *Journal of Latino/Latin American Studies* 6, no. 2 (2014): 81–96; Gina Ann Garcia, *Becoming Hispanic-Serving Institutions*; Patel, "Countering Coloniality"; Patel, "Nationalist Narratives, Immigration, and Coloniality," *Decolonization: Indigeniety, Education & Society Blog* (2015); Derrick Bell, "Racial Realism," *Connecticut Law Review* 24 (1991): 363.

39. Nancy Acevedo-Gil, "Toward a Critical Race Nepantlera Methodology: Embracing Liminality in Anti-Colonial Research," *Cultural Studies Critical Methodologies* 19, no. 3 (2019): 231–239.

40. Maldonado-Torres, "On the Coloniality of Being"; Patel, "Deservingness."

41. José F. Moreno. *The Elusive Quest for Equality: 150 years of Chicano/Chicana Education*, (Cambridge, MA: Harvard Education Press, 1999).

42. Patel, "Nationalist Narratives."

43. Anzaldúa, *Borderlands*.

44. Patel, "Countering Coloniality," 15.

45. The coloniality experienced by individuals of Mexican descent is complex because Mexico was colonized first by Spain and then by the United States. During colonial times, Spain used the education system to maintain a racial caste system through formal schooling; see Martha Menchaca, "The Treaty of Guadalupe Hidalgo and the Racialization of the Mexican Population," in *The Elusive Quest for Equality: 150 years of Chicano/Chicana Education*, ed. José F. Moreno (Cambridge, MA: Harvard Education Press, 1999), 3–30. Upon gaining independence from Spain, Mexico maintained the schooling and mission system in California and New Mexico; see David J. Weber, *The Mexican Frontier, 1821–1846: The American Southwest Under Mexico* (Albuquerque: University of New Mexico Press, 1982). After the US-Mexico war, "Mexican

Americans had no legal protections against the processes of racialization that were already in place for other people of color in the United States . . . [This] furthered the perception of Mexicans as 'other' in the context of U.S. society;" see Menchaca, "Racialization of the Mexican," 25.

46. Guadalupe San Miguel, "The Schooling of Mexicanos in the Southwest, 1848–1891," in *The Elusive Quest for Equality: 150 years of Chicano/Chicana Education*, ed. José F. Moreno (Cambridge, MA: Harvard Education Press, 1999), 31–51.
47. Moreno, *The Elusive Quest.*
48. San Miguel, "The Schooling of Mexicanos."
49. San Miguel, "The Schooling of Mexicanos"; Alemán and Luna, *Stolen Education.*
50. San Miguel, "The Schooling of Mexicanos," 44.
51. Moreno, *The Elusive Quest.*
52. Moreno, *The Elusive Quest*, 57.
53. Patel, "Deservingness," 16.
54. Patel, "Nationalist Narratives."
55. Patel, "Deservingness."
56. Patel, "Deservingness"; Anzaldúa, *Borderlands.*
57. Anzaldúa, *Borderlands*, 26.
58. US Department of Education, *The State of Racial Diversity in the Educator Workforce* (Washington, DC: US Department of Education, 2016).
59. Rita Kohli and Daniel G. Solórzano, "Teachers, Please Learn Our Names! Racial Microaggressions and the K-12 Classroom," *Race Ethnicity and Education* 15, no. 4 (2012): 441–462; Lindsay Perez Huber, Robin N. Johnson, and Rita Kohli, "Naming Racism: A Conceptual Look at Internalized Racism in US Schools," *Chicano-Latino Law Review* 26 (2006): 183.
60. Corey Mitchell, "How Much Can Schools Protect Undocumented Students?," *Education Week*, February 27, 2017; Gilberto Soria Mendoza and Noor Shaikh, "Tuition Benefits for Immigrants," National Conference of State Legislators, September 26, 2019, https://www.ncsl.org/research/immigration/tuition-benefits-for-immigrants.aspx.
61. Claudia G. Cervantes-Soon, "A Critical Look at Dual Language Immersion in the New Latin@ Diaspora," *Bilingual Research Journal* 37, no. 1 (2014): 64–82, 64.
62. Kohli and Solórzano, "Teachers, Please Learn Our Names!"; Perez Huber, Johnson, and Kohli, "Naming Racism."
63. Gary Orfield et al., *Brown at 62: School Segregation by Race, Poverty and State* (Los Angeles: Civil Rights Project-Proyecto Derechos Civiles, 2016).
64. John Rogers et al., *Educational Opportunities in Hard Times: The Impact of the Economic Crisis on Public Schools and Working Families* (Los Angeles: UCLA IDEA and UC/ACCORD, 2010); Lindsay Perez Huber et al., *Still Falling Through the Cracks: Revisiting the Latina/o Education Pipeline*, CSRC Research Report no. 19 (Los Angeles: UCLA Chicano Studies Research Center, 2015).
65. Anthony P. Carnevale and Jeff Strohl, *Separate & Unequal: How Higher Education Reinforces the Intergenerational Reproduction of White Racial Privilege* (Washington, DC: Center on Education and the Workforce at Georgetown University, 2013).
66. Gina Ann Garcia, *Becoming Hispanic-Serving Institutions.*
67. Cati V. de los Rios, "A Curriculum of the Borderlands: High School Chicana/o-Latina/o Studies as Sitios y Lengua," *Urban Review* 45, no. 1 (2013): 58–73; Elisa S.

Abes, "Theoretical Borderlands: Using Multiple Theoretical Perspectives to Challenge Inequitable Power Structures in Student Development Theory," *Journal of College Student Development* 50, no. 2 (2009): 141–156; Dolores Delgado Bernal, Enrique Alemán Jr, and Andrea Garavito, "Latina/o Undergraduate Students Mentoring Latina/o Elementary Students: A Borderlands Analysis of Shifting Identities and First-Year Experiences," *Harvard Educational Review* 79, no. 4 (2009): 560–586.

68. Considering the history of the education system in the US, a continual presence of racial segregation (Orfield et al., *Brown at 62*), whether it be de jure or de facto, reinforces that schooling represents a borderland for Chicana/o/x students. A key example of a physical boundary is represented by the prison-like fences and gates present outside and within majority Chicana/o/x schools. The presence of such physical boundaries signify that communities are "unsafe." See Yanira I. Madrigal-Garcia and Nancy Acevedo-Gil, "The New Juan Crow in Education: Revealing Panoptic Measures and Inequitable Resources That Hinder Latina/o Postsecondary Pathways," *Journal of Hispanic Higher Education* 15, no. 2 (2016): 154–181.

69. Patel, "Deservingness."

70. Anzaldúa, *Borderlands*, 26.

71. Patel, "Deservingness."

72. Gilberto Q. Conchas, "Structuring Failure and Success"; Frances Contreras, "Strengthening the Bridge to Higher Education for Academically Promising Underrepresented Students," *Journal of Advanced Academics* 22, no. 3 (2011): 500–526; Patricia C. Gandara and Frances Contreras, *The Latino Education Crisis: The Consequences of Failed Social Policies* (Cambridge, MA: Harvard University Press, 2009); Victoria MacDonald, *Latino Education in the United States: A Narrated History from 1513–2000* (New York: Palgrave Macmillan, 2004); Richard R. Valencia, *The Evolution of Deficit Thinking: Educational Thought and Practice* (London: Routledge, 2012); Garcia, *Becoming Hispanic-Serving Institutions*.

73. Patricia C. Gandara and Frances Contreras, *The Latino Education Crisis: The Consequences of Failed Social Policies* (Cambridge, MA: Harvard University Press, 2009); John Rogers et al., *Educational Opportunities in Hard Times: The Impact of the Economic Crisis on Public Schools and Working Families*, California Educational Opportunity Report (Los Angeles: UCLA Institute for Democracy, Education, and Access, 2010).

74. Rogers et al., *Educational Opportunities in Hard Times*, 7.

75. Maria Estela Zarate and Ronald Gallimore, "Gender Differences in Factors Leading to College Enrollment: A Longitudinal Analysis of Latina and Latino Students," *Harvard Educational Review* 75, no. 4 (2005): 383–408.

76. Davison Aviles et al., "Perceptions of Chicano/Latino Students Who Have Dropped Out of School," *Journal of Counseling & Development* 77, no. 4 (1999): 465–473; Luti Vela-Gude et al., "'My Counselors Were Never There': Perceptions from Latino College Students," *Professional School Counseling* 12, no. 4 (2009): 272–279.

77. Lorraine Kasprisin, "The School-to-Prison Pipeline: A Civil Rights and a Civil Liberty Issue," *Journal of Educational Controversy* 7, no. 1 (2013): 1; Victor Rios and Mario G. Galicia, "Smoking Guns or Smoke & Mirrors? Schools and the Policing of Latino Boys," *Association of Mexican American Educators Journal* 7, no. 3 (2014): 54–66.

78. Anzaldúa, *Borderlands*.

79. Anzaldúa, *Borderlands*.
80. Anzaldúa, *Borderlands*, 61.
81. Anzaldúa, *Borderlands*.
82. Anzaldúa, *Borderlands*, 39.
83. Anzaldúa, *Borderlands*.
84. Anzaldúa, *Borderlands*.
85. Anzaldúa, *Borderlands*, 61.
86. AnaLouise Keating, *The Gloria Anzaldúa Reader* (Durham, NC: Duke University Press, 2009); Anzaldúa, *Borderlands*, 39.
87. Anzaldúa defined *la facultad* for Chicanas; we acknowledge the role of intersectionality and intersecting forms of oppression, so we highlight that the marginalizing contexts vary by student identities. See Crenshaw, "Mapping the Margins."
88. Nancy Acevedo-Gil, "College-Going Culture in an Underresourced Urban High School: Examining Latina/o College Choice and Navigation" (PhD diss., University of California, Los Angeles, 2014); Nancy Acevedo-Gil, "College-Conocimiento."
89. Nancy Acevedo-Gil, "College-Conocimiento."
90. Muñoz, "Unpacking Legality," 78.
91. Cindy Cruz, "Toward an Epistemology of a Brown Body," *International Journal of Qualitative Studies in Education* 14, no. 5 (2001): 657–669; Cherríe Moraga and Gloria Anzaldúa, eds., *This Bridge Called My Back: Writings by Radical Women of Color* (New York: State University of New York Press, 2015); Dolores Delgado Bernal, "Learning and Living Pedagogies of the Home: The Mestiza Consciousness of Chicana Students," *International Journal of Qualitative Studies in Education* 14, no. 5 (2001): 623–639; Ruth Trinidad Galvan, "Portraits of Mujeres Desjuiciadas: Womanist Pedagogies of the Everyday, the Mundane and the Ordinary," *International Journal of Qualitative Studies in Education* 14, no. 5 (2001): 603–621; Luis C. Moll et al., "Funds of Knowledge for Teaching: Using a Qualitative Approach to Connect Homes and Classrooms," *Theory into Practice* 31, no. 2 (1992): 132–141; Tara J. Yosso, "Whose Culture has Capital? A Critical Race Theory Discussion of Community Cultural Wealth," *Race Ethnicity and Education* 8, no. 1 (2005): 69–91.
92. Yosso, "Whose Culture Has Capital?"
93. Tara J. Yosso and Daniel G. Solórzano, "Conceptualizing a Critical Race Theory in Sociology," in *The Blackwell Companion to Social Inequalities*, ed. Mary Romero and Eric Margolis (Malden, MA: Blackwell Publishing, 2005), 117–146.
94. Yosso and Solórzano, "Conceptualizing," 127.
95. Yosso and Solórzano, "Conceptualizing," 129.
96. Tara J. Yosso, "Whose Culture Has Capital?"
97. Yosso, "Whose Culture Has Capital?"
98. Dolores Delgado Bernal, "Using a Chicana Feminist Epistemology in Educational Research," *Harvard Educational Review* 68, no. 4 (1998): 555–583.
99. Yosso, "Whose Culture Has Capital?"
100. Tara J. Yosso, *Critical Race Counterstories Along the Chicana/Chicano Educational Pipeline* (New York: Routledge, 2013), 80.
101. Marcela G. Cuellar, Vanessa Segundo, and Yvonne Muñoz, "Assessing Empowerment at HSIs: An Adapted Inputs-Environments-Outcomes Model," *Association of Mexican American Educators Journal* 11, no. 3 (2018): 84–108.

102. Alejandra C. Elenes et al., "Introduction: Chicana/Mexicana Feminist Pedagogies: Consejos, Respeto, y Educación in Everyday Life," *International Journal of Qualitative Studies in Education* 14, no. 5 (2001): 595–602.

103. Crenshaw, "Mapping the Margins," 1241–1299; Ange-Marie Hancock, "When Multiplication Doesn't Equal Quick Addition: Examining Intersectionality as a Research Paradigm," *Perspectives on Politics* 5, no. 1 (2007): 63–79.

104. Delgado Bernal, "Pedagogies of the Home."

105. AnaLouise Keating, *The Gloria Anzaldúa Reader* (Durham, NC: Duke University Press, 2009), 300.

106. Gloria Anzaldúa, "Now Let Us Shift . . . The Path of Conocimiento . . . Inner Work, Public Acts," in *This Bridge We Call Home: Radical Visions for Transformation*, ed. Gloria Anzaldúa and AnaLouise Keating (New York: Routledge, 2002), 540–578.

107. Anzaldúa, "Now Let Us Shift," 549.

108. AnaLouise Keating, "New Mestiza, Nepantlera, Beloved Comadre: Remembering Gloria E. Anzaldúa," *Letras Femeninas* 31, no. 1 (2005): 13–20, 15.

109. Walter Mignolo, "Introduction: From Cross-Genealogies and Subaltern Knowledges to Nepantla," *Nepantla: Views from South* 1, no. 1 (2000): 2.

110. AnaLouise Keating, "From Borderlands and New Mestizas to Nepantlas and Nepantleras: Anzaldúan Theories for Social Change," *Human Architecture: Journal of the Sociology of Self-knowledge* 4, no. 3 (2006): 3.

111. Laura I. Rendón, Amaury Nora, and Vijay Kanagala, *Ventajas/Assets y Conocimientos/Knowledge: Leveraging Latin@ Strengths to Foster Student Success* (San Antonio: Center for Research and Policy in Education, University of Texas at San Antonio, 2014).

112. Rendón, Nora, and Kanagala, "Ventajas/Assets y Conocimientos/Knowledge."

113. Sue G. Kasun, "Hidden Knowing of Working-Class Transnational Mexican Families in Schools: Bridge-Building, Nepantlera Knowers," *Ethnography and Education* 9, no. 3 (2014): 313–327.

Chapter 2

1. AnaLouise Keating, *Gloria E. Anzaldúa: Interviews/Entrevistas* (New York: Routledge, 2000).

2. Immigrants and their children often develop a positive and hopeful outlook regarding their chances at intergenerational mobility based on immigrant narratives/optimism. Understanding their immigrant parents' struggles and sacrifices, 1.5- and second-generation youths develop a sense of appreciation and are motivated to do well in school (Min Zhou and Carl Bankston, *Growing Up American: How Vietnamese Children Adapt to Life in the United States* Russell Sage Foundation, 1998), achieve intergenerational occupational mobility (Grace Kao and Marta Tienda, "Educational Aspirations of Minority Youth," *American Journal of Education* 106, no. 3 (1998): 349–384; Maria Eugenia Matute-Bianchi, "Ethnic Identities and Patterns of School Success and Failure Among Mexican-Descent and Japanese-American Students in a California High School: An Ethnographic Analysis," *American Journal of Education* 95, no. 1 (1986): 233–255), and "give back" to their family and coethnic communities

to assist others' mobility (Jody Agius Vallejo and Jennifer Lee, "Brown Picket Fences: The Immigrant Narrative and 'Giving Back' among the Mexican-Origin Middle Class," *Ethnicities* 9, no. 1 (2009): 5–31). See Anne-Marie Núñez, "Employing Multi-level Intersectionality in Educational Research: Latino Identities, Contexts, and College Access," *Educational Researcher* 43, no. 2 (2014): 85–92. Moreover, immigrant narratives and optimisms of Chicana/o/xs often buttress their beliefs in achieving the American dream. *The American dream* refers to the meritocratic belief that individuals' hard work, anchored by individualism, self-reliance, and discipline, will lead to upward socioeconomic mobility, assuming equality in opportunities (Jennifer L. Hochschild, *Facing Up to the American Dream: Race, Class, and the Soul of the Nation* [Princeton University Press, 1995]; Vallejo and Lee, "Brown Picket Fences"). Mexicans' intergenerational mobility rate is much greater than their Asian counterparts, where the second-generation college graduate rate doubles that of their fathers and triples that of their mothers (Jennifer Lee and Min Zhou, "The Success Frame and Achievement Paradox: The Costs and Consequences for Asian Americans," *Race and Social Problems* 6, no. 1 (2014): 38–55.

3. Rita Kohli, and Daniel G. Solórzano, "Teachers, Please Learn Our Names! Racial Microaggressions and the preK–12 Classroom," *Race Ethnicity and Education* 15, no. 4 (2012): 441–462.

4. Hae Yeon Choo and Myra Marx Ferree, "Practicing Intersectionality in Sociological Research: A Critical Analysis of Inclusions, Interactions, and Institutions in the Study of Inequalities," *Sociological Theory* 28, no. 2 (2010): 129–149; Kimberle Crenshaw, "Mapping the Margins: Intersectionality, Identity Politics, and Violence Against Women of Color," *Stanford Law Review* 43 (1990): 1241; Leslie McCall, "The Complexity of Intersectionality," *Signs* 30, no. 3 (2005): 1771–1800.

5. Patricia Hill Collins, *Black Feminist Thought: Knowledge, Consciousness, and the Politics of Empowerment* (New York: Routledge, 2000).

6. Janice McCabe, "Racial and Gender Microaggressions on a Predominantly-White Campus: Experiences of Black, Latina/o and White Undergraduates," *Race, Gender & Class* (2009): 133–151; Gilberto Q. Conchas, *The Color of Success: Race and High-Achieving Urban Youth* (New York: Teachers College Press, 2006).

7. Dorothy E. Smith, *The Everyday World as Problematic: A Feminist Sociology* (Toronto: University of Toronto Press, 1987); Sandra G. Harding, *The Feminist Standpoint Theory Reader: Intellectual and Political Controversies* (New York: Routledge, 2004).

8. Nancy Acevedo-Gil, "College-Conocimiento: Toward an Interdisciplinary College Choice Framework for Latinx Students," *Race Ethnicity and Education* 20, no. 6 (2017): 829–850.

9. Ange-Marie Hancock, "When Multiplication Doesn't Equal Quick Addition: Examining Intersectionality as a Research Paradigm," *Perspectives on Politics* 5, no. 1 (2007): 63–79.

10. Gloria Anzaldúa, *Borderlands: La Frontera*, vol. 3. (San Francisco: Aunt Lute, 1987); Dolores Delgado Bernal, "Learning and Living Pedagogies of the Home: The Mestiza Consciousness of Chicana Students," *International Journal of Qualitative Studies in Education* 14, no. 5 (2001): 623–639.

11. Aida Hurtado, *The Color of Privilege: Three Blasphemies on Race and Feminism* (Ann Arbor: University of Michigan Press, 1996).

12. Delgado Bernal, "Pedagogies of the Home."

13. Oscar Lewis, *Five Families: Mexican Case Studies in the Culture of Poverty* (New York: Basic Books, 1959); Oscar Lewis, *La Vida: A Puerto Rican Family in the Culture of Poverty—San Juan and New York* (New York: Random House, 1966); Daniel Patrick Moynihan, *The Negro Family: The Case for National Action* (Washington, DC: Office of Policy Planning and Research, US Department of Labor, 1965).
14. Anzaldúa, *Borderlands*.
15. Aida Hurtado, Karina Cervantez, and Michael Eccleston, "Infinite Possibilities, Many Remaining Obstacles: Language, Culture, and Identity in Latino/a Educational Achievement," in *The Handbook of Latinos and Education: Theory, Research and Practice*, ed. Enrique G. Murillo Jr. et al. (New York: Routledge, 2010), 284–299.
16. Angela Valenzuela, *Subtractive Schooling: Issues of Caring in Education of US-Mexican Youth* (New York: State University of New York Press, 1999).
17. Jessica M. Rodriguez, "High Stakes Test" (PhD diss., University of Washington, 2020).
18. Nancy Lopez, *Hopeful Girls, Troubled Boys: Race and Gender Disparity in Urban Education* (New York: Routledge, 2003).
19. Miguel Muñoz-Laboy et al., "The 'Knucklehead' Approach and What Matters in Terms of Health for Formerly Incarcerated Latino Men," *Social Science & Medicine* 74, no. 11 (2012): 1765–1773.
20. Anzaldúa, *Borderlands*, 3.
21. Bernal, "Pedagogies of the Home."

Chapter 3

1. Gloria Anzaldúa, *Borderlands: La Frontera*, vol. 3, (San Francisco: Aunt Lute, 1987), 20–21.
2. Michal Kurlaender, "Choosing Community College: Factors Affecting Latino College Choice," *New Directions for Community Colleges* 2006, no. 133 (2006): 7–16; Ruth Zimmer Hendrick, William H. Hightower, and Dennis E. Gregory, "State Funding Limitations and Community College Open Door Policy: Conflicting Priorities?," *Community College Journal of Research and Practice* 30, no. 8 (2006): 627–640.
3. Mary Martinez-Wenzl and Rigoberto Marquez, *Unrealized Promises: Unequal Access, Affordability, and Excellence at Community Colleges in Southern California* (Los Angeles, CA: Civil Rights Project, 2012); Christopher M. Mullin, *Why Access Matters: The Community College Student Body*, Policy Brief 2012-01PBL (Washington, DC: American Association of Community Colleges, 2012).
4. Nancy Acevedo-Gil, Ryan E. Santos, and Daniel G. Solórzano, "Examining a Rupture in the Latina/o College Pipeline: Developmental Education in California Community Colleges," *PERSPECTIVAS: Issues in Higher Education Policy and Practice*, no. 3 (Spring 2014).
5. Nancy Acevedo-Gil et al., "Examining a Rupture"; Judith Scott-Clayton, *Do High-Stakes Placement Exams Predict College Success?*, CCRC Working Paper no. 41 (New York: Community College Research Center, Columbia University, 2012); Thomas Bailey, "Challenge and Opportunity: Rethinking the Role and Function of Developmental Education in Community College," *New Directions for Community Colleges* 2009, no. 145 (2009): 11–30; Anthony P. Carnevale and Jeff Strohl, *Separate &*

Unequal: How Higher Education Reinforces the Intergenerational Reproduction of White Racial Privilege (Washington, DC: Center on Education and the Workforce, Georgetown University, 2013).

6. Nancy Acevedo-Gil et al., "Latinas/os in Community College Developmental Education: Increasing Moments of Academic and Interpersonal Validation," *Journal of Hispanic Higher Education* 14, no. 2 (2015): 101–127; Carola Suárez-Orozco et al., "Toxic Rain in Class: Classroom Interpersonal Microaggressions," *Educational Researcher* 44, no. 3 (2015): 151–160.

7. Adrian H. Huerta, Shannon M. Calderone, and Patricia M. McDonough, "School Discipline Policies That Result in Unintended Consequences for Latino Male Students' College Aspirations," in *Educational Policy Goes to School*, ed. Gilberto Q. Conchas et al. (New York: Routledge, 2017), 157–172; Anthony A. Peguero, Jennifer M. Bondy, and Zahra Shekarkhar, "Punishing Latina/o Youth: School Justice, Fairness, Order, Dropping Out, and Gender Disparities," *Hispanic Journal of Behavioral Sciences* 39, no. 1 (2017): 98–125.

8. David Omotoso Stovall, *Born Out of Struggle: Critical Race Theory, School Creation, and the Politics of Interruption* (New York: State University of New York Press, 2016).

9. Damien M. Sojoyner, "Black Radicals Make for Bad Citizens: Undoing the Myth of the School to Prison Pipeline," *Berkeley Review of Education* 4, no. 2 (2013); Patricia Hill Collins, *Black Feminist Thought: Knowledge, Consciousness, and the Politics of Empowerment* (New York: Routledge, 2000); Samir Amin, *Eurocentrism: Modernity, Religion and Democracy: A Critique of Eurocentrism and Culturalism* (New York: Monthly Review Press, 1988).

10. Angela Davis, "Masked Racism: Reflections on the Prison Industrial Complex," *Indigenous Law Bulletin* 4, no. 27 (2000): 4; Chauncee D. Smith, "Deconstructing the Pipeline: Evaluating School-to-Prison Pipeline Equal Protection Cases through a Structural Racism Framework," *Fordham Urban Law Review* 36 (2009): 1009.

11. Anne Carson, "Prisoners in 2016," US Bureau of Justice Statistics, August 7, 2018, https://www.bjs.gov/content/pub/pdf/p16.pdf.

12. Bruce Western, *Punishment and Inequality in America* (New York: Russell Sage Foundation, 2006), 108–130; Pew Charitable Trusts, *Collateral Costs: Incarceration's Effect on Economic Mobility* (Washington, DC: Pew Charitable Trusts, 2010), http://www.pewtrusts.org/~/media/legacy/uploadedfiles/pcs_assets/2010/collateralcosts1pdf.pdf.

13. Matthew R. Durose, Alexia D. Cooper, and Howard N. Snyder, *Recidivism of Prisoners Released in 30 States in 2005: Patterns from 2005 to 2010* (Washington, DC: US Department of Justice, Office of Justice Programs, Bureau of Justice Statistics, 2014), https://www.bjs.gov/index.cfm?ty=pbdetail&iid=4986.

14. Michael M. O'Hear, "The Second Chance Act and the Future of Reentry Reform," *Federal Sentencing Reporter* 20, no. 1 (2007): 75–83.

15. Lois M. Davis et al., *Evaluating the Effectiveness of Correctional Education: A Meta-Analysis of Programs That Provide Education to Incarcerated Adults* (Santa Monica, CA: Rand Corporation, 2013).

16. David Skorton and Glenn Altschuler, "College Behind Bars: How Educating Prisoners Pays Off," *Forbes*, March 25, 2013, https://www.forbes.com/sites/collegeprose/2013/03/25/college-behind-bars-how-educating-prisoners-pays-off/#5e40cf3a2707.

17. Mary W. Byrne, Lorie S. Goshin, and Sarah S. Joestl, "Intergenerational Transmission

of Attachment for Infants Raised in a Prison Nursery," *Attachment & Human Development* 12, no. 4 (2010): 375–393.

18. Rosa Minhyo Cho, "Maternal Incarceration and Children's Adolescent Outcomes: Timing and Dosage," *Social Service Review* 84, no. 2 (2010): 257–282; John Hagan and Holly Foster, "Children of the American Prison Generation: Student and School Spillover Effects of Incarcerating Mothers," *Law & Society Review* 46, no. 1 (2012): 37–69.

19. Ashton D. Trice and JoAnne Brewster, "The Effects of Maternal Incarceration on Adolescent Children," *Journal of Police and Criminal Psychology* 19, no. 1 (2004): 27–35.

20. Emily B. Nichols, Ann B. Loper, and J. Patrick Meyer, "Promoting Educational Resiliency in Youth with Incarcerated Parents: The Impact of Parental Incarceration, School Characteristics, and Connectedness on School Outcomes," *Journal of Youth and Adolescence* 45, no. 6 (2016): 1090–1109.

21. Nichols, Loper, and Meyer, "Promoting Educational Resiliency," 1090–1109.

22. Barbara Gault, *Single Mothers in College: Growing Enrollment, Financial Challenges, and the Benefits of Attainment* (Washington, DC: Institute for Women's Policy Research, 2017).

23. Gault, *Single Mothers*.

24. Gault, *Single Mothers*.

25. Gault, *Single Mothers*.

26. Gault, *Single Mothers*.

27. Barbara Gault, Elizabeth Noll, and Lindsey Reichlin, *The Family-Friendly Campus Imperative: Supporting Success Among Community College Students with Children* (Washington, DC: Institute for Women's Policy Research, 2017), https://iwpr.org/publications/family-friendly-campus-imperative-supporting-successamong-community-college-students-children/; Cynthia Hess et al., *Supports That Matter in Workforce Development Programs: A National Client Survey on Access to Services* (Washington, DC: Institute for Women's Policy Research, 2017), https://iwpr.org/wp-content/uploads/2017/02/C452-Supports-that-Matter.pdf.

28. Hill Collins, *Black Feminist Thought*; Samir Amin, *Eurocentrism*.

29. Lindsey Livingston Runell, "Identifying Desistance Pathways in a Higher Education Program for Formerly Incarcerated Individuals," *International Journal of Offender Therapy and Comparative Criminology* 61, no. 8 (2017): 894–918, 913.

30. Kimberle Crenshaw, "Mapping the Margins: Intersectionality, Identity Politics, and Violence Against Women of Color," *Stanford Law Review* 43 (1990): 1241.

Chapter 4

1. AnaLouise Keating, *Gloria E. Anzaldúa: Interviews/Entrevistas* (New York: Routledge, 2000), 18.

2. Lauren Musu-Gillette et al., *Status and Trends in the Education of Racial and Ethnic Groups 2017*, NCES 2017-051 (Washington, DC: National Center for Education Statistics, 2017); National Center for Education Statistics, *Hispanics and STEM Education* (Washington, DC: White House Initiative on Educational Excellence for Hispanics, 2010), https://www2.ed.gov/about/inits/list/hispanic-initiative/stem-factsheet.pdf.

3. Hispanic Association of Colleges and Universities, *Fact Sheet: Hispanic Higher Education and HSIs* (San Antonio, TX: Hispanic Association of Colleges and Universities, 2019), https://www.hacu.net/hacu/HSI_Fact_Sheet.asp.

4. Lindsey E. Malcom, "Charting the Pathways to STEM for Latina/o Students: The Role of Community Colleges," *New Directions for Institutional Research* 2010, no. 148 (2010): 29–40.

5. Gloria Crisp and Amaury Nora, *Overview of Hispanics in Science, Mathematics, Engineering and Technology (STEM): K-16 Representation, Preparation and Participation* (San Antonio, TX: Hispanic Association of Colleges and Universities, 2012); Kevin Eagan, Sylvia Hurtado, and Mitchell Chang, *What Matters in STEM: Institutional Contexts That Influence STEM Bachelor's Degree Completion Rates* (Indianapolis, IN: Association for the Study of Higher Education, 2010); Gina A. Garcia and Sylvia Hurtado, *Predicting Latina/o STEM Persistence at HSIs and Non-HSIs* (Los Angeles: University of California, Los Angeles, 2011); Malcom, "Charting the Pathways to STEM."

6. Crisp and Nora, *Overview of Hispanics in Science*, 12.

7. Yanira I. Madrigal-Garcia and Nancy Acevedo-Gil, "The New Juan Crow in Education: Revealing Panoptic Measures and Inequitable Resources That Hinder Latina/o Postsecondary Pathways," *Journal of Hispanic Higher Education* 15, no. 2 (2016): 154–181.

8. Mary Elizabeth Hannah and Elizabeth Midlarsky, "Helping by Siblings of Children with Mental Retardation," *American Journal on Mental Retardation* 110, no. 2 (2005): 87–99.

9. Vincent Tinto, *Leaving College: Rethinking the Causes and Cures of Student Attrition* (Chicago: University of Chicago Press, 1993).

10. Gloria Anzaldúa, "Now Let Us Shift . . . The Path of Conocimiento . . . Inner Work, Public Acts," in *This Bridge We Call Home: Radical Visions for Transformation*, ed. Gloria Anzaldúa and AnaLouise Keating (New York: Routledge, 2002), 540–578.

11. Gilberto Q. Conchas, *The Color of Success: Race and High Achieving Urban Youth* (New York: Teachers College Press, 2006).

12. Tara J. Yosso, "Whose Culture Has Capital? A Critical Race Theory Discussion of Community Cultural Wealth," *Race Ethnicity and Education* 8, no. 1 (2005): 69–91, 77.

13. Taryn Ozuna Allen, Yi (Leaf) Zhang, and Enrique Romo, "Portraits of Ganas: The College-Going Pathways of Undocumented Students at a Texas HBCU," *Journal of Hispanic Higher Education* (2018): 1–19, https://doi.org/10.1177/1538192718797926; Nate Easley Jr., Margarita Bianco, and Nancy Leech, "Ganas: A Qualitative Study Examining Mexican Heritage Students' Motivation to Succeed in Higher Education," *Journal of Hispanic Higher Education* 11, no. 2 (2012): 164–178.

14. Melissa A. Martinez, "(Re)considering the Role Familismo Plays in Latina/o High School Students' College Choices," *High School Journal* 97, no. 1 (2013): 21–40.

15. Stephen J. Ceci and Wendy M. Williams, eds., *Why Aren't More Women in Science? Top Researchers Debate the Evidence* (Washington, DC: American Psychological Association, 2007); Catherine Hill, Christianne Corbett, and Andresse St. Rose, *Why So Few? Women in Science, Technology, Engineering, and Mathematics* (Washington, DC: American Association of University Women, 2010).

16. Sarah L. Rodriguez et al., "Becoming *La Ingeniera*: Examining the Engineering

Identity Development of Undergraduate Latina Students," *Journal of Latinos and Education* (2019): 1–20, https://doi.org/10.1080/15348431.2019.1648269.

17. Marguerite Bonous-Hammarth, "Pathways to Success: Affirming Opportunities for Science, Mathematics, and Engineering Majors," *Journal of Negro Education* 69, no. 1–2 (2000): 92–111; Sharon L. Fries-Britt, Toyia K. Younger, and Wendell D. Hall, "Lessons from High-Achieving Students of Color in Physics," *New Directions for Institutional Research* 2010, no. 148 (2010): 75–83; Jerilee Grandy, "Persistence in Science of High-Ability Minority Students: Results of a Longitudinal Study," *Journal of Higher Education* 69, no. 6 (1998): 589–620; Eagan, Hurtado, and Chang, *What Matters in STEM.*

18. Alberta M. Gloria and Sharon E. Robinson Kurpius, "The Validation of the Cultural Congruity Scale and the University Environment Scale with Chicano/a Students," *Hispanic Journal of Behavioral Sciences* 18, no. 4 (1996): 533–549; Sylvia Hurtado, "The Institutional Climate for Talented Latino Students," *Research in Higher Education* 35, no. 1 (1994): 21–41; Sylvia Hurtado and Deborah Faye Carter, "Effects of College Transition and Perceptions of the Campus Racial Climate on Latino College Students' Sense of Belonging," *Sociology of Education* (1997): 324–345; Sylvia Hurtado and Luis Ponjuan, "Latino Educational Outcomes and the Campus Climate," *Journal of Hispanic Higher Education* 4, no. 3 (2005): 235–251; Tara Yosso et al., "Critical Race Theory, Racial Microaggressions, and Campus Racial Climate for Latina/o Undergraduates," *Harvard Educational Review* 79, no. 4 (2009): 659–691; Eagan, Hurtado, and Chang, *What Matters in STEM.*

19. Jeffrey Mervis, "Data Check: US Producing More Stem Graduates Even Without Proposed Initiatives," *Science Insider,* June 30, 2014, https://www.sciencemag.org /news/2014/06/data-check-us-producing-more-stem-graduates-even-without -proposed-initiatives.

20. Rodriguez et al., "Becoming *La Ingeniera.*"

Chapter 5

1. Gilberto Q. Conchas, "Structuring Failure and Success: Understanding the Variability in Latino School Engagement," *Harvard Educational Review* 71, no. 3 (2001): 475–505; Hannah Rarden Kivalahula-Uddin, "Decolonization of the Mind: A Strategy to Improve Native American Student Achievement" (PhD diss., University of Hawai'i at Manoa, 2018); Gary Orfield and Erica Frankenberg, "Increasingly Segregated and Unequal Schools as Courts Reverse Policy," *Educational Administration Quarterly* 50, no. 5 (2014): 718–734.

2. Leigh Patel, "Nationalist Narratives, Immigration and Coloniality," *Decolonization: Indigeneity, Education & Society* (blog), September 17, 2015, https://decolonization. wordpress.com/2015/09/17/nationalist-narratives-immigration-and-coloniality/; Guadalupe San Miguel, "The Schooling of Mexicanos in the Southwest, 1848–1891," in *The Elusive Quest for Equality: 150 Years of Chicano/Chicana Education*, ed. José F. Moreno (Cambridge, MA: Harvard Education Press, 1999), 31–35.

3. Enrique Alemán and Rudy Luna, *Stolen Education*, directed by Rudy Luna (2013); Gilbert González, "Segregation and the Education of Mexican Children: The Legacy of Expansionism and the American Southwest," *Western Historical Quarterly* 16, no.

1 (1985): 55–76; Nancy Acevedo-Gil, "College-Conocimiento: Toward an Interdisciplinary College Choice Framework for Latinx Students," *Race Ethnicity and Education* 20, no. 6 (2017): 829–850.

4. Patricia Hill Collins, *Black Sexual Politics: African Americans, Gender, and the New Racism* (New York: Routledge, 2004); Kimberle Crenshaw, "Mapping the Margins: Intersectionality, Identity Politics, and Violence Against Women of Color," *Stanford Law Review* 43 (1990): 1241–1299; Hae Yeon Choo and Myra Marx Ferree, "Practicing Intersectionality in Sociological Research: A Critical Analysis of Inclusions, Interactions, and Institutions in the Study of Inequalities," *Sociological Theory* 28, no. 2 (2010): 129–149.

5. Crenshaw, "Mapping the Margins"; Leslie McCall, "The Complexity of Intersectionality," *Signs: Journal of Women in Culture and Society* 30, no. 3 (2005): 1771–1800.

6. Marc Zimmerman, "Testimonio," in *The SAGE Encyclopedia of Social Science Research Methods*, ed. Micahel S. Lewis-Beck et al. (Thousand Oaks, CA: SAGE Publications, 2003), 1118–1119.

7. Susana M. Muñoz, "Unpacking Legality Through La Facultad and Cultural Citizenship: Critical and Legal Consciousness Formation for Politicized Latinx Undocumented Youth Activists," *Equity & Excellence in Education* 51, no. 1 (2018): 78–91.

8. Gloria Anzaldúa, "Now Let Us Shift . . . The Path of Conocimiento . . . Inner Work, Public Acts," in *This Bridge We Call Home: Radical Visions for Transformation*, ed. Gloria Anzaldúa and AnaLouise Keating (New York: Routledge, 2002), 540–578.

Chapter 6

1. Leigh Patel, "Nationalist Narratives, Immigration and Coloniality," *Decolonization: Indigeneity, Education & Society* (blog), September 17, 2015, https://decolonization.wordpress.com/2015/09/17/nationalist-narratives-immigration-and-coloniality/; Guadalupe San Miguel, "The Schooling of Mexicanos in the Southwest, 1848–1891," in *The Elusive Quest for Equality: 150 Years of Chicano/Chicana Education*, ed. José F. Moreno (Cambridge, MA: Harvard Education Press, 1999), 31–35.

2. Enrique Alemán and Rudy Luna, *Stolen Education*, directed by Rudy Luna (2013); Gilbert González, "Segregation and the Education of Mexican Children: The Legacy of Expansionism and the American Southwest," *Western Historical Quarterly* 16, no. 1 (1985): 55–76.

3. Kimberle Crenshaw, "Mapping the Margins: Intersectionality, Identity Politics, and Violence Against Women of Color," *Stanford Law Review* 43 (1990): 1241–1299; Leslie McCall, "The Complexity of Intersectionality," *Signs: Journal of Women in Culture and Society* 30, no. 3 (2005): 1771–1800.

4. Patricia Hill Collins, *Black Sexual Politics: African Americans, Gender, and the New Racism* (New York: Routledge, 2004); Crenshaw, "Mapping the Margins"; Hae Yeon Choo and Myra Marx Ferree, "Practicing Intersectionality in Sociological Research: A Critical Analysis of Inclusions, Interactions, and Institutions in the Study of Inequalities," *Sociological Theory* 28, no. 2 (2010): 129–149.

5. Collins, *Black Sexual Politics*.

6. Gilberto Q. Conchas, "Structuring Failure and Success: Understanding the

Variability in Latino School Engagement," *Harvard Educational Review* 71, no. 3 (2001): 475–505.

7. Nancy Lopez, *Hopeful Girls, Troubled Boys: Race and Gender Disparity in Urban Education* (New York: Routledge, 2003); Grace Kao and Jennifer S. Thompson, "Racial and Ethnic Stratification in Educational Achievement and Attainment," *Annual Review of Sociology* 29, no. 1 (2003): 417–442; Robert C. Smith, "Gender, Ethnicity, and Race in School and Work Outcomes of Second-Generation Mexican Americans," In *Latinos: Remaking America*, ed. Marcelo M. Suárez-Orozco and Mariela M. Paez (Berkeley/Cambridge, MA: University of California Press/David Rockefeller Center for Latin American Studies, 2002), 110–125; Min Zhou and Carl Bankston, *Growing Up American: How Vietnamese Children Adapt to Life in the United States* (New York: Russell Sage Foundation, 1998).

8. Dolores Delgado Bernal, "Learning and Living Pedagogies of the Home: The Mestiza Consciousness of Chicana Students," *International Journal of Qualitative Studies in Education* 14, no. 5 (2001): 623–639.

9. Gloria Anzaldúa, *Borderlands: La Frontera*, vol. 3 (San Francisco: Aunt Lute, 1987).

Chapter 7

1. Gloria Anzaldúa, *Light in the Dark/Luz en lo Oscuro: Rewriting Identity, Spirituality, Reality*, ed. AnaLouise Keating (Durham, NC: Duke University Press, 2015).

2. Ana Clarissa Rojas Durazo, "Decolonizing Chicano Studies in the Shadows of the University's 'Heteropatriracial' Order," in *The Imperial University: Academic Repression and Scholarly Dissent*, ed. Piya Chatterjee and Sunaina Maira (Minneapolis: University of Minnesota Press, 2014), 187–214.

3. See folukeifejola, "Why I Say 'Decolonisation Is Impossible,'" *African Skies* (blog), December 17, 2019, https://folukeafrica.com/why-i-say-decolonisation-is-impossible/.

4. Nelson Maldonado-Torres, "Outline of Ten Theses on Coloniality and Decoloniality," Foundation Frantz Fanon, 2016, https://fondation-frantzfanon.com/wp-content/uploads/2018/10/maldonado-torres_outline_of_ten_theses-10.23.16.pdf, 4.

5. Craig Steven Wilder, *Ebony and Ivy: Race, Slavery, and the Troubled History of America's Universities* (New York: Bloomsbury Press, 2014).

6. Gloria Anzaldúa, "Now Let Us Shift . . . The Path of Conocimiento . . . Inner Work, Public Acts," in *This Bridge We Call Home: Radical Visions for Transformation*, ed. Gloria Anzaldúa and AnaLouise Keating (New York: Routledge, 2002): 540–578.

7. Anzaldúa, *Light in the Dark*, 82.

8. Anzaldúa, *Light in the Dark*, 82–84.

9. Anzaldúa, *Light in the Dark*, 82.

10. Stanley Sue et al., "Community Mental Health Services for Ethnic Minority Groups: A Test of the Cultural Responsiveness Hypothesis," *Journal of Consulting and Clinical Psychology* 59, no. 4 (1991): 533.

11. Anzaldúa, "Now Let Us Shift," 542.

12. Anzaldúa, *Light in the Dark*, 82.

13. Gina Ann Garcia, *Becoming Hispanic-Serving Institutions: Opportunities for Colleges and Universities* (Baltimore: Johns Hopkins University Press, 2019).

14. Elizabeth Zachry Rutschow and Emily Schneider, *Unlocking the Gate: What We Know About Improving Developmental Education* (New York: MDRC, 2011).
15. Nancy Acevedo-Gil et al., "Latinas/os in Community College Developmental Education: Increasing Moments of Academic and Interpersonal Validation," *Journal of Hispanic Higher Education* 14, no. 2 (2015): 101–127.
16. Maldonado-Torres, "Outline of Ten Theses on Coloniality."
17. Sylvia Hurtado and Deborah Faye Carter, "Effects of College Transition and Perceptions of the Campus Racial Climate on Latino College Students' Sense of Belonging," *Sociology of Education* 70, no. 4 (1997): 324–345.
18. Hurtado and Carter, "Effects of College Transition," 842.
19. Alberta M. Gloria, Jeanette Castellanos, and Veronica Orozco, "Perceived Educational Barriers, Cultural Fit, Coping Responses, and Psychological Well-Being of Latina Undergraduates," *Hispanic Journal of Behavioral Sciences* 27, no. 2 (2005): 161–183; Sylvia Hurtado and Luis Ponjuan, "Latino Educational Outcomes and the Campus Climate," *Journal of Hispanic Higher Education* 4, no. 3 (2005): 235–251.
20. Gilberto Q. Conchas, *The Color of Success: Race and High Achieving Urban Youth* (New York: Teachers College Press, 2006); Patricia M. McDonough, *Choosing Colleges: How Social Class and Schools Structure Opportunity* (Albany: State University of New York Press, 1997).
21. Kimberle Crenshaw, "Mapping the Margins: Intersectionality, Identity Politics, and Violence Against Women of Color," *Stanford Law Review* 43 (1990): 1241–1299; Gregory J. Palardy, "High School Socioeconomic Composition and College Choice: Multilevel Mediation via Organizational Habitus, School Practices, Peer and Staff Attitudes," *School Effectiveness and School Improvement* 26, no. 3 (2015): 329–353.
22. Laura I. Rendon, "Validating Culturally Diverse Students: Toward a New Model of Learning and Student Development," *Innovative Higher Education* 19, no. 1 (1994): 44.
23. Nancy Acevedo-Gil et al., "Latinas/os in Community College Developmental Education."
24. Christine E. Sleeter, *The Academic and Social Value of Ethnic Studies* (Washington, DC: National Education Association, 2011).
25. Julio Cammarota and Augustine Romero, "Encuentros with Families and Students: Cultivating Funds of Knowledge Through Dialogue," in *Raza Studies: The Public Option for Educational Revolution*, ed. Julio Cammarota and Augustine Romero (Tucson: University of Arizona Press, 2014), 122–134.
26. Sleeter, *The Academic and Social Value of Ethnic Studies.*
27. Sleeter, *The Academic and Social Value of Ethnic Studies*, xii.
28. Cati, V. de los Ríos, Jorge López, and Ernest Morrell, "Toward a Critical Pedagogy of Race: Ethnic Studies and Literacies of Power in High School Classrooms," *Race and Social Problems* 7, no. 1 (2015): 84–96.
29. Cammarota and Romero, "Encuentros with Families and Students"; Nolan L. Cabrera et al., "Missing the (Student Achievement) Forest for All the (Political) Trees: Empiricism and the Mexican American Studies Controversy in Tucson," *American Educational Research Journal* 51, no. 6 (2014): 1084–1118; de los Ríos, López and Morrell, "Toward a Critical Pedagogy"; Thomas Dee and Emily Penner, "The Causal Effects of Cultural Relevance: Evidence from an Ethnic Studies Curriculum," *American*

Educational Research Journal 54, no. 1 (2017): 127–166; Augustine Romero, Sean Arce, and Julio Cammarota, "A Barrio Pedagogy: Identity, Intellectualism, Activism, and Academic Achievement Through the Evolution of Critically Compassionate Intellectualism," *Race Ethnicity and Education* 12, no. 2 (2009): 217–233.

30. Tanya J. Gaxiola Serrano, Mónica González Ybarra, and Dolores Delgado Bernal, "'Defend Yourself with Words, with the Knowledge That You've Gained': An Exploration of Conocimiento Among Latina Undergraduates in Ethnic Studies," *Journal of Latinos and Education* 18, no. 3 (2019): 244.

31. Ashley Smith, "The Benefits of Ethnic Studies Courses," *Inside Higher Ed* (blog), July 9, 2018, https://www.insidehighered.com/news/2018/07/09/san-francisco-state-finds-evidence-ethnic-studies-students-do-better.

32. The field of ethnic studies includes but is not limited to Chicana/o studies, African American/Black studies, American Indian studies, and Asian American and Pacific Island studies.

33. Anne-Marie Núñez, Elizabeth T. Murakami, and Leslie D. Gonzales, "Weaving Authenticity and Legitimacy: Latina Faculty Peer Mentoring," *New Directions for Higher Education* 2015, no. 171 (2015): 87–96.

34. Kimberle Crenshaw, "Mapping the Margins."

35. Dolores Delgado Bernal and Enrique Alemán Jr., *Transforming Educational Pathways for Chicana/o Students: A Critical Race Feminista Praxis* (New York: Teachers College Press, 2017).

36. José L. Santos and Nancy Acevedo-Gil, "A Report Card on Latina/o Leadership in California's Public Universities: A Trend Analysis of Faculty, Students, and Executives in the CSU and UC Systems," *Journal of Hispanic Higher Education* 12, no. 2 (2013): 174–200.

37. Maldonado-Torres, "Outline of Ten Theses on Coloniality," 4.

38. Angelica Cortes, "The Experiences and Studying Practices of Community College Latin@ STEM Majors Taking Calculus I" (PhD diss., University of California, Davis, 2017).

39. Gina A. Garcia and Jenesis J. Ramirez, "Institutional Agents at a Hispanic Serving Institution: Using Social Capital to Empower Students," *Urban Education* 53, no. 3 (2018): 355–381; Silvia J. Santos and Elena T. Reigadas, "Latinos in Higher Education: An Evaluation of a University Faculty Mentoring Program," *Journal of Hispanic Higher Education* 1, no. 1 (2002): 40–50.

40. Rocío Mendoza, "En Comunidad: The Undergraduate Research Experiences of Students of Mexican Descent" (Unpublished PhD diss., Claremont Graduate University, 2020).

41. Matias Farre, "Spending Where It Matters: Exploring the Relationship Between Institutional Expenditures and Student Retention Rates at the California State University" (PhD diss., California State University, San Bernardino, 2019).

42. Farre, "Spending Where It Matters."

43. Carola Suárez-Orozco et al., "Toxic Rain in Class: Classroom Interpersonal Microaggressions," *Educational Researcher* 44, no. 3 (2015): 151–160.

44. Maldonado-Torres, "Outline of Ten Theses on Coloniality," 4.

45. Gloria Anzaldúa, *Borderlands: La Frontera*, vol. 3 (San Francisco: Aunt Lute, 1987), 71–87.

Appendix

1. Robert K. Yin, *Case Study Research and Applications: Design and Methods* (Thousand Oaks, CA: SAGE Publications, 2017).
2. Daniel Solórzano et al., *Pathways to Postsecondary Success: Maximizing Opportunities for Youth in Poverty* (Los Angeles: UC/ACCORD, 2013).
3. Johnny Saldaña, *The Coding Manual for Qualitative Researchers* (Thousand Oaks, CA: SAGE Publications, 2015).
4. Gina A. Garcia and Sylvia Hurtado, *Predicting Latina/o STEM Persistence at HSIs and Non-HSIs* (Los Angeles: University of California, Los Angeles, 2011).
5. Saldaña, *Coding Manual.*
6. Yvonna Lincoln and Egon G. Guba, *Naturalistic Inquiry* (Thousand Oaks, CA: SAGE Publications, 1985).
7. Saldaña, *Coding Manual.*
8. Lincoln and Guba, *Naturalistic Inquiry.*
9. Egon G. Guba, "Criteria for Assessing the Trustworthiness of Naturalistic Inquiries," *ECTJ* 29, no. 75 (1981).
10. Gilberto Q. Conchas et al., "The Chicana/o/x Promise: Testimonios of Educational Empowerment Through the Enactment of La Facultad Among First-Generation College Students," *CLEARvoz Journal* 5, no. 1–2 (2019); Dolores Delgado Bernal, Enrique Alemán Jr., and Andrea Garavito, "Latina/o Undergraduate Students Mentoring Latina/o Elementary Students: A Borderlands Analysis of Shifting Identities and First-Year Experiences," *Harvard Educational Review* 79, no. 4 (2009): 560–586; Lindsay Pérez Huber and Bert Maria Cueva, "Chicana/Latina Testimonios on Effects and Responses to Microaggressions," *Equity & Excellence in Education* 45, no. 3 (2012): 392–410.
11. Luz del Alba Acevedo, *Telling to Live: Latina Feminist Testimonios* (Durham, NC: Duke University Press, 2001).
12. Daniel G. Solórzano and Tara J. Yosso, "Critical Race Methodology: Counter-Storytelling as an Analytical Framework for Education Research," *Qualitative Inquiry* 8, no. 1 (2002): 23–44.
13. Dolores Delgado Bernal, Rebeca Burciaga, and Judith Flores Carmona, "Chicana/Latina Testimonios: Mapping the Methodological, Pedagogical, and Political," *Equity & Excellence in Education* 45, no. 3 (2012): 363–372.
14. Richard Delgado, "Storytelling for Oppositionist and Others: A Plea for Narrative Legal Storytelling," *Michigan Law Review* 87 (1989): 2411–2441.
15. Gloria Anzaldúa, *Borderlands: La Frontera*, vol. 3. (San Francisco: Aunt Lute, 1987).
16. Conchas et al., "Chicana/o/x Promise."
17. Sofia Villenas and Douglas E. Foley, "Chicano/Latino Critical Ethnography of Education: Cultural Productions from La Frontera," in *Chicano School Failure and Success: Past, Present, and Future*, 2nd. ed., ed. Richard R. Valencia (London: RoutledgeFalmer, 2002), 225–261.
18. Anzaldúa, *Borderlands*; Villenas and Foley, "Ethnography of Education."
19. Teresa Cordova, "Power and Knowledge: Colonialism in the Academy," in *Living Chicana Theory*, ed. Carla Trujillo (Berkeley, CA: Third Woman Press, 1998), 17–45; Sofia Villenas, "The Colonizer/Colonized Chicana Ethnographer: Identity,

Marginalization, and Co-optation in the Field," *Harvard Educational Review* 66, no. 4 (1996): 711–732.

20. Patricia Zavella, "Feminist Insider Dilemmas: Constructing Ethnic Identity with 'Chicana' Informants," *Frontiers: A Journal of Women Studies* 13, no. 3 (1993): 53–76.

21. Alan Peshkin, "In Search of Subjectivity—One's Own," *Educational Researcher* 17, no. 7 (1988): 17–21.

22. Joseph A. Maxwell, *Qualitative Research Design* (Thousand Oaks, CA: SAGE Publications, 2012); Martyn Hammersley and Paul Atkinson, *Ethnography: Principles in Practice* (New York: Routledge, 1983).

23. Anzaldúa, *Borderlands*; Gilberto Q. Conchas, *The Color of Success: Race and High-Achieving Urban Youth* (New York: Teachers College Press, 2006); Dolores Delgado Bernal, "Using a Chicana Feminist Epistemology in Educational Research," *Harvard Educational Review* 68, no. 4 (1998): 555–582; Francisca E. Gonzalez, "Formations of Mexicana ness: Trenzas de Identidades Multiples Growing up Mexicana: Braids of Multiple Identities," *International Journal of Qualitative Studies in Education* 11, no. 1 (1998): 81–102; Villenas and Foley, "Ethnography of Education."

24. Delgado Bernal, "Chicana Feminist Epistemology."

25. Delgado Bernal, "Chicana Feminist Epistemology."

Acknowledgments

W E ARE INDEBTED TO MANY in the writing of this book. Our profound gratitude goes to all of the young men and women who through interviews and *testimonios* shared their intimate struggles, successes, and the human spirit. This book is for you, about you, and your journeys in the educational borderlands will inform future generations to come.

This book is also about us. We are both proud first-generation college graduates; proud first-generation PhDs; and proud first-generation tenured college professors. We began our intellectual journey at UC Berkeley as first-generation undergraduates, where we discovered our passion for Chicana feminism and critical ethnic studies. It is through these initial experiences that fostered our own nepantlera/o/x critical consciousness that we hope to impact the research field, students, and our communities.

We express deep gratitude to our extremely supportive editor at Harvard Education Press, Jayne Fargnoli, who shared our passion for Chicana feminist theory and thus believed in this book from the minute we discussed it during a phone call two years ago. Thank you for listening to us and for taking this project on. We benefited tremendously from your careful reading and thoughtful feedback through the writing of the book.

Gil's Voice

After I, Gil Conchas, passed my summer remedial English course at Cal, I had the pleasure of fulfilling my English requirement by taking two semesters with renowned Chicana feminist and author Cherrie Moraga. I would like to thank Cherrie for teaching, introducing, and guiding me through important avant-garde feminist writings such as Moraga and Anzaldua's *This Bridge Called My Back: Writings by Radical Women of Color*, Anzaldua's *Borderlands: La Frontera: The New Mestiza*, Sandra Cisnero's *The House on Mango Street*, and Anna Castillo's *The Mixquiahuala Letters*. Thank you very much for teaching this barrio schoolboy and expanding my own mestizo consciousness.

At Cal, I would also like to acknowledge the many Chicanx/Latinx professors that contributed to my successful crossing of educational borderlands through their scholarship, teaching, and activism. Tomás Almaguer (who later became my dissertation advisor at the University of Michigan, colleague, and dear friend), Norma Alarcon, Mario Barrera, the late Robert Blauner, Carlos Muñoz Jr., Julie E. Curry Rodríguez, and Alex Saragoza are a few notable professors that I studied under as an undergraduate.

I also thank the extended network of Chicanx/Latinx scholars who have been instrumental supporters in my academic journey and *conocimiento* of the field of Chicanx/Latinx studies. Thank you, Eddy F. Alvarez, Patricia Baquedano-López, Lisa García Bedolla, Frances Contreras, Dolores Delgado Bernal, Eduardo Bonilla-Silva, Antonia Castañeda, Leo Chavez, Regina Deil-Amen, Cynthia Feliciano, Glenda Flores, Stella Flores, Patricia Gándara, Roberto Gonzales, Kris D. Gutiérrez, Alexandro Gradilla, Ramón Gutiérrez, Julian Vasquez Heilig, Aida Hurtado, Sylvia Hurtado, Gloria Martinez, Eduardo Mosqueda, Pedro Nava, Pedro A. Noguera, Leticia Oseguera, Katy Pinto, Laura I. Rendón, Maria Rendón, Rebeca Mireles-Rios, Victor Rios, Anna Ríos-Rojas, Vicki Ruiz, Louie F. Rodríguez, Sophia Rodríguez, Laura Romo, Chela Sandoval, Denise Segura, Daniel Solórzano, Ricardo Stanton-Salazar, Carola and Marcelo Suárez-Orozco, Eddie Telles, Rodolfo Torres, Abel Valenzuela Jr., Angela Valenzuela, James Diego Vigil, and Pat Zavella. You are all giants in the field, and I am happy to have had the opportunity to work with you in one way or another.

I am eternally grateful for all of the students who worked with me on the book and whose enthusiasm toward the topic was infectious. To my graduate students, Socorro Cambero, Vanessa Delgado, Gabby Gutierrez, and Jess Lee, and to my many undergraduate students, I thank you all for assisting me with the book at various stages. This book would not have been possible without the countless hours you spent working with me on the literature review, data collection, data analysis, and many chapter drafts. A special thank you to Socorro Cambero—my ardent undergraduate student turned into an even fiercer doctoral student—for her critical eye throughout the project, for assisting with the write-up of chapter 2, and for taking the initiative in formatting the entire manuscript. Through this process, you all taught me to be a better listener, a better mentor, and a much better scholar.

I would be remiss not to thank Nancy Acevedo for guiding me through the *nepantla* and the colonial educational borderlands. As a sociologist of education, the aforementioned scholar's and their writings have influenced my own work, but it took 30 years to pen a book that places Chicana feminist theory and critical ethnic studies as the core underpinnings of this book. Nancy has led the way from the very beginning and has taught me so much through the writing of this book. Nancy, you are a fierce Chicana scholar, mother, warrior, and friend. I am grateful for you and honored to call you my intellectual *comadre—hoy y para siempre! Gracias amiga mia.*

Nancy's Voice

I, Nancy Acevedo, thank Gil Conchas. Gil, when you served as a board member for UC/ACCORD, you provided me with mentorship and guidance as I prepared for the job market. Now, *estoy eternamente agradecida* for you walking me through the process of developing a book idea, securing a press, and doing the work. Thank you for your patience and support during this process. Writing this book with you has been an amazing experience, and I promise to pay it forward to the next generation of Chicana/o/x faculty.

I would like to thank the Chicano studies professors at UC Berkeley, many of whom were part-time faculty. I would not have considered the faculty route had it not been for you: Josefina Castillo-Baltodano, Josefina Parra, and Blas Guerrero. I also would like to thank Alex Saragoza, Ramon Grosfoguel, Lilia Soto, and Nelson Maldonado-Torres because through your courses, I was introduced to the history and theories of Chicano studies, including coloniality and the work of Gloria Anzaldúa. Martha A. Cabrales, thank you for being an amazing friend who helped me learn to study hard but to balance work with fun. Marcos Pizarro and Julia Curry, thank you for your support and encouragement in my preparation to pursue the PhD. I would like to thank Danny Solórzano for his mentorship all these years and for allowing us to use in this book the qualitative data from the UC/ACCORD Pathways to Postsecondary Success Project, which was funded by the Bill & Melinda Gates Foundation. Danny, you have taught me that we can foster various counterspaces within academia where we can uplift and support one another. I would also like to thank Kimberley Cousins for inviting me to serve as lead researcher of the Promoting Pre- and Post-transfer Success in STEM at Hispanic Serving Institutions project (Grant # 1644261), funded by the NSF S-STEM program. I am grateful for Jake Zhu and the College of Education at CSUSB for funding our writing retreat, in which Leslie Gonzales helped me overcome my fear of writing the first draft of chapter 1.

I would also like to thank my AAHHE *familia*, led by Loui Olivas; you all have been instrumental in my life since 2011. Leticia Oseguera, Louie. F. Rodriguez, Frances Contreras, and Victor Saenz, thank you for being mentors, colleagues, and friends on this journey; you have served as role models in balancing family with academia. To my writing group, Joanna Wong, Juliet Wahleithner, Jennifer Collett, and Funnie Hsu, thank you for our biweekly check-ins! They definitely motivated me and kept me going when I struggled to balance writing with everything else. Yanira Ivonne Madrigal-Garcia, Ursula Aldana, Qiana Wallace, José Aguilar-Hernandez, Maria Malagon, Sera Hernandez, and Marissa Vasquez, thank you for being honest and sharing advice; it was instrumental in my journey as I wrote this book. Most of my writing was done in coffee shops, and, just like with my dissertation, Tierra Mia Coffee is definitely a space where I can concentrate and write because I feel at home; I am grateful for spaces like this. Edwin Hernandez, thank you so much for providing the space so that I could wrap up final revisions and edits. While in the IE, I have found an amazing support system of *profesoras chingonas* and I am so thankful for you all: Edna Martinez, Liliana Conlisk Gallegos, Angie Otiniano Verissimo, Yvette Saavedra, Lorena Gutierrez, and Isabel Huacuja. Of course, to my *Valemadristas*, Noralee Jasso and Jessica Rodriguez, thank you for your daily texts and for lifting me up so that I could manage to balance academia with wellness.

The past two years, I have had support from so many individuals as I work to balance academia with motherhood. My parents, Rodimiro

Acevedo *y* Gloria Rivas de Acevedo, have provided unconditional love and support, *gracias a sus sacrificios, yo he podido lograr tanto.* I have been fortunate that my kids have had amazing teachers at the CSUSB Infant Toddler Lab School and the Children's Center; you have become part of our family. Angelina Saucedo, Mireya Olguin, Sabrina Murguia, and Becky Valle, thank you for your help with caring for my kids so that I can work. Finally, Diana Isabella and Victoria Linda, I love you: *ustedes son mi inspiración y motivación. Espero que este libro contribuye de una manera u otra para mejorar el sistema educativo que ustedes navegan; yo se que van a cambiar el mundo.*

About the Authors

GILBERTO Q. CONCHAS is the Wayne K. and Anita Woolfolk Hoy Professor of Education in the College of Education at Pennsylvania State University. Conchas's research unearths the triumphs of urban youth of color despite unequal school-community processes. He is the author and coauthor of nine books—including *The Color of Success, Streetsmart Schoolsmart, Cracks in the Schoolyard,* and *The Complex Web of Inequality*—numerous articles, book chapters, and policy reports. Dr. Conchas has been a professor at the Harvard Graduate School of Education and the University of California at Irvine and visiting professor at the University of Southern California, San Francisco State University, University of Washington, University of Barcelona, and the University of California, Berkeley and Santa Barbara.

NANCY ACEVEDO is an associate professor in the Department of Educational Leadership and Technology at California State University, San Bernardino. Acevedo uses critical race and Chicana feminist theories to examine transitions along the higher education pipeline for Latina/o/x students, with a focus on college access, choice, and transitions. She was a UC/ACCORD Dissertation Fellow and a Faculty Fellow for the American Association for Hispanics in Higher Education. Her research has received several recognitions, such as the 2019 American Educational Research Association Latina/o/x Research Issues Emerging Scholar Award.

Index

AB-540 students, 136–137
AB 705 (CA), 58, 159
AB 1460 (CA), 165
AB 2772 (CA), 26, 165
ableism, 113–119, 139–146
academic invalidations, 58
academic preparation, 164–165
accessibility issues, 143–144
Acevedo, Nancy, 7–12
Acevedo, Rodimiro, 8
advisors, 67, 161–163
Alejandra (testimonio), 46
Amelia (testimonio), 51–52
anchor babies label, 20, 119–124
Anzaldúa, Gloria
    atravesadas/os/x, 28–30
    borderlands and, 25–28, 53–54
    change and, 14
    la facultad and, 38
    helpfulness of theories of, 2–3, 11–12
    nepantleras and, 33–34
    praxis and, 156
    reflection and, 156–157
    self-awareness, 172
    socially just reality and, 158–159
Araceli (testimonio), 139–146
Arianna (testimonio), 46
arrebato (breakthrough), 10–11, 89, 100
Asian Americans, model minority
        typology, 42, 43–44
assimilation, 24–25, 140

atravesadas/os/x (transgressors). *See also*
        belonging; testimonios
    assimilation and, 140
    borderlands and, 27–28
    criminal records and, 70
    defined, 2
    disability status and, 141–142
    in prison, 61–62
    resistance causing, 120–121
    view as, 22
autism, 88–89, 91–92

bachelor's degrees, 18, 21, 27, 85
balance, 105–106
belonging. *See also* atravesadas/os/x
        (transgressors)
    curriculum and, 26
    disabilities, Students of Color with, 116
    ethnic studies classes and, 164–165
    ganas and, 103
    health conditions and, 98
    Hispanic-Serving Institutions and, 85,
        107
    lack of social support and, 88
    nepantla as, 161–170
    poverty and, 114
    pregnancy and, 74
    STEM education and, 103–104
    teacher impact on feelings of, 71–72
    validating experiences and, 65
bilingual education, 26

borderlands
  overview of, 23–28
  Anzaldúa and, 25–28, 53–54
  community college system and, 57–58
  defined, 23, 25–26
  marginalization and, 171
breakthrough (arrebato), 10–11, 89, 100
bridges, 2, 7. *See also* nepantleras/os/x
      (individuals navigating in-between
      spaces)
bullying, 120, 141–142, 147

California Community Colleges (CCC)
      system, 57, 159–160
California DREAM Act, 20
career internships, 168–170
career pathways, 61–63
Carlos (testimonio), 124–129
Casa Joaquin Murietta, 6
CCC (California Community Colleges)
      system, 57, 159–160
Christian (testimonio), 44
Christina (testimonio), 146–150
citizenship, 20
class, inequality and, 44–45
classroom climate, 167–168, 170
collaborative classrooms, 167–168, 170
college applications, 142–143, 148–149
college field trips, 72
college guidance, 61–63
coloniality
  criminalization and, 138
  critical race theory and, 22–23
  decoloniality, 154
  deservingness and, 25
  educational system and, 17–18, 24–25,
      112, 131, 133
  nepantlera/o/x praxis and, 155–161
  teacher characteristics and, 26
  US founded on, 23, 50
community college system
  overview of, 57–58
  Giselle's experience with, 71–81
  Javier's experience with, 60–71
  STEM education and, 85–86
  transition to, 88, 161–163

community cultural wealth, 31–32, 150,
      152
Conchas, Evelia, 4–5
Conchas, Gilberto, 4–7
Conchas, José, 4–5
confidence, 104–105
conocimentio, 6–7, 156–157
consciousness, stepping into, 155
COVID-19, 171
creative acts, reflexive engagement in,
      156
criminalization of Latinos, 19–20, 28, 125,
      127
criminal records, 70
critical consciousness, 32–33, 41, 160–161,
      164–167
critical race theory (CRT), 22–23, 31, 46
cultural factors, perceptions of inequality
      and, 40
culture of poverty, 43
curriculum, 24, 26, 133

DACA (Deferred Action for Childhood
      Arrivals), 20, 136
Danny (testimonio), 42
decoloniality, 154
decolonization, 154
Deferred Action for Childhood Arrivals
      (DACA), 20, 136
deficit versus asset lens, 31, 32–33, 50–51,
      156, 159
degree attainment, 18, 21, 27, 85
deservingness, 23–24, 25, 49. *See also*
      belonging
Diego (testimonio), 37, 38, 43–44
disabilities, Students of Color with, 21,
      113–119, 139–146
doctoral degrees, 85
DREAM Act, 20
dual-language immersion programs, 26

Early Academic Outreach Program, 148
education, 86–87, 111
educational outcomes
  advanced degrees, 85
  bachelor's degrees, 18, 21, 27, 85

factors impacting, 19
family education and, 45
educational system. *See also* community
    college system
  coloniality of, 17–18, 24–25, 112, 131,
    133
  degree attainment and unequal
    opportunities in, 18–19
  economic capital and, 52
  epistemology and, 21–23
  funding, 171
  inequality in, 111–112, 145
  resource availability in, 28
education-life balance, 105–106
Elena (testimonio), 37, 38
employment, criminal records and, 70
English language testing, 50
Enrique (testimonio), 49
epistemology, 21–23
Esteban (testimonio), 113–119
ethnic studies classes, 164–165
expectations, lower for Latina/o/x
    students, 28, 71, 87, 119–120
exposure to college, 72
extracurricular activities, 101–102, 117,
    144–145, 151

la facultad (seeing beneath the surface).
    See also inequality; testimonios
  overview of, 53–54
  borderlands and, 28–32
  community cultural wealth and, 31
  critical consciousness and, 32–33, 41,
    160–161, 164–167
  defined, 2, 29
  development of, 29–30
  disabilities and, 118
  hobbies and, 117
  machismo and, 129–130
  moving towards, 41–42
  nepantleras and, 33
  persistence and, 18, 96
  purpose of, 38
  resistance and, 3, 22
  skill development and, 30–31
  STEM and, 94–97

student-parents and, 82–83
undocumented status and, 30, 123–124
faculty. *See* professors
familial capital, 31
families. *See* parents and families
FAN. *See* Framework of Atravesada/o/xs
    Nepantleando (FAN)
feminism, 19, 42
feminist standpoint theory, 41
financial aid, 69, 74, 77–78. *See also*
    scholarships
four-year university, Chicana female
    students
  overview of, 133–134, 150–152
  Araceli, 139–146
  Christina, 146–150
  Rosa, 133, 135–139
four-year university, Chicano male
    students
  overview of, 111–113, 129–132
  Carlos, 124–129
  Esteban, 113–119
  Miguel, 111, 119–124
Framework of Atravesada/o/xs
    Nepantleando (FAN), 22, 32–35,
    37–38. *See also* atravesadas/os/x
    (transgressors); la facultad (seeing
    beneath the surface); nepantleras/
    os/x (individuals navigating
    in-between spaces)
Francisco (testimonio), 86–97
funding, 171

ganas, 103
gangs, 121–122
gay and lesbian students, 20–21, 124–129,
    146–150
gender. *See also* four-year university,
    Chicana female students; four-year
    university, Chicano male students
  intersectionality and, 19–20
  mothers, view of, 52–53
  perceptions of inequality and, 39–42,
    45, 48, 128
Giselle, 71–81
goals, 73–74

Guerrero, Blas, 10–11
guidance programs, 67, 161–163

HB 2281 (AZ), 26, 165
Head Start, 5
high school as not preparing for college, 88
Hispanic-Serving Institutions (HSI), 85, 107
hobbies, 117
homophobia, 1–2
hope, 3, 29. *See also* resistance
Houston Independent School District, 165
HSI (Hispanic-Serving Institutions), 85, 107

IDEA (Individuals with Disabilities Education Act), 114
IEP (Individualized Education Program), 114
illegal label, 135
immigration
    anchor babies label and, 20, 119–124
    assimilation and, 24–25, 140
    atravesadas/os/x and, 136–137
    illegal label and, 135
    labor exploitation of, 51–52
    opportunity and, 47–48, 51
    political climate and, 1
incarceration rates, 59
inclusive classrooms, 167–168, 170
individualism, 42–44, 48, 53
Individualized Education Program (IEP), 114
Individuals with Disabilities Education Act (IDEA), 114
inequality
    overview of, 53–54
    ability to see, 47–48
    defined, 37, 44–47
    educational system, 111–112, 145, 165–166
    gender differences in perceptions of, 39–42, 45, 48, 128
    intersectionality and, 38–39, 40
    opportunity and, 44, 45–46, 48

structures reproducing, 49–53
undocumented status and, 51–52
white privilege and, 47, 49
institutional resources, 95–96, 101, 170
intelligence, perceptions of, 103–104
internships, 168–170
intersectionality. *See also* four-year university, Chicana female students
    Chicana/o/x school experience and, 18–21, 133–134
    citizenship and, 20
    disability status and, 21
    gender and, 19–20
    guidance programs and, 162
    inequality and, 38–39, 40
    marginalization and, 18, 112, 131, 171
    mentors and, 166
    opportunity and, 46–47
    sexual minority status and, 20–21, 124–129, 146–150
    student-parents and, 83
IQ movement, racism and, 25
Ivonne (testimonio), 43

Jamie (testimonio), 43
Janet (testimonio), 51
Javier (testimonio), 60–71
Jesus (testimonio), 48
Jorge (testimonio), 45

knowledge, holders and creators of, 41, 42

labor exploitation of immigrants, 51–52
language, 49–51
Latinx population, 18, 57, 85
LGBT students, 124–129, 146–150
Lyme disease, 114

machismo, 19–20, 122, 129–130
Maldonado-Torres, Nelson, 167, 170
marginalization
    avoiding replication of structures for, 158
    coloniality and, 25
    educational system and, 23–24

la facultad and, 30
feminist standpoint theory and, 41
inequality and, 47–48
intersectionality and, 18, 112, 131, 171
non-native English speakers, 50
normativity and, 46
socially just reality and, 160
masculinity, 122. *See also* machismo
master's degrees, 85
Mathematics, Engineering, Science,
    Achievement (MESA) program,
    90, 101–102
MEChA (Movimiento Estudiantil
    Chicana/o/x de Aztlan), 123,
    144–145
mentors. *See also* nepantleras/os/x
    (individuals navigating in-between
    spaces); role models
    acting as, 11–12
    gang leader as, 121–122
    importance of, 7, 9, 95–96, 142–143
    intersectionality and, 166
    lack of as harmful, 98–100
    peer support, 104
meritocracy, 42–44, 48, 51, 53, 153
MESA (Mathematics, Engineering,
    Science, Achievement) program,
    90, 101–102
Miguel (testimonio), 111, 119–124
minoritized status, inequality and
    opportunity and, 47–48
Minority Opportunity Summer Training
    (MOST), 7
model minority typology, 42, 43–44
motivation, 71
Movimiento Estudiantil Chicana/o/x de
    Aztlan (MEChA), 123, 144–145

National Science Foundation (NSF), 90
nativism, 1–2, 119–124
navigational capital, 31–32
nepantla (in-between)
    defined, 2, 33
    polarity thinking and, 153
    as sense of belonging, 161–170
    student-parents and, 68

nepantleras/os/x (individuals navigating
    in-between spaces). *See also*
    borderlands; testimonios
    benefits of, 112–113
    defined, 2, 33–34
    disabilities and, 118–119
    la facultad and, 33
    praxis and, 155–161
    as role models, 66–67, 123
    in STEM, 93–94
    student-parents, 66–67, 80–81
non-native English speakers, 50
NSF (National Science Foundation), 90

occupational inequality, 45
opportunity
    abilities to see inequity of, 47–48
    as available for all, 44
    defined, 37
    immigrant status and, 51–52
    inequality and, 44, 45–46, 48
    intersectionality and, 46–47
othering, 24–28

parents and families. *See also*
    student-parents
    authoritative style and, 124–127
    educational attainment conflicting with
        responsibilities to, 70
    education to give back to, 137–138
    encouragement by, 120
    experiences of as guidance, 130
    impacts of becoming parents, 72–73,
        82
    impacts of going to college on, 92–93,
        137–138
    imprisonment of, impacts from, 59–60
    informal, 121–122
    as role models, 64–65
    single parents, 60
    as support system, 76–77, 93–94, 98,
        116, 151
patriarchy, 19–20, 122, 129–130
pay-it-forward mentality, 151–152
pedagogies of the home, 19, 32
peer support, 66–67, 78–79, 104, 167–168

persistence
disabilities and, 140–143
disabled status and, 117–118
la facultad and, 18, 96
as resistance, 82–83
policing of Latinos, 19–20, 28
postsecondary obstacles, anticipation of, 30
potlucks, 168
poverty, 113–114, 168
priorities, conflict between, 105–106
prison industrial complex, 59–60, 82. See also student-parents
professors. See also teachers
classroom climate and, 170
as representative of students, 96–97, 166–167
as resources, 95–96
validation from, 163–164
Proposition 227 (CA), 26

Queer Students of Color, intersectionality and, 20–21, 124–129, 146–150

racism, 1–2, 25
Rafael (testimonio), 49
recidivism, 59
recommendations
overview of, 154
academic preparation, 164–165
classroom climate, 167–168
dismantling of stereotypes, 155–156
educational resource distribution, 165–166
guidance counselors and advisors, 161–163
hiring practices, 166–167
internships, 168–170
marginalizing structures, avoiding replication of, 158
nepantla as sense of belonging and, 161–170
peer support, 167–168
reflexive engagement in creative acts, 156–158
socially just reality and, 158–161

validation from teachers and faculty, 163–164
reflexive engagement in creative acts, 156
religion, 125–126
research internships, 168–170
resistance. See also testimonios
atravesadas/os/x status due to, 120–121
community as, 150, 152
disabilities and, 117–118
la facultad and, 3, 22
pedagogies of the home and, 19
persistence as, 82–83
self-awareness as, 100–106
resistant capital, 31
resources in educational system, 28, 87, 165–166
Rivas, Francisco (Panchito), 8–9
Rivas de Acevedo, Gloria, 7–8
role models. See also mentors
nepantleras acting as, 66–67, 123
for students, 64–65, 95, 116–117, 149
Rosa (testimonio), 50, 133, 135–139

scholarships, 90–91, 102
school-to-prison pipeline, 58–59
science versus subjectivity, 85
Second Chance Act of 2007, 59
segregation, 24–25, 27
self-awareness, 89–90, 100–106, 172
self-confidence, 104–105
self-esteem, 141–142
self-reflection, 157–158, 160
sexism, increase of, 1–2
sexual minority status, 20–21, 124–129, 146–150
Shadow-Beast, 28–29
single parents, 60
social justice, 3, 19, 160
socially just reality, 158–161
social struggles, 88
socioeconomic status, 45, 113–114
Spanish language, 49–51
SSI (Supplemental Security Income), 114–115
STEM education
overview of, 85–86, 106–108

Francisco, 86–97
  White males as "normal" in, 106–107
  Yesenia, 97–106
stereotypes, 43–44, 49, 155–156
structural factors, 39–40, 42–44
student-parents
  overview of, 60
  Giselle, 71–81
  internships and, 169–170
  Javier, 60–71
subjectivity versus science, 85
success, 3–4, 106, 139, 159
Summer Academic Research Institute,
  6–7
Supplemental Security Income (SSI),
  114–115

teachers. See also professors
  belonging and, 71–72
  hiring, 166–167
  low expectations by, 71, 87, 119–120
  positive attention from, 148
  as predominantly white women, 26,
  166–167
  validation from, 163–164
testimonios
  Alejandra, 46
  Amelia, 51–52
  Araceli, 139–146
  Arianna, 46
  benefits of, 131
  Carlos, 124–129
  Christian, 44
  Christina, 146–150
  Danny, 42
  defined, 18, 112
  Diego, 37, 38, 43–44
  Elena, 37, 38
  Enrique, 49
  Esteban, 113–119
  Francisco, 86–97
  Gilberto Conchas, 4–7
  Ivonne, 43
  Jamie, 43
  Janet, 51
  Javier, 60–71

Jesus, 48
Jorge, 45
Miguel, 111, 119–124
Nancy Acevedo, 7–12
Rafael, 49
Rosa, 50, 133, 135–139
Vanessa, 45
Yesenia, 97–106
Zulema, 47
testing, 50
theories, impacts of, 17
tracking, 8–9, 10–11
transgressors. See atravesadas/os/x
  (transgressors)
transition to community college, 88,
  161–163
transition to four-year college, 91–92,
  104, 161–163. See also four-
  year university, Chicana female
  students; four-year university,
  Chicano male students
Trump, Donald, 1, 137

undocumented status
  anchor babies label, 20
  belonging and, 26
  la facultad and, 30, 123–124
  illegal label, 135
  inequality and, 48, 51–52
  Rosa's testimonio, 133, 135–139
University of California, Berkeley, 6
(un)learning, 156

validating experiences, 65, 67, 163–164
Vanessa (testimonio), 45
la verdad, 125–126
vocational programs, 63–68

white privilege, 42–44, 47, 49

xenophobia, 1–2

Yesenia (testimonio), 97–106

Zulema (testimonio), 47